The Soviet Novel

The Soviet Novel

History as Ritual

KATERINA CLARK

With a new Afterword
by the Author

The University of Chicago Press • Chicago and London

The University of Chicago Press, Chicago 60637
The University of Chicago Press, Ltd., London

Published 1981
Second edition 1985
Printed in the United States of America

94 93 92 91 90 89 88 87 86 85   5 4 3 2 1

Library of Congress Cataloging in Publication Data

Clark, Katerina.
   The Soviet novel.

   Bibliography: p.
   Includes index.
   1. Russian fiction—20th century—History and
criticism.   2. Socialist realism in literature.
I. Title.
PG3098.4C4   891.73'409   80–18758
ISBN 0–226–10767–1

For my mother and father

Contents

Contents

Preface

When, in some chance encounter at a professional gathering, I am politely asked what I "do," I find myself in the unhappy position of having to admit that I work on the Soviet novel. Usually my interlocutor tries to help me out at first by suggesting, if he knows anything about Soviet literature, that of course that must mean that I am working on one of the more respectable writers, such as Platonov, Bulgakov, Pasternak, or Solzhenitsyn. "No?...Well, I suppose even someone like Fedin....Not really?...Oh!" Then follows that dreadful pause when it all comes out: my work is on the *Soviet* Soviet novel, on those hundreds of unreadable texts that serve as examples of Socialist Realism. That is to say, I do not look at good novels that happen to have been published in the Soviet Union, or even at good examples from typical Soviet fiction, but actually at those works whose authors have *deliberately* followed the conventions of Socialist Realism. It is then that my leprous nose comes finally into view. My interlocutor's response is either to back out of the conversation or to mutter words of sympathy and amazement: "How do you ever manage to get through them!"

Soviet Socialist Realism is virtually a taboo topic in Western Slavic scholarship. It is not entirely taboo, for it can be discussed, but preferably only in tones of outrage, bemusement, derision, or elegy. Three main arguments underpin this collective judgment. First, it is felt to be intellectually suspect—or simply a waste of time—to analyze what is patently bad literature. The history of Soviet literature, it is felt, provides a classic case of that familiar pattern in which political revolution becomes cultural devolution. Between constant state interference in the business of literature and Socialist Realism's doctrine of mandatory *partijnost'* (or "Party-mindedness," i.e., the stipulation that all works be infused with the Party's point of view), literature's natural evolution was tampered with, and with disastrous results. Hence the bathetic decline from

the great prose works of a Dostoevsky or a Tolstoy to those of a
Nikolay Ostrovsky or a Gladkov. Second, it is argued that it is
virtually immoral to devote attention to a tradition that has developed at the cost of so many violations of intellectual freedom and
integrity, of so much human suffering. Finally, it is felt that Socialist
Realism is itself so lifeless and dull that any study of it would of necessity be hopelessly pedestrian (unless, of course, enlivened by tales of
infamy or by acerbic comments).

All three are very powerful arguments, and their impact has been
such that very few scholars have undertaken to write on Soviet
Socialist Realism per se. It is considered far more worthy to write
on dissidents or at least on the *less* conformist writers within Soviet
literature—on those who might be expected to show some spark of
originality or independent spirit.

Only a few topics are recognized as valid for those who want to
study mainstream Soviet literature rather than its dissident fringes.
One can, for instance, chronicle the literary politics in terms of rival
factions, interference from above, forced rewritings of manuscripts,
etc. Alternatively, one can describe the various theoretical positions
taken in that ongoing debate over what "Socialist Realism" really
means. Or, again, one can discuss why Socialist Realism is bad
literature. Or, finally, one can undertake a thematic study on the
grounds that this will either reveal the absurdity of most Socialist
Realism or provide useful data on changing Soviet attitudes, mores,
etc. Some supporters of this approach have even pointed out the
intelligence advantages of looking at Soviet novels: by reading *The
Regional Party Secretary* (1961), written by that arch "hard-liner"
Vs. Kochetov, for instance, one learns of a special hot line that
connects regional party managers directly with their bosses.[1]
There is also a place for a general history of Soviet literature, one
that sets out the various periods and describes the most important
works published in each; but Gleb Struve's *Russian Literature
under Lenin and Stalin, 1917–1953* already performs that function
very well.

While not denying the value of these various kinds of studies, I
would like to argue for a different approach, one that has thus far
gone largely unexplored.

The underlying assumption that has inspired most accounts of
Soviet Socialist Realism to date (other than those written by sym-

pathizers) is that the repressive climate of the Soviet Union has resulted in bad literature. Trying to determine whether Socialist Realism is or is not "bad literature" is not, however, the most fruitful approach. Some of the problems derive from applying Western "highbrow" literary criteria in studying a literature that was not intended to meet them. It is easy for us to compare works by Melville, Flaubert, and Dickens, because their novels perform a fairly homogeneous aesthetic function in the literary systems of America, France, and England. But there has always been a distinction between modern Russian and other Western literature, and this distinction became exacerbated under the Soviets. It is a cliché in talking about nineteenth-century Russian literature that it performed a social function not just as literature but also as a forum for intellectual and political debates, which the censor kept out of the more expected channels. In Soviet literature this extraliterary dimension has become so paramount that the texts themselves insist that they not be treated as high literature. Until recently Soviet critics rarely gave a work's "literary" merits more than a passing mention.

The Soviet novel performs a totally different function from the one the novel normally performs in the West, and this difference in function has given rise to a different kind of text. The differences extend right across the board—in the type of plot that is used, in mode of characterization, point of view, etc. Consequently, the body of methodology that has been developed for dealing with literature in the modern Western context is not self-evidently the most appropriate optic through which to view what is essentially a structurally different phenomenon. It would be more meaningful to ask whether the institution of Soviet Socialist Realism is adequate to its function than whether it has literary respectability. That question will not be engaged here, since the chosen task is to describe and analyze rather than to evaluate.

Rather than berate Ostrovsky for not being Henry James, we might get further if we discussed his novels in the context of types of literature that perform a more analogous function. The Socialist Realist novel was intended to be a form of popular literature (or, at most, middlebrow), and like most varieties of popular literature it is formulaic. It thus lends itself to a comparison with other varieties of popular formulaic literature, such as detective stories and serial novels. Unlike most such fiction, however, it is also highly didactic (but not unlike all: elsewhere I have compared it to the novels of Arthur Hailey, a comparison that works well in most respects),[2] and could thus be looked at as a case study in literary didacticism (a topic that has not in fact been taken up in this book). The Socialist Realist novel forms a tradition that rests on canonical exemplars. Consequently, medievalists who study the conventions of hagiography and other such texts tied to a canon will find much in common between the distinctive features of their texts and those of the Soviet novel. Finally, the Soviet novel's major function since at least 1932–34, the time when the canon was instituted, has been to serve as the official repository of state myths.[3] For this reason, studies of the Soviet novelistic tradition can be conducted in much the same ways as structural studies of myth.

In short, the arsenal of analytical tools developed for treating folkloric texts and other formulaic genres, such as serial novels and hagiography, seems to be more efficient for studying Soviet texts than the tools developed for analyzing modern highbrow literature. This book therefore has something of an anthropological bias and contains several quasi-structuralist studies of the Soviet novel. The methodology used is indebted to the Soviet medievalist D. S. Likhachev and the literary theorist M. Bakhtin, but it also draws on the work of a large number of anthropologists, including V. Propp, A. Van Gennep, M. Gluckman, V. Turner, and C. Lévi-Strauss, and on the scholar of myth M. Eliade.

As can be appreciated from the diverse approaches these names suggest, the methodology used here for analyzing Soviet texts has been eclectic. Indeed, no one methodology has been applied with sufficient rigor to please a structuralist purist. This is because the book's ultimate aim is not to produce a structural study per se— that is, a highly abstract and generalized ahistorical analysis of the conventional Soviet novel—but to give a *dynamic* account of the novel's evolution, seen in the general context of Soviet culture.

The question how a tradition as singular as that of the Soviet novel ever came to be is a very intriguing one. That is not, however, the only reason why this study eschews the temptation to rest with a purely synchronic analysis. The main reason for that is the limitations of a purely structural approach. When one considers the Soviet novel in a context that aligns it with other text types that are themselves manifestly dissimilar in some crucial respects (such as folklore, hagiography, and detective stories), much of the novel's singularity and specificity will clearly be lost. Additionally, in a strictly structural analysis an important dimension—the ideological—is left out. The problem of literature's relationship to its political and social environment, and the dependence of *meaning* on factors external to the texts themselves, cannot be treated properly without introducing a historical or extratextual dimension. The interrelationship of the intrinsic and the extrinsic is always an interesting question, but it becomes especially acute in the case of Soviet literature because of the marginal importance of the aesthetic function in texts and the unusually great importance of politics and ideology. In dealing with such aspects, however, it is not sufficient to demonstrate how, over time, official values have been imposed upon literature, *since these official values have themselves been culturally determined.*

Here anthropology once again provides useful analytical tools with which to study Socialist Realist texts.There is a need to look at Socialist Realism from the point of view of the semiotics of culture, to discriminate the meaning of texts and the tradition they form, as opposed to their brute structure, by appealing to differences in different culture systems. As Tynyanov and Jakobson pointed out in 1928, "the history of a system is in turn a system."[4] Thus, rather than a comparative study of the Socialist Realist novel and other text types, what I have attempted here is an interpretive cultural history that uses the novel (and novella) as its focus because the novel is *the* privileged genre of Soviet Socialist Realism, occupying the same structural slot as the opera does in China. I have done this by using a composite approach, involving methods from history, anthropology, and, to a lesser extent, literary theory. By anthropologizing history and historicizing anthropology, I have hoped to avoid both the excesses of the ahistorical scientism of most structuralisms, on the one hand, and, on the other, the monological mystifications of historical accounts, most of which labor under the disadvantages of a particularist naiveté.

In meeting the realities of present-day publishing I have had to make radical cuts in my original manuscript. I have tried to retain my basic ideas and the historical scope of the book at the cost of reducing the number of examples and the coverage of the most familiar aspects of Soviet literary history and politics. I have provided a bibliography of the most basic Western sources on these topics.

I cannot possibly thank all those who have helped me during the six years of this book's preparation. I owe a special debt of gratitude to Harry Rigby, who first made me aware of the questions about Soviet literature and society that I am still trying to answer. Others who have helped by reading the manuscript and making valuable comments include Grace Hucko, Geoffrey Hosking, Gary Saul Morson, Richard Pope, Jane Andelman Taubman, Robert Tucker, and Mikhail Ulman. Kay Stephenson deserves mention, not only for her superb typing but also for her editorial help, and I am grateful to Gianna Kirtley for pitching in, as usual, when things got hectic. I would also like to thank my husband, Michael, for doing all of the above things—and more. Finally, I would like to express my gratitude to two institutions: to Wesleyan University for its generous faculty research grants, which enabled me to make four trips to the Soviet Union to do research for this book, and to the University of Texas at Austin for a grant toward the cost of manuscript preparation.

Note on
Transliteration

This book uses two different systems of transliteration. In the text, Russian names and titles are rendered so that they will indicate for the nonspecialist the approximate Russian pronunciation (i.e., kh is used rather than x, zh rather than ž, hard and soft signs are not indicated, etc.). For Russian words cited in the text and for Russian sources in the Notes and Bibliography, however, the I.P.A. system is used. By this system the following special signs have the approximate values indicated below:

'   *soft sign,* indicating that the preceding consonant is "softened" (i.e., palatalized)
"   *hard sign,* indicating that the preceding consonant is not palatalized
c   *ts*
č   *ch*
j   *y* as in *yes*
š   *sh*
šč *shch*
x   *h*
y   *i* as in *bill*
ž   *zh*

The Soviet Novel

Introduction The Distinctive Role of Socialist Realism in Soviet Culture

What is Socialist Realism? It is not, first of all, a *single* doctrine. We now recognize that that old bogey, "monolithic communism," does not exist—that there are, instead, many different communisms. In much the same way, there are many different Socialist Realisms. Different countries, different political parties, and critics with different *partis pris* have each evolved different definitions of it.

Even if Socialist Realism is confined to the meaning "officially sponsored Soviet literature," it soon becomes apparent that among the various canonical accounts of it there is no *one* that is incontrovertible or in any sense comprehensive. Some official pronouncements on the theory of Socialist Realism have been important (e.g., that literature should be "optimistic," that it should be accessible to the masses, that it should be "party-minded"), but they are too general to have guided such a distinctive practice.

It is not in theoretical writings but in practical examples that one should look for an answer to the question What is Socialist Realism? Soviet scholars have been arguing since the term was coined in 1932 over what it means, and their debates are, in essence, mere academic hairsplitting. Scholars still argue, for instance, as to how much "realism" and how much "romanticism" it should entail.[1] In the meantime, Socialist Realism has long since evolved into a highly conventionalized literary practice. Consequently, instead of going into the Byzantine arguments that surround the question What is Socialist Realism?, I shall use a strictly pragmatic approach and define Soviet Socialist Realism as a canonical doctrine defined by its patristic texts.

Nowhere has Soviet Socialist Realism been more conventionalized than in the subject of this inquiry, the novel. Although the clichés of the novel are in some measure officially fostered, the source for them has not been theoretical pronouncements but, rather, official "model" novels. Ever since 1932, when the

Writers' Union was formed and Socialist Realism was declared
the sole method appropriate for Soviet literature, most official
pronouncements on literature, and especially the addresses that
open every Writers' Congress, have contained a short list of
exemplars (*obrazcy*) that are to guide the writers in their future
work (see Appendix B). Each new version of the list contains as its
core the official classics of Socialist Realism; a few recently published works are then added on. No two lists are exactly the same,
and additions to earlier lists tend to be left out in later versions.
However, there is a core group of novels that are cited with
sufficient regularity to be considered a canon. These include
M. Gorky's *Mother* and *Klim Samgin;* D. Furmanov's *Chapaev;*
A. Serafimovich's *The Iron Flood;* F. Gladkov's *Cement;* M. Sholo-
khov's *Quiet Flows the Don* and *Virgin Soil Upturned;* A. Tolstoy's
The Road to Calvary and *Peter the First;* N. Ostrovsky's *How the
Steel Was Tempered;* and A. Fadeev's *The Rout* and *The Young
Guard.*

   These canonical works have been a crucial factor in determining
the shape of the Soviet novel. There was a good deal of external
stimulus for following these exemplars besides the mere fact that
they were cited by authoritative voices. In the early thirties a literary
institute was founded to train new writers to follow the models. A
preferential scale of royalty payments and other positive inducements, such as dachas and "creative" stays at writers' Houses
of Rest, were dangled before the writer as positive inducements to
follow the developing official traditions of the Soviet novel. In other
words, when authoritative voices cried out "Give us more heroes
like X [the hero of some model novel]," the cry did not fall on
entirely deaf ears.

   As a result, the business of writing novels soon became comparable to the procedure followed by medieval icon painters. Just as the
icon painter looked to his original to find the correct angle for a
particular saint's hands, the correct colors for a given theme, and so
on, so the Soviet novelist could copy the gestures, facial expressions,
actions, symbols, etc., used in the various canonical texts.

   The Soviet writer did not merely copy isolated tropes, characters,
and incidents from the exemplars; he organized the entire plot
structure of his novel on the basis of patterns present in the exemplars. From the mid-thirties on, most novels were, *de facto,* written

to a single master plot, which itself represents a synthesis of the plots of several of the official models (primarily Gorky's *Mother* and Gladkov's *Cement*). This shaping pattern does not account for everything in a given Soviet novel. Despite the frequent Western charge that the Soviet novel is clichéd and repetitive, it is not actually true that every novel is nothing more than a reworking of a single formula. In any given novel one must distinguish between, on the one hand, its overarching plot or macrostructure and, on the other, the microstructures, the smaller units, which are threaded together by this shaping formula—the digressions, subplots, and so on. If a novel is looked at in terms of these smaller units, much of it will be found to be somewhat journalistic and topical; it may, for instance, be geared to praising a recent Soviet achievement or to broadcasting or rationalizing a new decree or official policy. In other words, much of it is based on ephemeral material.

The overarching plot of a given novel is not ephemeral—that is, it is not tied to a particular time. If its plot were stripped of all references to a specific time or place or to a particular theme of the novel, it could be distilled to a highly generalized essence. This abstract version of a given novel's plot is the element that is, in effect, shaped by the master plot.

If a novel is to be written to the canon, this master plot controls the most crucial moments of the novel—its beginning, climax, and end. For the rest it may provide no more than general guidelines, together with a range of symbols, motifs, etc., to be used in certain formulaic situations. However, the most common variety of Soviet novel, the production novel, uses the full version of the master plot (see Appendix A): canonical functions in this case determine the whole course of the novel.

Not all Soviet novels follow the master plot. Not even all novels listed in the canon follow it completely. That official classic, Sholokhov's *Quiet Flows the Don*, for example, shows only occasional traces of the master plot, and these primarily in connection with lesser characters.[2] Thus, even though statistically my hypothetical master plot has been followed to a greater or lesser degree by the overwhelming majority of Soviet novels (or Stalinist novels, at any rate), its status as a defining trait of the novel tradition does not depend on the actual percentage of novels patterned on it, for the master plot is not random or arbitrary in the sequence it sets up: it illustrates major tenets of ideology.

The master plot is the one constant that links most novels of the Stalin period and, to a lesser extent, those of the post-Stalin era as well. I would go so far as to say that it *is* Socialist Realism: in order for a Soviet novel to be Socialist Realist, it must replicate the master plot.

What are the sources of the master plot? Surely it did not evolve *in vacuo?* Did Soviet writers of the thirties know *which* gestures, tropes, etc., to copy from the disparate novels assigned as models? Did they know how to put all the pieces together to make a coherent narrative frame, and, if so, *how* did they know these things?

The evolution of the Socialist Realist tradition owes some debt to artistic ingenuity on the part of the writers themselves, but the process was larger in scope than its purely literary context. Obviously, politics played some part. One cannot analyze either the dynamic of the master plot's evolution or the meanings of its formulaic components without looking at its relations both to politics and ideology, on the one hand, and to literary traditions on the other. On the whole, the Western approach has been to assume that the contents of Soviet novels have in some way been "handed down" by the authorities or else have slavishly been designed to be pleasing to them. Westerners see this as an unnatural state of affairs, since they conceive it as normal for literature to be fairly autonomous; in this view, Soviet literature, if it achieves the lofty role the Russian intelligentsia has *traditionally* prescribed for it, should itself "hand down" ideas to society. Of course this "unnatural state of affairs" did not come into being without resistance. Western observers tend to see Soviet intellectual history as a long, epic struggle between "the regime" and "the intellectuals" or, among Soviet intellectuals, between the "diehards" or "conservatives," who support the regime, and the "liberals," who want less "straitjacketing" (e.g., being obliged to follow the master plot)—who want, perhaps, to express a more complex, even Western, account of reality. But the prominence of ultrarightest views among the most recent crop of Soviet dissidents should give us pause.

The trouble with this historical model is not that its categories are inaccurate but that it is an illusion to think that the two parties—

the "regime" versus "the intellectuals"—could in any circumstances be completely autonomous and free systems. They are implicated with each other more closely than in most other cultures. Moreover, in the Soviet Union there is not something extrahistorical called "the government" or "the Party." Both are subfunctions of the larger system of the complete culture to which they belong. Indeed, the Party itself is in a sense only one group of that larger class called the intelligentsia. Moreover, it houses within its confines much internal debate and has been known on occasion to adopt values previously held by a dissident group. Likewise, there is no such thing as an independent literary system, as we are increasingly beginning to suspect.

Thus, the master plot was not merely "handed down" to the Soviet writers from above. It is of course true that the leadership fostered the canonization of the master plot, and it is also true that they saw to it that the spectrum of possible literary approaches became very narrow. Nevertheless, the movement from politics and ideology to literature was far from being a one-way street.

The relationship of literary to extraliterary factors is always a complex one. Literature is, on the one hand, an autonomous series, having its own traditions and generating new forms within those traditions; on the other hand, it can never be completely independent of the extraliterary aspects of its own culture, for, if it were, its signs would have no meanings. Literature interacts with *many* other aspects of culture, not just with politics and ideology. I say "interacts with," because literature never merely "reflects" extraliterary matter; it always adapts it to fit its own traditions. Bakhtin ("Medvedev") sees the process of interaction as dialectical:

> The artistic work is . . . drawn into the . . . conflicts and contradictions [within the ideological horizon]. It is penetrated by and absorbs some elements of the ideological environment and turns away other elements external to it. Therefore, in the process of history, "extrinsic" and "intrinsic" dialectically change places, and, of course, do not remain unchanged as they do so. That which is extrinsic to literature today, is an extra-literary reality, can enter literature as an intrinsic, constructive factor tomorrow. And that which is literary today can turn out to be an extra-literary reality tomorrow.[3]

In the Soviet Union the interaction between literary and nonliterary worlds has been even closer than is generally the case; the borders between literature and journalism, for instance, are often difficult to perceive. This is so because modern Russian literature and the functions of the forum have traditionally been close, and the political powers have actively promoted an intensification of this relationship. Still, "politics" or "ideology" should not be identified as some monolithic entity with which literature has interacted. Not only has the process of interaction been dialectical rather than a one-way street, but the "extraliterary" pole of the dialectic has been made up of several distinct components, each of which has in turn interacted with the others—and again dialectically.

There are at least six major elements in Soviet society and culture that play a part in the generative process of literature. First, there is literature itself; second, there is Marxism-Leninism; third, there are the Russian radical intelligentsia's traditional myths and hero images, which the Bolsheviks brought with them when they took power in Russia in 1917; fourth, there are the various nonliterary forums through which the official viewpoint is disseminated (the press, the political platform, theoretical writings, official histories, and the like), which I shall refer to in this book by the general term "rhetoric"; fifth come political events and policies; and, sixth, there are the individual persons who are the principal actors in these political events, together with their roles and values. In some respects, any change in any one of these elements is the product of ongoing trends within its own "series"; but for the most part they are interdependent, and change in any one of them *potentially* affects changes in any or all five of the others (even Marxism-Leninism can be changed).

In short, it is too much of a simplification to see the symbols or master plot of Soviet literature as having come from politics via the refracting medium of rhetoric. The principal actors on the political scene were themselves caught up in acting out roles suggested to them by revolutionary lore, and much of that lore, in turn, originated in literature. Ultimately, the question What caused what? must be a chicken-and-egg question.

The elements that make up the master plot come, at one level, from within literature itself. In general the master plot continues one strand of prerevolutionary literature: it reworks the prevailing myths and tropes of Russian radical fiction and rhetoric of the second half of the nineteenth and early twentieth century. Also carried over has been some influence from folk and religious literature (though pre-Soviet radical texts used these sources, too). But the master plot is by no means an isolated or purely literary phenomenon. Indeed, it could not have survived solely on its literary merits or role. The master plot plays a distinctive role for the entire Soviet culture.

Socialist Realism is essentially a name applied to Soviet culture's literary system rather than to a way of writing that is particularly "socialist" or "realist." Indeed, the "socialist" aspects and "realist" aspects of Soviet literature are more functions of the "superstructure" than they are of the "base." The "base" is the master plot.

The one invariant feature of all Soviet novels is that they are ritualized, that is, they repeat the master plot, which is itself a codification of major cultural categories. Here I mean "ritual" in the same sense as it is used by anthropologists. Ritual is a term for those social acts that are felt by the participants to concentrate the greatest amount of cultural meaning in them (with respect to the Soviet novel's master plot, this does not, of course, necessarily mean that the participants are personally in accord with these "meanings"). Rituals are that part of the language of culture in which signs achieve the lowest degree of arbitrariness. This is somewhat paradoxical, because they are, at the same time, the most conventionalized. All rituals have form, and they are successful in focusing otherwise diffuse cultural energies precisely in the degree to which they are formulaic. They provide a kind of shaping force to the energies that are most powerfully abroad in the society; they are a focusing lens for cultural forces.

The one thing that rituals have in common in any culture, as anthropologists from Van Gennep to Victor Turner have pointed out, is a concern for transformation of various kinds. Rituals personalize abstract cultural meanings and turn them into comprehensible narrative. This is the way they make specific meanings that would otherwise be general. The subject of the ritual "passes" from one state into another, well-known examples being the progression from boyhood to manhood or from foreigner to citizen.

The primary function of the master plot is very similar to that of ritual understood in these terms. It shapes the novel as a sort of parable for the working-out of Marxism-Leninism in history. The novel takes as its focus a relatively modest figure, usually a Soviet worker, administrator, or soldier. This subject is known as the "positive hero." However modest he may be, the phases of his life symbolically recapitulate the stages of historical progress as described in Marxist-Leninist theory. The novel's climax ritually reenacts the climax of history in communism. This crucial role played by the positive hero is, indeed, the reason he has received so much attention from critics. When the cry goes out "Give us more heroes like X!" one may be sure that the novel in which the stages of X's life are portrayed shows skillful use of the master plot.

The ritual form of conventional Soviet novels comprises both iconic signs for positive heroes and a catalogue of plot functions they normally perform. Both the signs and the plot functions are encoded symbols, derived largely from prerevolutionary lore but with meanings that ultimately derive from Marxism-Leninism. The master plot is, however, much broader in the range of meanings it encompasses and is not confined to Marxism-Leninism for its subtext.

It is by now a commonplace of Western histories of the Soviet Union that during the thirties all public activity became more highly ritualized and that much of it was geared to legitimizing the hegemony of the Stalinist leadership by identifying its links with Lenin and Leninism. This development more or less coincided with the institutionalization of Socialist Realism (which occurred between 1932 and 1934). Not suprisingly, therefore, the signs and functions of the master plot that had meanings in Marxist-Leninist historiography also acquired established associations with the Soviet leadership and its connection to Lenin. Soviet novels became simultaneously parables of Marxism-Leninism and myths for maintaining the status quo.

In view of the novel's role as repository of official myths, extraordinary measures were taken to ensure that the purity of the formulas be preserved from book to book. It was, for instance, not merely political caprice that motivated the Party's spokesman Zhdanov, in 1946, when he called for strict adherence to doxology.[4]

In Stalinist novels, whatever the context, whatever the year, events can be relied upon to follow the prescribed pattern. The symbolic forms of literature are remarkably constant because this very constancy affirms "Leninist" continuity.

Thus it would seem that the Soviet novel offers perfect material
for making a structural analysis of the master plot in terms of its
formulaic phases, somewhat as Propp has done for the Russian
folktale.[5] That is, one could adduce a "grammar" of the Soviet
novel. I have, in fact, provided something like a "grammar" of this
kind in Appendix A. I have relegated it to this peripheral position
because to provide a mere "grammar" of forms, an unvarying
structural pattern in Soviet novels, ignoring contextual consid-
erations, is to ride roughshod over the dimension of meaning,
which, in the Soviet context, is all important.

The constancy with which the same signs recur in Soviet novels is
in part deceptive. Continuity in the use of symbols need not be an
accurate index to continuity of values. If, as most linguists now
agree, the relationship between sign and meaning in ordinary language is not fixed but dynamic, then, surely, when language is used
symbolically, this potential for change is increased. And in fact in
the Soviet novel many of the formulaic tropes have, over time,
changed or have at least been modified in their meanings.

The political anthropologist Abner Cohen has written about the
relationship between political symbols (using "political symbols" in
the extended sense as objects, concepts, or linguistic formations)
and the changing world and power structure they are meant to
support. Cohen cautions against seeing symbols as "mechanical
reflections, or representations, of political reality" or of thinking
that "Power relations and symbolic formations are...reducible
one to the other." As he points out, power relations and symbolic
formations are relatively autonomous, and the relations between
the two are complex. "Symbols...stand *ambiguously* for a mul-
tiplicity of disparate meanings," and the same symbol can thus be
used in different contexts to mean the same thing; we must "distinguish between symbolic *forms* and symbolic *functions*" or meanings. He continues:

> Symbols achieve a measure of continuity-in-change by their am-
> biguity and multiplicity of meanings. A ceremonial may be re-
> peated over and over again in the same form though its symbols
> may be charged with different meanings to accommodate new
> developments. Thus there is a continuous process of action and
> counteraction between the symbolic order and the power order
> even when there is no significant structural change.[6]

In other words language—and highly symbolic language *a fortiori*—is multivalent. Symbols can have several meanings, even at the same time, and they can often be used ambiguously. Shalom Spiegel has shown how a major symbolic text of the Jewish people, the biblical story of Abraham and Isaac, or Akedah, has been variously interpreted. Although the events of the story have remained substantially the same in each retelling, at various points in the history of the Jews the story has been interpreted in new ways, colored by their current aspirations and experiences.[7] Something like this occurred with the Soviet novel. During the different phases of the Stalin era various clichés of the novel were interpreted in different ways. Some changes were made in the master plot, too, but these changes were on the whole semantic rather than formal.

The symbolic forms of Socialist Realism have not been used as a medium of expression for the official viewpoint alone. The intellectuals are, after all, more immediately involved in the business of literature than the leadership is, and they have also been able to profit from the multivalence of literature's iconic signs.

The traditional role of Russian literature has been, since at least Belinsky,[8] to provide a forum for the most advanced ideas of the age, to bear witness to the grim realities of Russian life not admitted to in official sources; the self-image of Solzhenitsyn in our time provides a good example of this tradition. Most people in the West would contend that the various institutional controls placed on Soviet literature have all but robbed creative writing and criticism (at least that published through official channels) of this particular dimension. But they have certainly not done so entirely, and there is an incipient tension in fiction between its function as occasional writing and propagator of official myths and values, on the one hand, and, on the other, its more traditional role in modern Russia of standing in the forefront of intellectual life. This tension is not readily apparent, for it is expressed in the most delicate nuances.

When the formulaic patterns of the Soviet novel became fixed in the thirties, a system of signs became the core of the Socialist Realist system. These signs are polysemic in themselves, but, when incorporated in the master plot, they take on very definite, specific meanings. Nevertheless, as words, they must retain the potential for other meanings, and a skillful writer can play on this.

If a writer wanted his novel to be published, he had to use the
proper language (epithets, catch phrases, stock images, etc.) and
syntax (conventional ordering of events in accordance with the
master plot). To do so was effectively a ritual act of affirmation of
loyalty to the state. Once the writer had accomplished this, his
novel could be called "party-minded." But he had room for play in
the ideas these phenomena expressed because of the latent ambiguities of the signs themselves.

Each novel was written in a context affected by change, controversy, and even the author's own position. All these factors bear
upon the individual work and have the power to change its meanings. New meanings can come from within the system of signs
by the slightest rearrangement or emphasis or shading—meta-
phasis—of the standard signs and sequences. Such changes may
be scarcely perceptible to an outsider not schooled in the tradition, but they would be striking to most Soviet readers. The
system of signs is, simultaneously, the components of a ritual and a
surrogate for the Aesopean language to which writers resorted in
tsarist times when they wanted to outwit the censors. Thus,
paradoxically, the very rigidity of Socialist Realism's formations
permits freer expression than would be possible if the novel were
less ritualized.

The formulaic signs of the Soviet novel have been used as a
medium for debates to this day. When Stalin died in 1953, many
writers set about to criticize his legacy, including the stiltedness of
Socialist Realist fiction. Yet when they produced fiction containing
critiques of Stalinism, they often used the ready-made code or system of signs of the Socialist Realist tradition. Inevitably, the system
of signs was modified as a result; some epithets, for instance,
changed their value import from positive to negative. Nevertheless,
the changes came from within the tradition the writers were opposing. In the post-Khrushchev era, literature became more varie-
gated in style and approach, yet one can still sense the presence of
the Socialist Realist tradition even in much unofficial literature
(underground publications and literature published in the West).

It would be too glib to conclude that this lingering attachment to
the tradition was due to Soviet citizens' having been inculcated in its
language for so long that they could not throw it off. But then one
must ask why the conventions of Socialist Realism have this power.

I would suggest that the reason so many of the symbols of Socialist Realism continue to resonate is that they ring not just for the Bolsheviks. They are sufficiently broad and flexible to contain most of the separate currents that make up Soviet culture. When Socialist Realism was launched in the early thirties, it led to the homogenization of Soviet literature. A major effect of this homogenization was that all writers henceforth began to use the same language. However, just as all speakers of English can express differing views while using roughly the same language, so likewise (although of course to a more limited extent) all Soviet writers could express varying views via the "language" of Socialist Realism. The linguistic imperialism that occasioned the influx of so many new speakers into the language group of the Bolsheviks had an effect not uncommon in cases of linguistic imperialism: while the writers were being issued the "uniform" of the new power, the agents of this power were simultaneously receiving the "mufti" of their new subjects. The ideas and values of divergent groups within the intelligentsia began to color the associations of the various elements of the official language. The result was a dynamic of cross-fertilization that involved not just literature but also five other major elements of Soviet culture, which, as I said above, interacted with it to produce Socialist Realism: Marxism-Leninism, revolutionary lore, rhetoric, political policies, and historical events, together with the actors within them.

For this exchange to occur, there had to be an effective medium for focusing it. This brings us back to our earlier remarks about ritual. The formulaic signs of the Soviet novel have proved so tenacious over time because they catch some of the burning issues and beliefs of the entire culture, not just of the official culture. The master plot is not merely a literary plot or even the formula for a literary plot. It is the literary expression of the master categories that organize the entire culture.

The problem posed in this book is thus a variant of the perennial question of continuity and change. Because the Soviet government is ideologically conservative and anxious to establish a "Leninist" connection for the current leadership, the novels written during its regime have used, to a remarkable degree, the *same* signs over the years, signs whose origins can in fact be traced back to well before 1917. But when are these signs really the *same,* and when are they *different* (because differently deployed)?

The signs of Soviet literature do not remain the same just because, as a ready-made code, they can be used as pawns in the
ongoing contest between "conservatives" and "liberals," nor do
they represent empty affirmations of allegiance to the status quo. In
this book I hope to show that the *same* signs are used with such
frequency because they encapsulate the polemics and dilemmas of
the Russian intelligentsia that have been constant from at least the
mid-nineteenth century to the present day. Bolshevism made its
contribution to these polemics, and it promised a way out of these
dilemmas; but the debate continues. Bolshevism simply gave it a
new focus and a new language.

The "Spontaneity"/"Consciousness" Dialectic as the Structuring Force That Shapes the Master Plot

Rituals, as pointed out above, always involve some kind of transformation: the subject of the ritual goes from one state to another,
and his progress, or "passage," enacts some central idea of the
culture. Since the master plot of the Soviet novel provides a
ritualized account of the Marxist-Leninist idea of historical progress, one might expect that the transition charted would involve
movement from a class society through proletarian hegemony and
on into that ultimate state, the classless society, i.e., communism.
Actually, however, the class struggle per se has not been a consistent theme of the Soviet novel and has certainly not provided the
structuring force for the novel's master plot.

The subtext that does shape the master plot is another fundamental idea of Marxism-Leninism, one that is a somewhat déclassé
and more abstract version of the class-struggle account of history.
In this version, historical progress occurs not by resolving class
conflict but through the working-out of the so-called spontaneity/
consciousness dialectic. In this dialectical model, "consciousness" is
taken to mean actions or political activities that are controlled,
disciplined, and guided by politically aware bodies. "Spontaneity,"
on the other hand, means actions that are not guided by complete
political awareness and are either sporadic, uncoordinated, even
anarchic (such as wildcat strikes, mass uprisings, etc.), or can be
attributed to the workings of vast impersonal historical forces
rather than to deliberate actions.

According to the Leninist model for historical progress, society from its earliest days has been locked in a dialectical struggle between the forces of "spontaneity" (which predominate in the earliest, most primitive social forms) and the forces of "consciousness" (which are present from the very beginning, although largely only as a potential). This dialectic provides the driving force of progress and leads to history's end in communism. It affects a series of increasingly higher-order syntheses ("leaps forward," or revolutions) resulting in ever-higher forms of both "spontaneity" and "consciousness." The ultimate stage of historical development, communism, is reached in a final synthesis, which resolves the dialectic once and for all. That final synthesis or ultimate revolution will result in the triumph of "consciousness," but the form of "consciousness" will then be such that it will no longer be in opposition to "spontaneity"; there will no longer be conflict between the natural responses of the people and the best interests of society. In other words, the end synthesis will resolve the age-old conflict between the individual and society.

The task of literature as generator of official myths is to provide object lessons in the working-out of the spontaneity / consciousness dialectic. As is generally true of ritual forms, the master plot personalizes the general processes outlined in Marxist-Leninist historiography by encoding them in biographical terms: the positive hero passes in stages from a state of relative "spontaneity" to a higher degree of "consciousness," which he attains by some individual revolution.

It has been possible to allegorize the spontaneity / consciousness dialectic because of the range of meanings these two terms can encompass. In the narrower context of the individual human being, as distinct from society at large, "consciousness" means political awareness and the complete self-control that enables the individual to be guided in all his actions by his awareness, whereas "spontaneity" refers to purely visceral, willful, anarchic, or self-centered actions. The great historical drama of struggle between the forces of spontaneity and the forces of consciousness is unfolded in a tale of the way one individual mastered his willful self, became disciplined, and attained to an extrapersonal identity. Thus, if you discount such trappings as the factory or kolkhoz setting and the Party meeting, the Socialist Realist novel might in effect be seen as a politicized variant of the *Bildungsroman,* in which the hero achieves greater harmony both within himself and in relation to his society. Such a comparison cannot be taken very far, however, because the Socialist Realist novel is so highly ritualized that the hero's progress is neither individual nor self-valuable.

Why did the Socialist Realist novel end up with the spontaneity / consciousness dialectic as its underlying subject rather than the class struggle? This outcome can scarcely be described as having been sought "consciously" (rather than arising "spontaneously"), yet it was far from random or arbitrary. The answer to this question—an answer that is actually twofold—explains why the Soviet novel is a key document in Soviet cultural history.

In the first place, the spontaneity / consciousness dialectic is itself not an innocent doctrine, for it has always been at the center of the main controversies within Russian Marxism. Initially, when the first Russian Marxist groups were formed in the 1890s, the debate centered around what is often described as the voluntarist / determinist controversy, that is, briefly stated, the question whether history is made by the conscious efforts of people, or whether historical change occurs of its own accord ("spontaneously") as a result of changes in such extrahuman factors as, for instance, the means of production.

In classical Marxism the voluntarist / determinist dichotomy was already problematical. In general, however, the Marxist sense of history favored the notion that historical change occurred as the result of vast, transpersonal forces rather than by the action of "self-consciousness," "spirit," or outstanding figures. In his accounts of history Marx emphasized the determining role of transpersonal material forces. Nevertheless, he did allow for some interaction—for the notion that not only do "circumstances make men" but that "men [also] make circumstances."[9]

For the Russian Marxists this question was more than a purely speculative one. It was central to the major issues of political practice. This was because Marx's observations were based on the relatively advanced industrial society of western Europe, where the notion of a "proletarian" revolution seemed more plausible. But Russia had not yet evolved to a point where it met the Marxist preconditions for a communist revolution. The country was at least four-fifths peasant, and even the relatively small working class comprised largely persons of recent peasant origins. The educational level of both workers and peasants was poor; indeed, most were illiterate. In short, it was unlikely for a significant segment of the population to have revolutionary consciousness. Some Russian Marxists argued that a revolution would therefore have to wait until the proletariat was larger and more developed; others believed that there could be a shortcut to the revolution by raising worker consciousness and by other deliberate actions.

This debate came to a head in 1903, when Lenin's treatise *What Is to Be Done?* (1902) split the Social Democratic (Marxist) Party into the Bolshevik (Leninist) and Menshevik factions. In this treatise Lenin introduced his highly controversial departure from the original Marxist theory (or addition to it, depending on one's point of view): the doctrine of the "vanguard." Lenin contended that it was possible to get around the various ways in which contemporary Russia did not meet the canonical Marxist preconditions for communist revolution by forming a "vanguard of the proletariat," comprising a small group of highly "conscious," disciplined, and dedicated revolutionaries who would guide the less "conscious" masses first to greater "consciousness" and then to revolution. The division in the Russian Marxist movement over these issues became exacerbated once again in 1917, when Lenin returned from exile after the initial (February) revolution and declared, in his April Theses, that this first, "bourgeois," revolution should be pushed further into a communist revolution. Many opposed this view, including prominent Bolsheviks, because they felt Lenin was being too rash and impatient.

It might be expected that the success of the October Revolution would have put an end to this controversy. This was far from the case, however, and Soviet Russians are still debating whether the revolution was premature and whether history can be "made" to any significant degree. Moreover, once the revolution had occurred, the continued reliance on the "vanguard" as an agent of control, in the sense of a centralized controlling elite, made it difficult to reconcile Soviet practice with that central Marxist doctrine, the "withering away of the state." Lenin himself believed that, once the revolution had occurred and the masses had become even more "conscious" in the postrevolutionary environment, the need for the "vanguard" as an agent of control, discipline, and enlightenment would end. The vanguard and the apparatus of state control (police and the like) would then progressively "wither away" as, Marx had stipulated, they should in a "classless" society.

Perhaps "circumstances" were against them, but the Bolsheviks fell somewhat short of realizing this prediction. In the early post-revolutionary years, various internal and external threats to Bol-shevik hegemony (such as the Civil War and the Allied intervention) made it necessary for them to build up the institutions of state control rather more than they had envisioned. Later, under Stalin, there was less external threat (except during World War II) and, arguably, less internal threat as well; yet under him the state ap-paratus became larger and more powerful than before. Although public controversy over political questions was virtually impossible in those years, it is clear that the state's resistance to its scheduled "withering away" troubled even the leadership. One symptom of their discomfiture is the fact that in the thirties almost every issue of the Party's bimonthly theoretical organ, *Bolshevik,* contained an article that directly or indirectly tackled the questions of why the state had not begun to "wither away" and when it might be ex-pected to do so.

Since the Bolsheviks were always more exercised by polemics with their detractors in the left-wing movement than they were by right-wing adversaries, it is not surprising that, instead of providing edifying tales about the class struggle, official Soviet literature gen-erated myths for rationalizing the Bolshevik position in the peren-nial radical controversy over the roles of consciousness and spon-taneity in history. Indeed, literature's de facto role as apologist increased over time. The Socialist Realist tradition began with par-ables (such as *Mother*) illustrating the workings of the spontaneity / consciousness dialectic, but, under Stalin, extra conventions were added to the master plot so that it also affirmed symbolically that the progress to communism was specifically assured under the pres-ent Soviet leadership.

While all this is true, it represents a somewhat limited explana-tion of the master plot's role in Soviet society. The role of the spontaneity / consciousness opposition as *the* subtext of Socialist Realism must not be viewed solely in the context of Russian Marx-ist controversies and the machinations of the Leninists or the Stalinists. Literature is not merely the handmaiden of politics, not even in times of severe repression. Moreover, the Party did not have a fixed interpretation of the dialectic to impose on literature, even if it were possible to impose one.

If one follows Bolshevik discussions of the spontaneity/consciousness dialectic over time, one will be struck by three features: ambivalence, controversy, and polysemy. I would suggest that this semantic diffuseness results from the fact that the spontaneity/consciousness opposition is broader in resonance than its place in Marxist-Leninist doctrine would imply. It is one of the key binary oppositions in Russian culture, comparable to, for instance, the ideal/real oppostion in Scholasticism or the subject/object distinction in nineteenth-century German thought.

The spontaneity/consciousness dichotomy was particularly well adapted to the ritual needs of the entire country. It is perhaps no accident that its scheme for historical progress is very like the Hegelian model for the working-out of *Geist* in history (Hegel had a profound influence on the Russian intelligentsia during its formative period in the mid-nineteenth century). More important, the opposition provides master tropes that focus major cultural energies and order the key dilemmas of the Russian intelligensia. The dialectic is a natively Russian version of the dynamic known to Western thinking as the nature/culture opposition, which has attracted a great deal of attention among contemporary anthropologists. We can detect Russia's root ambivalence on modernization lurking behind the various controversies concerning the Leninist model of historical progress. The spontaneity/consciousness oppostion was, in effect, an efficient formula for transcoding German Marxism into Russian culture.

The Leninist version of historical development did not differ from Marx merely in degree—by a change of emphasis, let us say, from Marx's view of historical change as effected 90 percent by necessity and 10 percent by deliberate actions, to ascribing the giant's share of the influence to the forces of "consciousness" (i.e., the vanguard). A more fundamental change had occurred.

The Russian Marxists began by adopting a *German* ideology to solve *Russia's* chronic social dilemmas (such as poverty, autocracy, and inequality). This ideology, once transplanted in Russian soil, became "russified." Marxism was an ideology that came out of an advanced industrial society. It was to be applied in a backward,

peasant society with very different political and intellectual conditions. Inevitably, Russia's culture colored its version of Marxist
ideology; as a result, it became less and less a western European
political program and more and more the ideology characterizing a
certain branch of the Russian radical intelligentsia.

A surface indicator of the differences between the two views is
the change in terminology. In classical Marxism the spontaneity /
consciousness opposition does not exist *as such*. Marx did describe
an analogous model for historical development, but he discussed it
in terms of the dialectic between "freedom," where men rationally
regulate their interchange with Nature, and "necessity," i.e., the
circumstances that effect historical development.[10] Marx also gave
a central place in his theories to the concept of "consciousness"
(*Bewusstsein*); but, though the concept "spontaneity" can be found
in Marxist writings (as *"Spontanität"*), it is much less central than
"consciousness" and is certainly not its explicit opposite.

When the Russian Marxists of the 1890s and the early twentieth
century argued about the way forward for Russia, their debates
centered not around the roles of "freedom" and "necessity" but on
"consciousness" and "spontaneity," which, in Lenin's *What Is to
Be Done?* (1902), became the two poles of the primary dialectic of
historical development. Moreover, whereas "consciousness" and
"spontaneity" in classical Marxism were relatively technical terms
(this is less so for "consciousness," *Bewusstsein*, which had Enlightenment connotations), the two words the Russian Marxist
chose for rendering these concepts both had connotations that
identified the terms with ongoing preoccupations of the Russian
intelligentsia.[11] The word chosen for "consciousness," for instance,
soznatel'nost', has the coloration of something inspired by one's
conscience and could hence be associated with the intelligentsia's
tradition of assuming the role of Russian society's conscience.

The most striking instance of transcoding is the word chosen
for "spontaneity," *stixijnost'*, which carries with it a vast range of
connotations—both positive and negative—all of which were central to the existential dilemmas of the Russian intelligentsia. The
root of *stixijnost'*, *stixija*, means "element" (as in "elemental"); the
word can thus be used both in expressions like "in his element,"
with positive valorization, and to mean wild, uncontrollable
"forces" (such as storms in nature and human rage). Thus it can

mean both what is natural and good, as distinct from something artificial, alien, or constricting, or, alternatively, it can connote what is wrong with what are termed the "blind forces of nature"; it can connote things that are out of control and even menacing. When the word *stixijnost'* was placed together with *soznatel'nost'* in a binary opposition, that opposition potentially embraced all the most obsessive dilemmas confronting the Russian intelligentsia. This was in large measure because of the rich and even contradictory associations that the word *stixijnost'* conjured up for them, associations that were all germane to its existential concerns. The oppostion suggests, for instance, that much-celebrated gulf in Russia between the vast, uneducated peasant masses (the "spontaneous") and the educated elite (the "conscious") or, to put it slightly differently, between backward rural Russia (the realm of "spontaneity") and modern urban Russia (the realm of "consciousness"), or, again, between those seething masses, capable of spontaneous popular uprisings, and the autocratic, heavily bureaucratized, and hierarchical state, which seeks to control these masses and direct them.

The spontaneity / consciousness opposition can also be seen as a schematization of some aspects of the old Slavophile versus Westerner controversy, i.e., the question whether the way forward for Russia could be found in Western models and ideas, in bringing reason, organization, order, and technology to this backward, anarchic country, or whether Western civilization was sterile and spiritually impoverished as compared with the native Russian or Slavic ethos, which was antirational, spontaneous, instinctive, perhaps even antiurban and against state order. Many favored a return to the social order of traditional peasant Russia, based on the village commune or *mir;* others developed a cult of the folk rebel or *buntar'.* The latter maintained that the dry theorizing of the intellectuals was sterile and that the most potent and effective forces for bringing about positive change in Russia were contained in those broad, illiterate peasant masses (the "spontaneous"), who had not been corrupted by Westernized education or by working for the autocratic state and could therefore express that pure, gut "rage" of the Russians against the defilement of their land by alien forces. For every intellectual who favored a "folk" remedy for Russia's dilemmas (whether in the folk rebel or in the traditional way of life) there was another who saw the way forward in terms of making those "spontaneous" masses more "conscious," in bringing enlightenment and culture to the darkness of the ignorant and wretched peasants.

Lenin himself was strongly on the side of "consciousness" in the sense of favoring reason, order, control, technology, and guidance and enlightenment for the masses. His rhetoric is full of imagery about bringing "light" to the "darkness" of the Russian people. Lenin's wife, Krupskaya, was to make her major contribution to the Soviet cause by dedicating herself to the literacy campaign and other programs for raising the cultural and educational level of the masses.

And yet, although Lenin favored "consciousness" over "spontaneity," he, like the intelligentsia class from which he came, was himself ambivalent about "spontaneity" and its role in history. Although "spontaneous" elements could, in his analysis, indeed be retrograde and dangerous if left unchecked or unguided, he did not see "spontaneity" as an essentially negative category. In *What Is to Be Done?* he maintained that, even in its most primitive expressions, "spontaneity" contains a sort of "embryonic" potential for "consciousness."[12] Moreover, being a shrewd tactician, Lenin was able to recognize the crucial role the peasantry would play in any Russian revolution; one therefore periodically finds in his speeches extremely flattering references to that "spontaneous" element.[13]

This equivocation did not end with Lenin, for it has continued in official rhetoric down to the present day. The terms "spontaneity" and "consciousness" and the meaning of their dialectic have been differently interpreted with each major change in political culture.

Thus the spontaneity / consciousness opposition is, on the one hand, a defining tenet of Leninism and the locus of the greatest controversies about how to put theory into practice. On the other hand, it catches some of the Russian intelligentsia's obsessive dilemmas. Indeed, Leninism, being itself in large measure a Russian ideology, also reflects the intelligentsia's own ambivalences.

This pattern of complexity is ramified when one looks at the role the spontaneity / consciousness dialectic plays in the Socialist Realist novel, i.e., as the shaping force behind the master plot. There it certainly serves the Party's interests by turning novels into ideological parables and, very often as well, into myths of maintenance for the status quo. Yet, paradoxically, it also provides some sort of medium, however reduced, for discussion and even for self-expression. The richly evocative terms "spontaneity" and "consciousness" not only provided an umbrella under which that eternal debate about Russia's way forward could continue; they also reverberated with some pervasive themes of Russian literature itself. These include such unlikely views—for Soviet literature—as the one commonly found in nineteenth-century literature, that surface reality is a mere semblance, a veneer; the notion that the underlying reality is in the grip of dark, elemental forces; and that cult of libidinous expression that one can find in literature from at least Appollon Grigoriev through Dostoevsky, Blok, and Bely, and on, even past the Revolution, into Scythianism. Although such views could of course never become actual themes of Socialist Realism, they often colored the symbols conventionally used for translating the spontaneity/consciousness opposition into novel form.

Thus, by studying the changing contours of the master plot and the complexity of forces that interact with it, this book will follow the broad patterns of Soviet culture through several transitions. Moreover, it will follow not only official culture but also, to a lesser extent, the dissident Russian voices that are in dialogue with it. In the finite context of the master plot, with its ideological underpinnings, the book will chart the vagaries of the dialectic between sign and meaning and the dialectic between what is intrinsic to literature and what is extrinsic to it. In this way it will provide a dynamic model of cultural change in the Soviet period.

I

Socialist Realism
before 1932

1

What Socialist Realism Is and What Led to Its Adoption as the Official Method of Soviet Literature

Socialist Realism *as such* did not exist until the Revolution was at least fifteen years old, for the term was not presented to the Soviet public until 1932. The first record of its use is in a speech made by Gronsky, the president of the Organization Committee of the newly founded Writers' Union, on May 17, 1932.[1]

The theory of Socialist Realism was not formulated until after the term had been coined. Gorky (the First Secretary of the Writers' Union) and other authoritative literary figures began to clarify the term in articles and speeches in 1932–34, and the first plenum of the Organizational Committee, in October, 1932, was devoted to that topic; but it was not until 1934, when the First Writers' Union Congress was held, that Socialist Realism acquired a canonical formulation. Ever since then, *the* official sources of the doctrine have been Lenin's 1905 article "Party Organization and Party Literature" (*locus classicus* for the doctrine of mandatory "party-mindedness"), Gorky's articles in his book *On Literature*, published in 1933 (and in later redactions of the same book), and the speeches made to the congress itself by Gorky and A. A. Zhdanov (chief representative of the Party's Central Committee).

Yet the consensus of Soviet literary history is that Socialist Realism was the dominant method (or theory) of Soviet literature *before* the term was ever invented. The second volume of the *Academy History of Soviet Russian Literature* of 1967 states: "By the thirties . . . the time socialist realism [was] given a theoretical formulation, in practice it was already the main method of Soviet literature. It arose naturally in the process of the development of literature."[2] Such authoritative sources also cite as evidence that Socialist Realism had evolved before 1932 such pre-nineteen-thirties novels as Gorky's *Mother* and *Klim Samgin*, D. Furmanov's *Chapaev*, A. Serafimovich's *The Iron Flood*, A. Fadeev's *The Rout*, F. Gladkov's *Cement*, and A. Tolstoy's *Road to Calvary*.

This list of official precursors is the pride and joy of official histories, where it is not merely quoted as a list of generative exemplars, but where the paradigms are given their own genealogy. The Social Realist tradition developed, as it were, not just "naturally," as the Academy history suggests, but even familially. Not only do the histories draw up a line of succession for the masterpieces; they give one for the positive heroes and even for the authors themselves. Just as histories claim that book *A* was modeled on book *B*, which was in turn modeled on book *C*, they also suggest that Pavel Vlasov (of *Mother*) begat Gleb Chumalov (of *Cement*), who begat Pavel Korchagin (of Ostrovsky's early thirties' classic, *How the Steel Was Tempered*), who begat Oleg Koshevoy (Fadeev's *The Young Guard*, a novel of the forties), who....[3] Historians also insist that virtually every author of a Socialist Realist classic learned from some earlier master in the putative line. Above all, each author of a Socialist Realist classic is represented as some sort of apprentice at the feet of the original master, Gorky, who in turn is said to have consulted Lenin while writing *Mother* and also to have benefited from the ideas Lenin expressed in "Party Organization and Party Literature."

What a tidy scenario! But it does not correspond very well to historical reality. Most of the authors involved were locked in bitter rivalries in both theory and practice. Even the classical master and apprentice team of the Soviet literary histories, Gorky and Gladkov, were neither as close nor as enthusiastic about each other's Socialist Realist classics as was later claimed. If Gladkov learned from Gorky, then it does not seem likely that *Mother* would have been the text he studied; for Gladkov said at one point that *Mother* was so "utilitarian and pedestrian" that he could not finish reading it. Moreover, his was far from a lone voice; for, until 1928 (when Gorky began his series of triumphal, officially sponsored return trips to the Soviet Union), most Party, proletarian, fellow-traveler, and *avant-garde* critics—in short, most critics and writers—expressed serious reservations about *Mother*. Even Gorky was not enthusiastic about the novel, which he described as a purely propagandistic piece, written in a moment of spleen.[4]

The claim that this list represents a single tradition is more valid if one resists all temptations to tell it as a tale of luminous masters and inspired apprentices. Soviet authors are auxiliaries to the

Socialist Realist tradition; their particular antipathies, allegiances, and even their aesthetic views do not have any necessary bearing on a given Socialist Realist novel. The most dramatic case is Gorky, who did not really like *Mother* but was prepared to assume the role of head of a literature that used *Mother* as its emblem.

The procrustean bed of Socialist Realism can accommodate strange bedfellows, but only if viewed *ex post facto*. The process by which the many and disparate became the one is important for understanding not only the evolution of Socialist Realism but its very nature.

Some light can be thrown on this dynamic by drawing an analogy with some observations made by Jorge Luis Borges in an essay he published in 1951, "Kafka and His Precursors." Borges contends that Kafka had as precursors authors and texts from a wide range of periods and traditions, including Zeno, a Chinese author of the ninth century, and a poem by Browning. He concludes:

> Kafka's idiosyncrasy, in greater or lesser degree, is present in each of these writings, but if Kafka had not written we would not perceive it; that is to say, it would not exist. The poem "Fears and Scruples" by Robert Browning is like a prophesy of Kafka's stories, but our reading of Kafka refines and changes our reading of the poem. Browning did not read it as we read it now . . . each writer *creates* his precursors. His work modifies our conception of the past, as it will modify the future.[5]

Similarly, if Socialist Realism had not been created in the early thirties, many of the official paradigms from the twenties would always have been seen as representing rival modes of writing. Just as Borges sees the later works of Kafka as having more in common with their "precursors" than with those of the early Kafka, so the Socialist Realist novels V. Kaverin wrote in the thirties and forties (*The Two Captains* and *The Open Book*) have in many crucial respects more in common with, say, Gladkov's *Cement* of 1925 than with Kaverin's own novels of the twenties, written to oppose "proletarian" literature (*The Troublemaker* and *Artist Unknown*).

Once the tradition of the Socialist Realist novel was "created" in the thirties, then, to use Borges' terms, it could be "perceived" in the official precursors because the tradition *was* these works. Yet, after Socialist Realism was "created," these exemplars became

other than they had been when they were written. *Mother* of 1906
is not *Mother* of 1936; *Chapaev* of 1923 is not *Chapaev* of 1933.
And so on. Even though almost every one of their authors aspired
to write a Socialist Realist classic, in the sense that he wanted to
write a novel that would be a model for writers committed to the
Bolshevik cause, the specifically Socialist Realist quality of each
novel was not created until 1932 or so. In each novel there is much
the author intended to be an important contribution to the quest for
a kind of writing adequate to the new age, but the "contribution"
was never adopted for Socialist Realism. When these novels were
pronounced exemplars, the number of possible features a model
Soviet novel might have became more finite, and in each novel those
aspects not envisaged in the canon became incidental, not germane
to its quality of being Socialist Realist.

One has to recognize the dual identity of each exemplar written
before Socialist Realism was officially established. They are both
precursors and exemplars. Fadeev's *The Rout* as precursor is not
the same as *The Rout* as exemplar. One sees this distinction in V.
Kirpotin's remarks in his official speech to the first Writers' Union
plenum of October, 1932. Kirpotin suggested that *The Rout*'s hero,
Levinson, though a good model for the positive hero, is depicted
with too much exploration of the inner man and his doubts.[6] Thus,
in *The Rout* as exemplar, these aspects are nonaspects (by analogy
with "nonpersons"). In this way, novels that seem to have been
plucked from different literary orientations acquired affinity.

As the term "nonaspects" suggests, politics were of course important in this process. In Soviet literature in the early thirties there
occurred a major political-cum-institutional-cum-theoretical upheaval (analogous upheavals occurred in most other areas of intellectual life): a *single*, centralized writers' organization was
formed (the Writers' Union) to which all writers were obliged to
belong; literature was required to be responsive to the Soviet political platform and policies; and a single doctrine or method for the
making of literature (Socialist Realism) was mandated to all writers. This development has to be compared with the process known
as *Gleichschaltung,* or homogenization, to which culture is said
to be subject in totalitarian societies. It is from this aspect that
Western commentary has tended to view the evolution of Socialist Realism.

If Soviet historians have suggested that their Socialist Realist

tradition developed "naturally," most Western commentators, by
contrast, have contended that its dominance in literature has been
an *unnatural* state of affairs. They suggest that it was only by
tampering with literature's "natural" development that the Party
could impose Socialist Realism on Soviet literature: by interference
(such as the 1932 decree abolishing all independent writers' organizations), by political pressures that intensified over the thirties to
the point where only the few could resist them, and by material and
other positive incentives.

It was in the cards that, sooner or later, Soviet literature would
become centrally organized and controlled. But, as Sinyavsky pointed
out in "On Socialist Realism," there is no necessary connection
between restrictive and normative controls in literature and poor or
even uninspired creative work.[7] What is most interesting about
what happened between 1932 and 1934 is not *that* there was a sort
of *Gleichschaltung,* but *what* was *gleichgeschaltet* and *how* and
why? Why was the particular type of writing permitted by the state
so narrow and restrictive in literary—as distinct from ideological—terms, and why was that particular type chosen and not
one of the other varieties of writing proposed from the platform
by loyalist and zealous groups?

If one looks at these questions from the standpoint of the twenties themselves, one will find the outcome much more difficult to
predict than has since been supposed. The literary world was very
complex, new alliances and antagonisms were constantly being
formed, and the fortunes of the various literary groups and writers
were subject to some surprising reversals. Even the Party was very
divided on literary questions.[8]

Until approximately 1927, the Soviet literary scene was *rea-
sonably* fluid, and the outcome of the various literary struggles was
by no means assured. By the end of 1927 the literary world had begun
to change rapidly. In that year Stalin consolidated his power and
launched the "cultural revolution" and the First Five-Year Plan.
"Proletarianization" of the professional classes and cultural institutions became official policy, and this made the status of
fellow-traveler literature problematical, the more so as Trotsky (a
cultural liberal) had lost his power struggle with Stalin in the previous year. From then until 1932 the literary battles became progressively dirtier and more dire in their consequences for the losers. And
RAPP (the most powerful and militant group in this "proletarian"

literature) became a sort of monster that seemed to be swallowing the small independent writers' organizations one by one.[9] In short, the situation became less open-ended. From 1927 on, the possibility that Soviet literature would have a wide range of literary schools or would opt for experimental, *avant-garde* writing became palpably weaker with each day. Elsewhere I have described how the reorganization of literature between 1932 and 1934 initially brought greater literary independence for the writer and more regard for literary quality.[10] Nevertheless, this ebbing of the 1928–32 tide of "proletarianization" did not bring Soviet literature back to the point where it was in 1927, for literature was now more closely controlled, and a narrower range of literary approaches was allowed.

One should not assume that this outcome was inevitable or that Socialist Realism was the only type of literature that could have been mandated to the writer. The history of Soviet literature from 1917 to 1932 raises a whole series of questions of the type Trotsky himself raised in his history of the Revolution, a series of What-ifs?: "What if Lenin had not died in 1924?"; "What if Trotsky had not lost the power struggle which brought Stalin to power"; "What if . . .," "if . . . ?"

A final What-if? might be "What if RAPP had not been disbanded in 1932 but had been given monopoly control over Soviet literature, as seemed about to happen as late as 1931?"[11] The major consequences would have shown themselves not merely in the high-handed, overbearing type of administration the RAPP leadership might have been expected to set up, judging from its performance to date (they might well have calmed down, once in power), but also in the type of literature mandated to the Soviet writer. With the demise of RAPP came the demise, or partial demise, of its particular brand of literature, "proletarian realism." Ironically, since RAPP's recipe for literature called for large dollops of verisimilitude and psychological portraiture but cautioned against exaggerating heroism, many Western critics would have found it preferable to Socialist Realism, even though RAPP's politics and tactics were decidedly unacceptable to them.

The upheavals in Soviet literature between 1932 and 1934 did not mean just the end of RAPP. Actually, one of RAPP's leaders, Alexander Fadeev, went on to hold an official position in the newly formed Writers' Union and ultimately assumed Gorky's old post as first secretary between 1939 and 1954. Moreover, RAPP did have some impact on Socialist Realism. Two RAPP novels, Fadeev's *The Rout* and Furmanov's *Chapaev*, figure on that short post-1932 list of canonical exemplars. Zhdanov in his official address to the First Writers' Congress in 1934 said most explicitly that Socialist Realism represented a fusion (or compromise?) between (RAPP's) proletarian realism and the rival proletarian literary theory, revolutionary romanticism. But it would be wrong to focus our attention here on the extent of RAPP's defeat.

What really happened in 1932 was not that RAPP, the player who up to that point seemed to be winning the game of Soviet literature, suddenly lost, but rather that another player entered the game, the pieces were swept off the board, and a new game was begun. In 1931 Maxim Gorky returned to the Soviet Union from exile (having been courted to do so for years). Inasmuch as Gorky was made titular head of Soviet literature—first secretary of the Writers' Union—it could be said that, when RAPP was disbanded in 1932 and the Writers' Union was formed, Gorky had the board cleared for him. (Incidentally, I refer here to the role Gorky played in literature rather than to what he himself actually did. It is difficult to ascertain what policies can be ascribed to the historical figure Gorky as opposed to the institution of "Gorky" as head of Soviet literature, although there seems to have been considerable overlap in the first few years.) Our final What-if? might therefore be "What if Gorky had not returned to the S.U. and had the board cleared for him in 1932?"

Although the analogy with a chess game is purely figurative, it is useful because it provides for the fact that the game itself was new although played with a selection of the old pieces. Strictly speaking, the only thing that was absolutely new about Socialist Realism was the term itself. Even this had numerous precedents. In the twenties most literary groups and several individuals tried to coin a name for the type of literature they wanted to see in the new society, and several of them were rather similar to Socialist Realism (e.g., "sociorealistic literature" and "communist realism").[12]

Socialist Realism was put together with pieces from several existing platforms for Soviet literature, primarily from RAPP's "proletarian realism" and a rival "proletarian" theory, "revolutionary romanticism," itself somewhat analogous to platforms put forward by A. Tolstoy, Lunacharsky, and Gorky himself. The result

of this assemblage can be seen in the Zhdanov capsule formula for
Socialist Realism: "a combination of the most matter-of-fact,
everyday reality with the most heroic prospects."[13] The RAPP concern for verisimilitude was to be combined with the belief of those
who championed revolutionary romanticism (and also the belief of
Gorky and others) that the writer should "anticipate the future
shape of man" and "heroize," "monumentalize," "romanticize," or
"exaggerate" him.

In practice, the balance was actually tilted in favor of revolutionary romanticism, with its exaggeration and grand scale, and
away from verisimilitude. This may have been because Gorky, who
was playing from strength, came to the table already an advocate of
exalting the heroic in fiction. It could be surmised that Stalin, who
liked Gladkov's revolutionary romantic works and seems to have
had a passion for heroes in general, favored that orientation, too.
However, this sort of speculation could go on forever, and the
results would never be very conclusive.

For one who is seeking causes for the shift in the dominant Soviet
literary mode from proletarian realism's lust for verisimilitude to
"romanticization" and exaggeration, it is best to look not in the
narrow context of literary politics but at Soviet society as a whole.
It seems to have been true that those who presided over Soviet
literature from 1932 to 1934, and even Stalin himself, favored a
very specific kind of writing, which they called "Socialist Realism,"
and also that they had the political power to legislate their norms.
But it is also true that much the same political situation had obtained during the previous three years, 1928–31 (in fact, some
would say that writers were *more* coerced during those years), and
yet the type of writing favored then was in many respects diametrically opposed to Socialist Realism: it was antiheroic and
mired in facts and statistics.[14] This literary orientation reflected the
cultural values of what was a starkly "proletarian" and positivist
age. But, from 1931 on, most of the values of the First Five-Year
Plan were debunked. The shift in literature legislated in 1932—a
shift from emphasis on the "real" to emphasis on the "heroic," not
to say the mythic—represents a systematization of major cultural
changes that encompassed literature as well. Politics were a major
factor in the institution of Socialist Realism, but they cannot provide a sufficient answer to the question posed earlier: Why was

that particular type [of literature] chosen, and not any of the other varieties of writing proposed from the platform by loyalist and zealous groups?

This 1931 shift in cultural values will be charted in Part Two. My concern in this and the next two chapters will be the prehistory of those individual "pieces," or official paradigms, that were put together in 1932–34. These pieces provided a sort of do-it-yourself kit for the aspiring Socialist Realist writer, who was encouraged to glue elements of one novel to elements of another, shape them with his own topic, and—abracadabra!—a new Socialist Realist novel would appear. As early as 1932, writers were instructed in how to construct one: the official exemplars were set out in special leaflets, which were circulated to members of the newly formed Writers' Union; authors of novels deemed outstanding were sent on lecture tours to the provinces to tell others how they wrote; authoritative speakers cited good and bad examples of writing in their speeches to writers; and so on.[15]

The list of exemplars mandated to writers in these various ways was, then, made up of an unlikely combination of works representing different literary orientations and written by writers most of whom would not, at the time they were written, have countenanced any suggestion that their writing had much affinity with many of the other official models of Socialist Realism. Lumping these disparate works together seems almost like a bad joke, the more so when we remember that the theory or method behind the list of exemplars, Socialist Realism, involves combining what hitherto seemed uncombinable: verisimilitude and mythicization. Yet one should not go to the extreme of assuming that the list itself was random or that it comprised merely the preferences of Gorky, Stalin, or some other influential figure or body; for among these pre-thirties classics of Socialist Realism that do not strike one as being remarkably similar there are coherences that tell us a great deal about the nature and function of Socialist Realism: about *why* those particular texts were chosen as models and about *how* the many and disparate were homogenized into the one. Let us look first for an answer to the questions How does Socialist Realism combine the seemingly uncombinable? and How do Soviet novelists manage to use "realism" in what is essentially a rhetorical rather than a fictive narrative? This is a defining paradox of the Socialist

Realist novel, a paradox that raises questions about the representation in utopian or partisan fiction (which is, after all, what Socialist Realism is).

The Socialist Realist Novel: A Case of Modal Schizophrenia

Most critics maintain that there is something wrong with the Soviet novel, not just in its informing ideology, but actually as literature. They charge that its characters are stilted and one-dimensional, its plots unconvincing, and the overall effect vulgarized, clichéd, and confused. In short, it is the sort of kitsch that you would not read even if you were stranded for twenty-four hours at an airport and nothing else was available.

Whatever the specific criticisms, sooner or later most detractors will describe the Soviet novel as a hodgepodge, riddled with incongruities and, above all, plagued by disastrous generic incompatibility. The Soviet novel's incongruities might be ascribed to the excessive ambition of those responsible for formulating Socialist Realism between 1932 and 1934. The leadership of that time wanted to generate a new literature to match in significance the place they believed Marxism-Leninism occupied in the evolution of human thought. All previous world systems had produced a great literature, and it was time to show the world what Soviet communism could do.

The Soviet novel was to be a sort of eclectic *summa* of all great literature (this is clear from the examples cited as models in official speeches of this period). The only kinds of writing to be specifically excluded were so-called formalist writing (e.g., parody, experimentalism, and varieties born of literary self-consciousness), decadent or erotic writing, "pessimistic" literature, and writing colored by the values of rival world systems, such as Christianity.

Yet the official formulators of Socialist Realism, Gorky especially, also wanted to create a great, universal, and *simple* form. This, of course, had been Tolstoy's dream before them; in many of his aesthetic tracts and in his later writings he tried to call an end to the self-indulgent verbosity of modern literature, to rise above all that into a literature of essential essences, accessible to all.

Into this great, universal, and simple form the novelists were to pour elements from many different literary genres, plus a good deal of semijournalistic and public relations material. In consequence, we find in most conventional texts a form that is at once simple and complex. By this I do not mean that the Soviet novel is the product of a sort of juggling act—of trying to fit as many substructures as possible under the one simple overarching structure, for "simple" does not refer merely to the number of plots, subplots, protagonists, etc. Those who founded Socialist Realism envisaged a literature somewhat like that of premodern society. They believed that their proselytizing aims would best be served in "simple forms" like the parable and the tale. In the modern day it is of course very difficult to achieve the purity of such simple forms; the effort to do so produced much of the incongruity seized upon by critics.

In most Soviet novels one finds a whole series of seemingly contradictory general features. To name a few: the novel is traditional / it is modern; its structure is simple / it is complex; its characters are individuals and are given psychological portraits / they are depersonalized or barely disguised sociological-ideological categories, or they are emblematically virtuous.

One can reduce most of these oppositions to a single dichotomy and characterize the novel's "fatal split" in terms of mode: the novel depicts "what is" (i.e., it uses the realist mode) / the novel depicts "what ought to be" (i.e., it idealizes reality, the utopian or mythic mode).[16]

This particular dichotomy is not some misguided trend that emerged in the course of literary practice; it was actually built into the definition of what was to be distinctive in Soviet Socialist Realism. It is especially apparent in the instructions Zhdanov gave writers in 1934 (to show "a combination of the most matter-of-fact, everyday reality, and the most heroic prospects").

Here we are at the heart of what most critics find difficult to stomach in the Soviet novel: not its mongrel pedigree, its datedness, and all that kitsch, but its modal schizophrenia, its proclivity for making sudden, unmotivated transitions from realistic discourse to the mythic or utopian. Most critics want a given novel to opt for one mode or the other; they want the Soviet novelist to remove from his text *either* "what is" *or* "what ought to be."[17]

Two modern theorists of the novel who were close to the Soviet experience, Bakhtin and Lukacs, have provided a framework for pursuing this paradox further. Both have shown that "what is" and "what ought to be" represent two irreconcilable stages of cultural development and that these stages are in turn characterized by two different text types, the epic and the novel. I shall draw my examples here from Bakhtin.

In his essay "Epic and Novel," Bakhtin, in describing these two forms, says that they are not merely two different genres with their own formal characteristics; they are expressions of two diametrically opposed senses of reality. The epic, he says, depicts a completed, perfected world, one that is separated from the world of the author and his audience by a so-called absolute epic past, which is unbridgeable. By the world of an "absolute epic past" Bakhtin does not mean merely a past age, for its actual location in time is not as important as the valorization of it, its closedness and "perfectedness." The epic is told as legend; it is sacred and incontrovertible. Thus "epic," in the sense that Bakhtin uses it, bears comparison with one half of the Soviet novel's fatal split: depicting what "ought to be." This entails showing "future prospects," whereas the epic normally describes the past; but the two are still comparable because they share the crucial characteristics of closedness and "perfectedness." "What ought to be" is legend-like in that it is told as history; it is also incontrovertible and "sacred" (partyminded).

Bakhtin sees the novel, by contrast, as the genre of an imperfect, incomplete world. It is constantly generating new forms and, unlike other major genres, cannot be pinned down to any set of formal characteristics (in other words, it is formally as incomplete as the world it depicts). There are, however, defining features of the novel, and these flow from the fact that it stands for the opposite of the epic's closedness and "perfectedness." Whereas in the epic the inner selves of characters are in complete harmony with their outer selves and social roles—there is no interiority and no complex point of view—in the novel a crucial feature is the multiple possibilities for both point of view and for discrepancy between the inner and outer selves of characters, between their capacities and their lot in life, and so on.

Bakhtin actually sees the rise of the novel as a product of the breakdown of the epic world view, which came about when writers began to parody and mock the styles, heroes, and world view of the

old forms. It was this intrusion into the closed epic world that led to
the disintegration of the holistic world view, brought about the
disjunction between the inner and outer man. The genre thus
generated—the novel (or rather the new sensibility, novel-ness)—is
therefore, by its very nature, forever iconoclastic, forever questing.

These ideas of Bakhtin's can provide us with a theoretical
framework for diagnosing the Soviet novel's modal schizophrenia.
Its juxtaposition of "what is" and "what ought to be" represents
the combining of two diametrically opposed time-value systems.
This, in Bakhtin's view, is impossible, because to create any kind of
bridge over the gulf between the epic past and the present is to
destroy the essence of the genre.[18]

But we can go beyond this. What sets the Soviet novel apart from
most other serious modern novels is the absence in it of those
features that can be seen as exploration or celebration of the
objective/subjective split: parody, irony, literary self-consciousness, and creative or complex use of point of view. If the Soviet
novel lacks this multiplanar dimension, it is not, in Bakhtin's view,
a true novel. Or, to put it another way, though it may have a
questing hero, it lacks a "questing form."

The question arises: if some crucial aspects of novel-ness are
absent, do we have a true collision of incompatible temporalities? Is
it not perhaps the case that the "present," or novelistic dimension,
is emasculated by this absence of its most dynamic components—
mockery, irony, parody, etc.—and thus defers to its antagonist, the
absolute epic past?

Something like this is in fact the case. The generic incompatibility
that most critics find in the Soviet novel is not as acute for those
who share its informing values. For them there is an ontological
hierarchy in which things of the "present," or novelistic, time-value
dimension, are subordinated to an absolute epic past.

The is/ought-to-be dichotomy in Soviet novels is a reflection of
the peculiar Stalinist cosmology abroad in the 1930s, when the
traditions of Socialist Realism were formed. The sense of reality
informing the official rhetoric of that time is very like the one Eliade
describes in his accounts of traditional societies. I am referring to
Eliade's theory of the dual sense of time characterizing these cultures: traditional man on the one hand looks to a mythic Great
Time and, on the other, recognizes the present as a form of profane

time. The Great Time provides a transcendent reality, and objects and events of the present, profane world acquire their reality and identity only to the extent that they participate in this transcendent reality by imitating a mythical archetype. Although Eliade regards this pattern of the two times as characteristic of traditional societies, he allows that it is present in many modern movements, and especially in messianic movements, which usually locate their Great Time in both the past and the future.[19]

In Stalinist rhetoric of the thirties one finds an ontological hierarchy very like the temporal hierarchy Eliade describes. The 1917 Revolution, the Civil War, and certain crucial moments in Stalin's life became a kind of canonized Great Time that conferred an exalted status on all who played a major part in them (World War II has since been added to the list). Likewise, the future, as represented in the official version of history—History—functioned in rhetoric as another Great Time, a time when life would be qualitatively different from present-day reality (and even from life in the time immediately preceding that quantum leap into Communism). There was an absolute cutoff between actual historical reality and the "reality" of these official Great Times. No event of the present time could transcend its profaneness unless it could be dignified by some identification with a moment either from the official Heroic Age or from the Great and Glorious Future. The meaning of all present-day reality was derived from its relationship with these mythic times. Stalinist epistemology was an idiosyncratic variety of neo-Platonism.

Thus the Stalinist novel was supported by a world view that tended to annul time, to write off that unbridgeable distance between its own kind of absolute epic past and the present. Fictional, historical, and actual experience were homogenized insofar as they all tended to be refracted through the lens of myth to form one of the archetypal patterns. There is no collision in the novel between "is" (or "present") and "ought to be" (or "epic past"—or future), or, by extension, even between simple and complex. A complex form is merely a more prolix and diffuse version of the simple. And those sudden, unmotivated transitions from realistic description to idealized vision, which so often offend the critics, can be seen as analogous to what happens when myth is used in the Platonic dialogues and the argument moves from rational dialectic to mythic assumptions.

All this raises questions about the integrity of the real-life material in any Soviet novel. Since material from present-day reality is, ideally, to provide a lesser example of something more grandly present in the Great Time, it is not really valuable in itself and need not be particularized. This subordination of historical reality to the preexisting patterns of legend and history bridged the gap between "is" and "ought to be." Soviet literature got its tractors and its transcendence too.

This conception of the nature and function of the Socialist Realist novel helps us to find more definitive answers to the questions posed above about the official pre-thirties models of Socialist Realism: *Why* was the particular type of writing permitted by the state so narrow and restrictive in literary, as distinct from ideological, terms? And if it was to be narrow, *why* was that particular type chosen rather than one of the other varieties of writing proposed in the platforms of loyalist and zealous groups? The question can be posed in more specific terms: Why does the list of Socialist Realist exemplars not include certain other major novels of the twenties, such as K. Fedin's *Cities and Years*—novels that remain classics of Soviet literature to this day? (That is, they are novels that have not fallen into official disfavor but are discussed with pride in official histories as quality Soviet literature.)

One is tempted to answer this question in terms of two factors. The first would be the political rating of the author at the time the canon was drawn up. Most of the canonical exemplars can be accounted for in these terms. The problem is that the author's political standing at the time does not always yield a valid reason why certain works were *not* included. Fedin's *Cities and Years* is a case in point. Fedin was probably closer to Gorky than any of the new Soviet generation of writers, and he also held office in the Writers' Union; yet the fiction he wrote in the twenties was bypassed.

A second possible factor would be something like "popularity with readers" or even "literary merit." It seems probable that these criteria *were* relevant, since, for each work included in the canon, there were many others, written to more or less the same recipe, that were not included. Publication figures from the twenties suggest that most of the works on the official list were widely read, although, since the market did not really determine print runs, it is impossible to ascertain to what extent these figures reflect real popularity.[20]

Neither of these two explanations is, however, very satisfactory. The choice of exemplars can be accounted for much more conclusively in terms of the way the classics of the twenties meet two major criteria brought out in the above discussion of Socialist Realism's modal schizophrenia: first, the demand that Socialist Realism produce a literature that would be internationally acclaimed as literature yet remain accessible to the masses, and, second, that it endow secular literature with the power of myth.

The institutionalization of Socialist Realism between 1932 and 1934 can be regarded as an act of synthesis of major cultural contradictions. When the Bolshevik Revolution occurred, there were two major discrepancies confronting all those who wanted to create a truly Soviet literature. The first of these was evident in the gulf between, on the one hand, the main types of literature written by Party members and fellow-traveling writers, who published in *literary* journals, and, on the other, the sort of literature actually published in the Party press. The second was that celebrated gulf between the educated classes and the broad masses of the illiterate and semiliterate, who made up about four-fifths of the population. In their own way the events of 1932–34, willy-nilly, bridged these gaps.

The nature of the problem can be demonstrated quite graphically by comparing the sort of literature published in *Pravda* between 1917 and 1919 with the writing done in the same years by some of the recipients of major government funding and, *a fortiori,* by the Futurists. The mainstay of *Pravda* literature in those years was highly rhetorical poetry, written in clumsy imitation of one of two senses of literary *kultura,* such as might have been culled from a tsarist schoolroom or study group. One finds either the eighteenth-century neoclassical occasional ode, with heavy use of archaic language and dripping with Enlightenment symbolism, or a sort of secondhand Lermontovism, singing of "storms," "waves," and other surging forces.[21] This kind of writing has to be contrasted with what might be described as cultural elitist avant-gardeism, that is, with writings that confronted the dated cultural modes in a bemused, parodistic, or iconoclastic spirit. In extreme forms, such as "trans-sense poetry" or abstract canvases, Futurist art was, to Bolshevik sensibilities at any rate, lacking in content. And while these self-styled cultural radicals contended that the aesthetic revolution of which they were the avant-garde was a necessary companion or even precondition of the political revolution, the mass and Party response to their works was largely one of incomprehension and bewilderment.

The twenties saw the progressive closing not only of the gulf between the literature of the Party press and other varieties of committed literature but the gulf between high culture and popular culture as well—between highbrow literature and Party rhetoric. This was largely achieved administratively, in the sense that between 1932 and 1934 Soviet literature became centralized and placed under Party dominance. It was also achieved at a literary level: the gulf between the type of literature published in the Party press and most other committed fiction was gradually bridged. However, the major advances on the literary front were made well before the most crucial administrative changes; for the pre-Stalinist novels, which became cornerstones of Socialist Realism, led the way, yet all were published before the end of 1927, that is, they were published before the Party made much effort to bridge the gulf by "administrative" means.

All of the pre-thirties novels on the list of official exemplars were undoubtedly chosen because they were harbingers of the later mythologization and symbolization of all public language in the thirties, which made possible the close interaction between the press and public platform, on the one hand, and imaginative literature, on the other. It is no accident that the authors of almost all these classics have in common the fact that they worked both in the Party sphere (most commonly in its press) and in literature. Some began in literature and then spent some time in Party work, from which their Socialist Realist novels emerged (e.g., Serafimovich, Gorky, and Gladkov). Others, like Fadeev and Furmanov, took the reverse course and entered literature after a spell in Party administration and journalism.[22] In either case, three impulses met in their work. The first was to mythologize literature from the Bolshevik point of view (this was especially true in the early twenties, when writers of this type tried to counter the popular myths of the Revolution in works by writers like Pilnyak).[23] The second was to make more literary the myths and notions to be found in Bolshevik rhetoric, and no matter how stodgy these writers might have seemed to the contemporary *avant-garde*, they did bring Party literature a little closer to contemporary European norms. The third impulse was to popularize ideology, to disseminate it in a form both attractive and accessible to the masses.

It is because of these authors' primary commitment to Bolshevik myth[24] that their texts became part of the canon, whereas works written in the twenties by authors like Fedin, Babel, and Leonov, who were more committed to describing the *experience* of the revolution, did not. But the commitment to mythmaking alone is not the mark of their Socialist Realism. The point of convergence that makes these disparate works form a single tradition is the informing scheme of human biography that underlies each work and has its roots in Marxist-Leninist historiography and revolutionary lore. This curious aspect of Socialist Realist composition is demonstrated most strikingly in two official classics that are autobiographical: D. Furmanov's *Chapaev* (1923) and N. Ostrovsky's *How the Steel Was Tempered* (1932–34). In these novels the author's own life was deindividualized as he patterned it to recapitulate the great legends of the revolutionary hero. Autobiography became autohagiography.

It was this biographical pattern that was to provide the formulaic master plot. In the precursors of Socialist Realism (i.e., the pre-thirties exemplars) it is present only potentially, in imperfect or incomplete form. Although the common biographical pattern might not have been apparent in the twenties when one compared, for instance, *The Rout* and *Cement*, it could be "perceived" (to use Borges' term) once the tradition had been established in the thirties. One factor that obscures the affinity between the two novels is the different modes that dominate each work (*The Rout* is more "real-ist," *Cement* more "mythical"); but, as has been established, in the different cultural climate of the thirties, mode became a more purely surface phenomenon in fiction than is generally the case.

Underlying the pre-thirties exemplars are two major biographical patterns, one positive and one negative. The positive pattern has a proletarian, or Party, positive hero, as in *Mother, Chapaev, The*

Iron Flood, Cement, and *The Rout.* The negative pattern has an
intellectual or bourgeois hero whose psychological and ideological
makeup puts him out of step with the new age. Prime examples of
this negative hero are to be found in the protagonists of Gorky's
Klim Samgin and in A. Tolstoy's *Road to Calvary.* Since, by the
mid-thirties, Soviet society had evolved to the point where most
remaining bourgeois and intellectuals were deemed either class
enemies or socialized to a degree, the negative pattern was rather
poorly represented in novels from then on. In other words, although
Gorky's and A. Tolstoy's epics, written in the twenties, are official
classics of Socialist Realism, they have been productive primarily as
supplying paradigms for subplots and lesser characters and will
therefore receive little attention in this book.[25]

   Thus the Socialist Realist tradition did not, as Soviet historians
claim, grow up in a family-like atmosphere of writers helping each
other as they worked toward a common cause. Nor, on the other
hand, was it merely an incongruous medley "imposed from above,"
as we in the West are tempted to think. The official models for
Socialist Realism have in common a biographical pattern, which
structures them. Although it might not, and probably could not,
have been perceived at the time by the authors of the various
exemplars, it was this pattern that provided the basis for the
Socialist Realist tradition that was established by administrative fiat
in 1932.

The Positive Hero in Pre-revolutionary Fiction

The "positive hero" has been a defining feature of Soviet Socialist Realism. The hero is expected to be an emblem of Bolshevik virtue, someone the reading public might be inspired to emulate, and his life should be patterned to "show the forward movement of history" in an allegorical representation of one stage in history's dialectical progress. A novel's positive hero(es) stand primarily for "what ought to be," and it is left for lesser protagonists, or sometimes for "negative characters," to represent "what is." Not surprisingly, Western critics consider the positive hero the main culprit in the Soviet novel's modal schizophrenia, and he has been treated by them with almost universal scorn.

However, the positive hero has always played a role in the great tradition of Russian literature (consider, for example, the heroes of Dostoevsky). This reflects the greater moral fervor to be found in modern Russian literature than in the West. Since the mid-nineteenth century, Russian critics have joined Russian writers in setting out two tasks for literature that, although found in Western literature, have certainly not characterized it for roughly the past hundred years. These tasks were, first, to draw "typical" characters—characters who were not so much individuals as representatives of commonly found social types through which the writer was to present a critique of Russian life—and, second, to set forth models of behavior who might, by their example, show the way out of Russia's social ills.

The Socialist Realist hero is not merely a successor to the positive hero of nineteenth century fiction. Although he became a cornerstone of Socialist Realism, the idea behind the positive hero—that he should be "typical," should exemplify moral and political (or religious) virtue, and should show the "way forward" for Russia—was, as happened so often when an intelligentsia convention was adopted into Soviet culture, interpreted with great literalism, extremism, and rigidity. The nineteenth-century positive hero was necessarily, because of his didactic function, less individualized (more "typical") than his counterpart in Flaubert or James, and this was even truer of the Socialist Realist hero; he was, in fact, so deindividualized that he could be transplanted wholesale from book to book, regardless of the subject matter.

Despite the Socialist Realist hero's *surface* resemblance to a nineteenth-century epigone, he is actually so deindividualized that he seems closer to a figure in one of the various genres of the Old Russian written tradition that tell the virtues of some positive figure. His image is reminiscent not just of hagiography, which tells of a saint's religious virtue as illumined in his life, but also of those sections of the old chronicles that tell of the secular virtues of princes, of the feudal sense of honor, duty, valor, and service to one's country. Whether the text told of a saint or a prince, the biographies were in both cases historicized. If actual historical figures were chosen as subjects, the details of their lives were pruned, embellished, or even ignored in order to make the subject fit the conventional patterns of the virtuous life.

Much Soviet literature and history has also been written in this way. Although an amazing number of Socialist Realist classics are based on actual events, their protagonists' lives always manage to follow the conventionalized stages of the master plot. One can compare the portrait of the Socialist Realist hero and that of his counterpart in medieval texts not just in function and genre but (as will be shown below) even in terms of the actual clichés used to characterize them.

The saints' lives were arguably a much more formative element in modern Russian culture than in the West (in Russia, people were still often brought up on them). Thus it is not surprising to find continuities when we compare the clichés used to describe medieval positive heroes with the clichés that describe both their Socialist Realist counterparts and the heroes of nineteenth-century revolutionary fiction.

I point these similarities out not merely to posit some line of genealogy or influence linking Christian iconology with the revolutionary or Bolshevik iconology, for one must be wary of seeing too much significance in continuity (or similarity) of signs. Still, one can trace a process whereby new meanings and new layers of complex-

ity were added to the original signs as they were taken up in a new
context (a staggered system). In medieval texts the clichés for the
prince or saint formed a relatively simple system (indicating Christian virtue and/or civic virtues appropriate to social status and,
possibly, the role of martyr). In nineteenth-century radical texts
there was an influx of new intellectual influences (such as utopian
socialism) that modified the meanings of the old clichés and introduced new ones into the pool as well; there was also a change in
the nature of the texts in which they were deployed (i.e., noveliza-
tion), so that the signs were used more randomly than before. In
Bolshevik-inspired Socialist Realism, this revised roster of clichés is
used again, giving Bolshevik literature the stamp of carrying on the
old intelligentsia traditions; but the signs now carry several extra
layers of meanings, which they acquired progressively, over time.

There were two important moments in this sequence. First, with
Gorky's *Mother* (1907), the clichés of nineteenth-century radi-
calism acquired significances in terms of the Bolshevik model
for historical deveopment, the spontaneity/consciousness dialectic.
Later, from the thirties on, they took on two new sets of functions:
they were used to legitimize both Stalinist succession and the reign
of terror and to reinforce the new hierarchical social structure. The
clichés became both highly codified and multifunctional.

This, then, is why the positive hero is so important in Soviet
Socialist Realism: not because he is so "positive" but because he is
society's official mandala. In this chapter we will follow his evolution through his first major transformation, in Gorky's *Mother*.

Pre-Bolshevik Models

During the second half of the nineteenth century the assorted radical groups in Russia sought to convert large numbers to their cause.
To this end they began to produce works of fiction that painted an
inspiring picture of the radical activists and their good works. These
works were of two different kinds: tracts and novels. The tracts
were written for the masses and were geared to counteracting the
influence of the so-called *narodnye izdanija,* which were mostly
penny dreadfuls or religious chapbooks. To this end, authors strove
for accessibility and so for the most part imitated genres they believed would appeal to the masses: folktales, folk epics (*byliny*),

short stories narrated as if told by a peasant or worker, and religious writings.

Most of these tracts were relatively short, but the various radical movements also produced some novels intended to inspire the educated classes (people like themselves) rather than the masses. The two most seminal of these have proved to be N. Chernyshevsky's *What Is to Be Done?* (1863), written to inspire the idealist populists of the 1860s and 70s, and A. Stepnyak-Kravchinsky's *Andrey Kozhukhov* (1889), written to inspire the populists' successors, the revolutionary terrorists.

Generically, these novels were very different from the short, popularized tracts that the radicals also produced (their *narodnye izdanija*). Nevertheless, both novels and tracts drew on the same store of myths and symbols of revolutionary lore, and the three types of symbolic patterns that were also common to them should be mentioned here because they were later to play a major role in Bolshevik myth.

In the first of these symbolic patterns, the particular political movement being championed is directly or indirectly identified with a "family." Often, and especially in the case of movements influenced by utopian socialists, this "family" was to supplant members' natural families; their ties were to be redirected to this "higher" family.[1]

The second is the pattern in which a relatively naive person is brought to see the light by some emissary of the new enlightenment. The stages of the conversion process often structured an entire work of fiction, and the two actors in this process were usually identified explicitly as "mentor" and "disciple" (*učitel'* and *učenik*).[2]

Third, an almost ubiquitous element in radical fiction was some kind of martyrdom. Minimally, the revolutionary hero was expected to lead an ascetic life of extraordinary dedication and self-deprivation. There were many conventionalized ways of providing palpable evidence of this, such as the hero's working late into the night while ordinary mortals slept.[3] Ideally, however, the hero should make the supreme sacrifice of his life, and this event was commonly followed by a secularized version of the Christian death-and-transfiguration pattern: the hero's "resurrection" in the ongoing movement, often symbolized by one of his comrades picking up the fallen banner.[4]

This penchant for depicting martyrdom is related to the second
feature common to both varieties of radical fiction, their religiosity.
Scarcely a text can be found that is not rich in biblical and liturgical
language and imagery. Many are even stylized along the lines of
traditional religious genres (sermons, saints' lives, and religious
songs). Whatever the genre ostensibly used, a heavy-handed didacticism and religiosity soon entered the narration; consequently
most radical fiction (including even the pseudo-folk and simulated
low style / oral) soon surrendered its generic identity to the language
of rhetoric and the church.

Despite the martyrology and religiosity, nineteenth-century radical
fiction never became what one could call hagiography or even secular hagiography. It was never sufficiently formalized, and its
heroes never attained that essential timeless guise. They were too
individualized for that; that is, the texts were too "novelistic." This
can be sensed even in that most famous segment of all Russian
revolutionary fiction, the life of the revolutionary superhero
Rakhmetov in N. Chernyshevsky's *What Is to Be Done?* Rakhmetov's life provides a good test case because it follows very closely
the pattern of a popular Russian saint's life, *The Life of Aleksey, A Man of God* (earliest version C12).[5] In both texts an
upper-class dandy undergoes a conversion, gives away his property,
leaves his home, eschews worldly success and true love, dedicates
himself to the faith, and uses incredible means of self-mortification
to drive out temptations to waver in his resolve (Rakhmetov trains
his will by lying on a bed of nails).

The practice of inserting a section of pseudo-hagiography was
quite common in fiction of the late nineteenth century: consider the
life of Father Zosima in Dostoevsky's *The Brothers Karamazov*
(1880), which is very self-consciously hagiographic. Other varieties
of medieval biography were also used in literature. For instance, the
poet N. Nekrasov attempted to write a folk-epic hero (Savely the
bogatyr') into his long poem "The Red-nosed Frost" (1863). This
trend must be seen as an attempt to appropriate the semantic over-
tones of the medieval text; authors hoped in this way to conjure up
the lionhearted hero who helps his fellow men (a *bogatyr'*) or the
truly dedicated champion of the faith (a saint).

When the saints' lives were inserted into fiction, the purity of the
original form was never recaptured because of the tension between
its aim of depicting a timeless hero and the novel's centrality of

idiosyncrasy and contingency. In the novel, at every point in the
"saint"'s life his actions could equally well realize or violate the
conventions of the *vita*. Dostoevsky essentially demonstrates this
freedom at the end of Zosima's life, when Zosima's stinking corpse
contravenes the formal expectations that, after death, the saint's
body should exude an aura or occasion some miracle.

Rakhmetov's character and actions are open to change, however
slight. The possibility that he will surprise us is reinforced by the
playful and self-conscious narrative tone of the text. The reader
senses the presence of a narrator who frequently interpolates his
own jesting speculations on the reader's probable reactions and
expectations of what is to follow. Moreover, Chernyshevsky leaves
the end of Rakhmetov's life as "open-ended" as his narrative:
Rakhmetov disappears without trace.

The various radical movements' essays in hagiography failed to
take them far from contemporary fictional norms because they
lacked that essential ingredient for epic genres—a completed historical world view. Merely to see the way forward as assured by
following a particular revolutionary program is not to provide that
total, unambiguous account of reality that makes possible, in protagonists, complete consonance between their individual identity
and their social role. Without this, there could be considerable
overlap between the two genres but never absolute correspondence.

Nineteenth-century radical fiction may have been different generically from Socialist Realism, but, paradoxically, its myths and
imagery were the mainstay of official Soviet lore and hence of
Socialist Realism. This paradox is only seeming, because there is a
distinction between, on the one hand, isolated event and the meaning of that event in its isolated context and, on the other, the same
event when put into the context of Socialist Realism's interdependent semantics and morphology.

This paradox is most strikingly caught in the case of *What Is to
Be Done?* The life of Rakhmetov (and, to a lesser extent, that of
Andrey Kozhukhov) was consistently cited by the founding fathers
of the Soviet nation as the text that had most inspired them in their
revolutionary work.[6] Every Soviet schoolchild has been brought up
on Rakhmetov's life. Yet one is hard pressed to find any specific
parallels between its formal features and those of a Socialist Realist
novel.

The general impact of the nineteenth-century radical tradition on

Soviet culture was considerable, but only as single elements, not as
a total system. Its influence can be felt even in the lives of the
nation's leaders. When, for instance, Lenin is said to have been
"simple like the truth" (prost kak pravda), this is not just empty
rhetoric, for Lenin in his extreme dedication seems to have felt
role-bound to lead the austere life of the revolutionary and also be
accessible to the common man. And when, as Solzhenitsyn shows
graphically in the opening chapter of The First Circle, Stalin would
stay up until all hours working on affairs of state, this may not have
been a sign of madness or that "conscience robs him of his sleep,"
but an acting-out of the role of the revolutionary leader of radical
myth.

Gorky's Mother

Most Soviet historians describe Mother as the novel that spawned the
numberless Socialist Realist progeny.[7] This metaphor, though appropriate to the book's title, does not take into account Mother's
relationship to earlier revolutionary fiction. I prefer to use another,
borrowed from Pushkin, who once described translators as the
"post-horses of civilization." Mother was that post, or station,
where Bolsheviks coming out of the old intelligentsia tradition were
able to stop and take on fresh horses to bear them on into Socialist
Realism itself. Mother provided a system for translating the clichés
of tsarist radicals into the determining formulas of Bolshevism.

The plot of Mother fuses historical reality and revolutionary
myth in a coherent political allegory. The novel describes an actual
incident, a May Day demonstration that took place in the Volga
town of Somov in 1902 and was broken up by the police. Those
arrested insisted on conducting their own defense at the trial. This
event heartened the Social Democratic (i.e., Marxist) party, for they
took it as evidence of growing consciousness among workers.
Gorky's attention was attracted to the incident; he spent some time
with the defendants and their families and then wrote about one of
their leaders, Pavel Zalomov (who appears in the novel as Pavel
Vlasov), and his mother.[8]

The story has been idealized somewhat. Pavel Zalomov complained, for instance, that his mother was both more daring and
more intelligent than the mother in the novel.[9] Also, if one com-

pares the transcripts of the actual Somov trial with the trial
speeches in *Mother,* one can see that Gorky made his Pavel much
more politically conscious than Zalomov was.[10] In part these
changes can be seen as adjustments made so that the story would fit
the stock patterns of the preceding generation of revolutionary
fiction. In order to create the conventional mentor / disciple pair, for
instance, Pavel (the mentor) had to be more conscious than in reality, and his mother (the disciple), less. Additionally, as can be seen
in the following plot outline, Gorky worked into the story such
familiar radical symbols as the "family" of revolutionaries, the
picking-up of the fallen banner, and martyrdom:

> Pavel Vlasov, born into an oppressed, working-class family,
> has a bitter drunkard of a father and a pious, submissive mother,
> who suffers endless beatings from her husband. Even as a child
> Pavel stands up to his father. A factory accident brings the father
> to an early grave, and the young Pavel has to go out to work.
> Initially he seems destined to repeat his father's bad habits (he
> starts to drink, etc.). But Pavel escapes this fate when he is at-
> tracted to a small group of underground socialists: he stops
> drinking and begins to dress neatly. Gradually, his mother be-
> comes curious about Pavel's interests. He explains some of his
> new beliefs to her, and she is shocked by his sacrilege in presum-
> ing to go against God and tsar. Then she meets his comrades and
> is attracted to them as people. When Pavel is imprisoned, her love
> for him leads her to help his comrades in his absence. This begins
> her gradual transformation from illiterate and pious housewife to
> inspired radical activist. As she changes, so does her sense of
> family change from one comprising merely Pavel and herself
> to one embracing the entire revolutionary group. At a May Day
> demonstration Pavel bears the red banner and is arrested again.
> His mother picks up its remnants and carries them home. Pavel is
> sentenced to exile for his role as leader of the demonstration, but
> by then his mother has become a convinced and fearless revolu-
> tionary. The novel closes as she is being beaten to death for her
> beliefs, defiant to the end.[11]

Not all the discrepancies between historical reality and *Mother's*
version of the Somov affair derive from *earlier* revolutionary
clichés. Some come from a stock of discernibly new conventions.
For example, the historical Pavel, Pavel Zalomov, complained
about Gorky's having killed off the mother at the end of the novel,

pointing out that his own mother had continued as a political activist well into her eighties.[12] In this instance Gorky's embellishment reflects changing times. Whereas earlier a martyr had normally been a male revolutionary leader, in recent fiction the vogue had favored political melodrama with beloved family members (very possibly females) as the sacrificial victims. Most radical authors of *Mother*'s times centered their plots around a particular family, selecting members of it to play "mentor" and "disciple" and ending the work with a mass demonstration at which a close relative would be killed.[13]

One such contemporary novel, A. Mashitsky's *In the Fire* (1904), seems to anticipate the plot of Gorky's *Mother* almost exactly: a drunk worker is killed in a factory mishap, his pious wife is converted to the revolutionary cause by her son, named Pavel. The son carries the banner at a May Day demonstration. His mother is beaten to death by the police, but the novel closes on an optimistic note: the revolution goes on.[14] It is generally assumed that Gorky did not know *In the Fire* at the time he was writing *Mother*.[15] Even if he did not have the benefit of its example, however, there were enough other works with similar plots for it not to be surprising that, in treating the Somov affair in fiction, he chose to focus on a mother and son rather than on the revolutionary group itself or just one revolutionary, that he charted the mother's gradual conversion through her son, and that he embellished her actual biography with a premature, martyr's death.

In comparing the conventions of revolutionary fiction from Gorky's time with earlier examples from the nineteenth century, one is struck by how much more coherently the various elements of the older radical tradition were now organized. The old standard motifs ("family," "mentor" / "disciple," and "martyr") all became part of one narrative strand in works like *In the Fire*. With *Mother* this streamlining process went even further, and a single myth emerged. This development made possible the single master plot of Socialist Realism, which patterns the various motifs into one sequence.

This process was not just a matter of depicting with ever greater skill the same features in the same landscape, for *Mother* represents a radical *generic* departure from the sort of fiction written before (including *In the Fire*) in the service of the cause. That revolutionary

fiction had been "novelistic"; with *Mother,* a new variety of secular
hagiography was introduced.

Several biographical reasons make it almost logical that Gorky
would cast his revolutionary fiction as a form of secular hagiography. At the time he wrote *Mother,* for instance, he was already
gravitating toward the position he articulated in 1907, when he
espoused the Bolshevik heresy known as "God-building."[16] The
adherents of God-building believed that in communism man would
attain such heights of human development that he would become as
God. And so, to Gorky, Bolshevism was *literally,* and not just func-
tionally, a secular substitute for religion.

Mother's heroes seem to share Gorky's views, for when Pavel and
a revolutionary friend explain their new beliefs to Pavel's mother,
they say, "We have to change our god," for in truth man is like
god.[17] And throughout the novel Gorky has used his ingenuity to
provide secular substitutes for most of the major symbols and institutions of Christianity.

Besides Gorky's attraction to the God-building heresy, he came
to consciousness surrounded by an environment drenched in Russian iconology. Among the many jobs he had in his youth was one
in an icon factory. In his childhood his grandfather had seen to it
that he had a thorough grounding in the saints' lives, and Gorky
even learned by heart the particular saint's life on which Chernyshevsky seems to have patterned Rakhmetov's biography, *The
Life of Aleksey, A Man of God.*[18] But despite all this, the plot of
Mother contains very few identifiable parallels with the formulaic
stages of the saint's life.

Nevertheless, *Mother* was more hagiographic than Chernyshevsky's *What Is to Be Done?* or, indeed, than any of the quasi-religious writing that had emerged thus far out of the various Russian
revolutionary movements. While Chernyshevsky used hagiographic
patterns to create something superficially like a saint's life, which
served as a substitute, Gorky broke ground for a new and distinctive
Bolshevik tradition of secular hagiography, which bore less surface
resemblance to the old tradition but was closer to it on a deeper level.

What has converted *Mother* from an idealized biography to a
ritualized one is the pervasive presence of the Bolshevik account of
history. One can sense the axial role played by the spontaneity/
consciousness dialectic in both character and plot. This is not to

make claims for the novel's genesis. It need not follow that *Mother* was consciously written by a Bolshevik to illustrate the dialectic. After 1907 *Mother* became a more or less official Bolshevik tract. Thus, whether or not Gorky was much of a Party man at the time he wrote it (a moot point),[19] thereafter—to reinvoke Borges' term used in the last chapter—the distinctive patterns of *Mother* could be "perceived" as encoded representations of the Bolshevik model for historical development.

A good way to get at the differences between *Mother* and earlier fiction would be to compare it with two comparable texts, Stepnyak-Kravchinsky's *Andrey Kozhukhov* and the Rakhmetov biography in Chernyshevsky's *What Is to Be Done?* The three texts are comparable because in each a young male hero (Pavel Vlasov, Andrey Kozhukhov, and Rakhmetov, respectively) becomes the true revolutionary. What differs in each case is *how* he becomes the true revolutionary, and these differences catch important distinctions between the text types.

In both *Andrey Kozhukhov* and Rakhmetov's life the relationship between the hero's inner and outer selves is a crucial factor in his progress. *Andrey Kozhukhov,* for instance, stresses the contrast between the two. Andrey is a man of seething passions, of uncontrollable emotions and violent jealousy, but, by supreme efforts on his part, he is able to appear outwardly calm, strong, and dedicated to the cause. In Rakhmetov's case the relationship between the inner and outer man is not so much one of conflict and discrepancy; rather, it is from the inner self that the outer gains its power. Rakhmetov's conversion or "rebirth" is effected by dint of sheer will and "working on himself."[20]

Chernyshevsky shows the before and after of Rakhmetov as he undergoes his conversion, but Gorky keeps the personality of Pavel fairly consistent throughout. Pavel remains to the end that strong and fearless character the reader first saw when Pavel, at the age of fourteen, forbade his father to lay a hand on him. He did change, first when he went to work and began to drink, and then again when he was converted, but Gorky does not *show* his hero during that time; he gives only sketchy reports of his hero's early activities. Gorky presents a full portrait of Pavel only after his conversion, and so the picture we get of him remains fairly stable.

Pavel's mother is not so static a figure. Indeed, the novel is ostensibly about her development. In this sense *Mother* might be called a *Bildungsroman,* with the mother as the one being "formed." But, unlike a *Bildungsroman* hero, her final incarnation has already been determined when she begins her progress to "consciousness." She merely assumes in her turn the likeness her son had assumed before her (but modified in her case by the essential "motherliness" she retains to the end and by her relative lack of education).

Rakhmetov and Andrey Kozhuknov *make themselves,* whereas Pavel and his mother are inspired by others to *assume their likeness;* their development is not, strictly speaking, one of character, for their inner selves play no significant role in it. The strength of the outer self is derived from *extrinsic* factors. In part it is due to the instruction and example of others, but these amount to no more than a ritual conferral of "consciousness." The dialectic of passion and reason that in earlier novels was played out in terms of divided selves has in *Mother* been transformed into an impersonal dialectic (between "spontaneity" and "consciousness") in which "characters" are merely a symbolic medium.

The crucial differences between the two varieties of revolutionary biography do not derive just from the fact that the more "novelistic" hero effects changes in himself by willpower and that his outer self is his own achievement. Nor do they derive even from the fact that the heroes of *Mother* are not in danger of becoming passion's slaves. The differences are based rather on the extraordinary degree to which the depiction of heroes in *Mother* is depersonalized.

This depersonalization has left its mark on the actual mechanics of character depiction. In *Mother* one can detect a shift to greater abstraction as compared with earlier revolutionary fiction. Two main techniques are used to draw the positive heroes in *Mother.* One is a technique also commonly used in earlier radical fiction: symbolization of physical features. The furrowed brow or pinched face, for instance, are signs of the revolutionary's dedication and sacrifice. The other technique is the use of code words, or epithets: a select group of adjectives that indicate moral political qualities and / or corresponding nouns or adverbs (e.g. *ser'ëznyj,* "serious").

Such epithets are widely used to describe positive heroes both in earlier revolutionary fiction and in *Mother,* but there is a crucial difference in the function they perform in the two types of text. In revolutionary fiction they are essentially just the tersest of the various symbolic attributes that make up the roster of clichés. In *Mother*, on the other hand, the revolutionaries' portraits are so depersonalized that they are reduced almost completely to functions of their roles, which are themselves ideologically determined. As a result, the epithets (which are used much more frequently than in the early revolutionary fiction) do not simply constitute a pool of indiscriminate associations, available to be deployed. Instead, they form a system. They stand for ideas, already covered at greater length in theoretical writings, which they represent in more economical form. They have ceased to be really descriptive and have become cryptological.

This mode of sketching the positive hero by means of sparse, formulaic details is reminiscent of the way the saint or ideal prince was depicted in medieval texts. The medieval scribe usually limited his written portraits to a catalogue of virtues plus an account of the subject's face and general mien. The motifs used were not only conventionalized but were restricted to a very select number. These motifs were themselves geared to showing the subject in a generalized, timeless guise—as he should be. As is frequently pointed out, his aspect was eminently comparable to that of a saint or prince on an icon.[21] In fact, passages describing a saint or prince are often called "word icons."

As mentioned earlier, the similarities between the portrait of the positive hero in medieval texts (the saint or prince) and in *Mother* extend beyond the techniques employed and include, to a significant degree, the actual clichés used. The Soviet medievalist D. S. Likhachev cites a portrait of the Ryazan prince as a prototype, and I will use it here as a source of examples (the passage is actually from a chronicle of the thirteenth or fourteenth century).

Before I introduce the prince's portrait, some qualifications must be made. One obvious difference between the portrait of the medieval prince and that of the modern revolutionary hero is that the former served Christ while the latter serves the revolution. A second one lies in the prince's *joi de vivre* as compared with the revolutionary's asceticism. This asceticism and the revolutionary's lust for martyrdom are in fact reminiscent of medieval saintly conventions, but medieval texts did not distinguish absolutely be-

tween civic and religious virtue; saints often exemplified civic virtues and princes saintlike virtue. Thus the revolutionary hero and
Pavel could best be compared with a saintlike version of the
medieval prince. A revised version of the Ryazan prince's portrait,
one pruned of the most clearly inapplicable attributes, would read:

> Loving Christ [cf. revolution], loving toward his brothers, fair of
> face, with shining [*svetly*] eyes, and a stern [*grozny*] countenance,
> extraordinarily brave, good-natured [alternative translations of
> this epithet—*serdcem legky*—include "open" and "simple" in the
> positive sense], good [*laskovy*] to his men [actually, "retainers"],
> majestic, strong in mind, stands for truth, keeps himself pure in
> body and soul.[22]

The roster of clichés used for the positive hero of nineteenth-
century radical fiction, of *Mother*, and, ultimately, of Socialist Realism itself is amazingly similar to the ones in this abbreviated list.

One suspects that initially, in the nineteenth century, the saints'
vitae were spectral presences guiding revolutionary writers in their
choice of epithets. This can be sensed in the following examples of
revolutionary portraits taken from both novels and chapbooks.
Note that in all of the examples of revolutionary portraits, I have
supplied in brackets the Russian words I regard as epithets and have
consistently given the same English translation for each epithet in
order to indicate recurrence, regardless of how stilted the resulting
translation might seem.

The first example comes from *What Is to Be Done?* Significantly,
Chernyshevsky does not provide us with a portrait of Rakhmetov;
the description below is of another revolutionary, Lopukhov.

> With a proud [*gordyj*] and brave [*smelyj*] look. "He's not bad
> looking [she thinks] and must be very goodly [*dobr*] but a bit too
> serious [*ser'ëzen*]." ... It's a long time since anyone has led such a
> stern [*stroguju*] life.[23]

Compare this with the description of a mentor, from a populist
tract of 1874:

> His large, dark brown eyes had a fine look, which was brave
> [*smelyj*] and open [*otkrytyj*].[24]

Finally, in a pseudo-folktale, a simple peasant woman describes her
mentor:

The more I looked at him, the more my heart was drawn to him. I have never seen a face more goodly [*dobroe*] and intelligent [*umnoe*]. His brown eyes shone [*svetilis'*] with light and were full of intelligence [*uma*] and goodliness [*dobroty*] . . . [he is] loving [*laskovo*] and calm [*spokoen*].[25]

In these quotations a typical nexus of attributes emerges: the hero is good-looking, serious, stern and calm, proud and brave, with a light in the eyes, yet also open and full of an infectious human warmth and of intelligence and goodness. These attributes bear comparison with the following, exemplified by the Ryazan prince: fair of face, stern, majestic (proud equals majestic minus the role of potentate), brave, open (as one of the alternative meanings of "good-natured"), with shining eyes, good to others, strong in mind. Incidentally, nineteenth-century revolutionaries—and Pavel Vlasov—also "kept themselves pure in body and soul" and axiomatically "stood for truth." In addition to the general correspondences of the epithets, in two cases the same epithet was used: "shining eyes" (*svetlyj*) and "loving" (*laskovyj*), in the sense of a loving father.

There are also differences. The epithets are, for instance, deployed more randomly. Also, the revolutionary hero is "serious" and "calm," qualities the prince did not have explicitly. These epithets are of course signs of the hero's revolutionary dedication, but they also mark an important shift that occurred in the modern period, a shift in the way characterization is conceived. They indicate something about the relationship of the inner man to either his outer self or action: "serious" tells us something about his attitude to the cause, and "calm" something about how he has mastered his inner self.

The roster of epithets used for Pavel in *Mother* is, generally speaking, closer to those of revolutionary fiction than to hagiography. This can be appreciated from the following representative sample of passages describing Pavel after his conversion to the revolutionary cause.

[He has become] simpler [*prošče*] and gentler [*mjagče*].

[His mother thinks to herself:] My he's stern [*strog*].

[Pavel explains his beliefs to her:] Without looking at her, he

started talking sternly [*strogo*]; for some reason . . . he looked at
her and answered softly and calmly [*spokojno*]. . . . His eyes
glowed with determination [*uprjamo*].

Her son's eyes shone attractively and brightly [*svetlo*].

. . .[his] swarthy, determined [*uprjamoe*] and stern [*strogoe*] face.

His calmness [*spokojstvie*], his gentle [*mjagkij*] voice and the
simplicity [or "openness": *prostota*] of his face gladdened the
mother's heart.

He said seriously [*ser'ëzno*].[26]

This selection from *Mother* provides considerable overlap with
the first group, from revolutionary fiction. Some of the epithets are
the same—"loving," "calm," "stern," "serious," and "with shining
eyes"—and some are near equivalents, such as "determined" for
"brave" ("determined" was actually commonly found in
nineteenth-century radical texts) and, possibly, "simple" for
"open." There are also some differences. For instance, Pavel is not
described as "intelligent." The fact that he is not so described gets
at a basic difference between the function of these epithets in
Mother as compared with earlier revolutionary fiction. No matter
how conventionalized "intelligent" may have been, it suggests a
degree of individuation that is not present in hagiography.

Every epithet used in *Mother* also has to have a meaning in terms
of the Bolshevik model for historical development. In consequence,
even when the *same* epithet is used in both text types, this sameness
is illusory, for in the different context it must have a different
meaning. By the time *Mother* was written, "calm," for instance,
had become such a highly charged word that it could not be used
casually: *only* if the hero was politically "conscious" could he be
called "calm"; in fact the word's primary function was to indicate
that this was so.

The epithets in *Mother* are not only more abstract; they are also
more systematized. If we delete "shining eyes," a traditional sign of
grace, which in *Mother* is used more or less as the sign of Pavel's
positivity, we find that most of the remaining epithets fall naturally
into two groups: on the one hand, there are signs indicating Pavel's
dedication and discipline, such as "serious," "stern," and "de-

termined," and, on the other, there are signs indicating his human
warmth, such as "gentle," "simple," and "loving." This dichotomy
is not merely latent; it is quite often brought out in the text when
Pavel is said to change his expression from one involving a combination of epithets from the first group to one involving some combination of epithets from the second. The following quotations
provide examples:

> ... his blue eyes, which were always serious [*ser'eznye*] and stern
> [*strogie*], now burned so gently [*mjagko*] and lovingly [*laskovo*].

> His stern eyes shone more gently, and his voice sounded more
> loving [*laskovo*], and he became more simple [*prošče*]
> altogether.[27]

This dichotomy translates the spontaneity/consciousness opposition into patterns formed by systematizing the epithets. This is not
to say that the dialectical opposition is directly translated into the
dichotomy. It is not the case that the group "serious," "stern," and
"determined" means "conscious," whereas the group "simple,"
"gentle," and "loving" means "spontaneous." Rather, the two
clusters of epithets represent alternative external guises, which are
not in conflict. This is because Pavel is the incarnation of higher-
order, Bolshevik "consciousness," one in which the dialectical
tension between "spontaneity" and "consciousness" (or tension
between individual interests and the collective good) has been resolved in a state where "consciousness" prevails and is nevertheless
in harmony with "spontaneity." In Pavel there is a dichotomy between two contrasting (but not conflicting) aspects of the one
higher-order "consciousness"; although he is completely dedicated
to the interests of the collective, he has not lost his capacity for
human interaction.

The primary sign of Pavel's consciousness is the epithet "calm."
As can be sensed in the following two quotations (also cited earlier),
"calm" can be used in combination with epithets from either side of
the dichotomy:

> Pavel talked sternly ... he ... answered ... calmly. ... His eyes
> glowed with determination.

> His calmness, his gentle voice, and the simplicity of his face glad-
> dened his mother's heart.

That it can be so used is of course due to the fact that "consciousness" must be present in both of the hero's two guises. Historically,
however, "calm" has indicated the hero's triumph in transcending
his turbulent inner self to appear externally calm.[28] In *Mother*,
interiority is not a significant element, and the inner / outer split has
been transformed into a much milder, and totally external, *contrast:* the "loving" / "stern" dichotomy. At the same time, thanks to
its prehistory, the epithet "calm" still carries some of the aura of
triumph over dark, inner forces.

The other epithets used for Pavel are also signs of his "consciousness" first and foremost, although at the same time they retain some
of their customary meanings and some of the more metaphorical
meanings they had acquired in the nineteenth-century revolutionary
texts. The narrator could not, for instance, say that Pavel looked
"stern," when it was not feasible that he should look "stern." Thus
one can trace, over time, a gradual process of abstraction in the
meanings of the clichés and of accretion of new layers of meaning.

The semantic prehistory of the patterns of verbal symbols found
in *Mother* does not begin with the nineteenth-century radical texts.
The epithets used in characterizing medieval stereotypes probably
cast their semantic shadows over Pavel's portrait, enhancing his
role as a quasi-religious figure who stands firm in the faith. This
possibility is particularly present in that characteristic dichotomy in
Pavel's portrait, the stern / loving opposition. This dichotomy corresponds to the old dual image of the prince (and later the tsar) as a
figure both stern (or statesmanlike) and loving (or paternal), which
is now virtually a commonplace in Western conceptions of traditional Russian popular attitudes to their heads of state.[29] One can
see this dualism reflected in the above example of the typical prince,
who is said to be loving, generous, hospitable, and good-natured,
but also stern and majestic. Since Pavel, a Bolshevik revolutionary,
was both an emblem of "consciousness" and a leader of the masses,
his portrait conflates the traditional Russian sense of the authority
figure with that of an incarnation of Bolshevik virtue. The traditional leader image left its mark on the depiction of "consciousness," providing yet another instance of a general dynamic to be
followed in this book: how basic Marxist concepts, once transplanted in Russian soil, tended to be shaped by native habits of
mind.

Pavel's portrait is not unique in the novel: it is depersonalized and is in large measure a function of his political (rather than individual) identity. *All* "conscious" revolutionaries in *Mother*, qua "conscious" revolutionaries, are given identical and highly formalized portraits. Gorky goes to some pains to differentiate their physical appearance, but only in such minor externals as "blue eyes" and "a swarthy complexion" (in the case of Pavel). There are no external signs indicating a distinctive inner self.

Mother is thus more austere in its characterization, more economical in its expression, than its forebears in revolutionary fiction were or even many of those short pieces in the populists' chapbooks. Where earlier one might find prolix character description or homily, now one most often found terse verbal symbols involving several layers of meaning.

In the plot of *Mother* there is also a high degree of abstraction and ritualization. This is quite striking in the novel's martyrological patterns.

Martyrdom, a recurrent motif in *Mother*, was a commonplace of earlier radical fiction and lore. From at least Turgenev's Insarov in *On the Eve* (1860), virtually all revolutionary novels ended with the hero dying of tuberculosis, moldering in prison or exile, or expiring from a mortal wound inflicted by the revolution's oppressors (even the tuberculosis victim was a martyr, for he had given his health to the cause). But, no matter how myth-inspired this convention was in committed literature, its execution was novelistic in the sense that the martyrdom was the hero's individual feat, that supreme moment when he rose above his worldly ties, silenced the storms within, and stood, fearless, to confront his fate. When, for instance, Andrey Kozhukhov made an unsuccessful assassination attempt on the tsar, knowing that he would in all probability be executed and never see his true love again, he might just as well have echoed Carton's words from *A Tale of Two Cities:* "It is a far, far better thing I do. . . ."

The "conscious" heroes of *Mother*, by contrast, always wear the mask of one who has transcended selfhood, and their acts of self-abnegation are consonant with, and even logical for, their static identity. The mother, for instance, is actually less in revolutionary virtue than her son, but she outdoes him in martyrdom in the sense that she pays the supreme sacrifice (her life). Yet this sacrifice does not elevate her above the others: hers is essentially not an individual

act of sacrifice in the name of the many (as is Andrey Kozhukhov's)
but one that might equally well have been performed by any one of
the characters who embody "consciousness." To use Propp's terms,
then, the action is a function. The mother's having performed it
enhances not just her image but the image of all the others in the
novel who exemplify "consciousness."

The structure of *Mother* is comparable with that of a saint's life in
that it is teleological: in *Mother* the hero's goal is a state of grace
(albeit revolutionary rather than religious) enhanced by sacrifice,
and all the stages of the novel's plot are subordinated to that end.
Gorky wrote this pattern into a fictionalized version of an actual
uprising by ill-educated workers in a minor provincial industrial
town in early twentieth-century Russia. But in the novel neither the
setting nor the local identities of the protagonists are important
(except that they are proletarian), for Gorky has given them a
timeless guise, like that of the saints and princes in medieval icons
and manuscripts.

The plot of *Mother* represents a departure from medieval hagiography in that it uses twinning: not just one protagonist reaches out
toward grace, but two. But the two are not equal, for mother and
son are to each other as disciple and mentor. Although that particular relationship was common, even explicit, in revolutionary
fiction, in earlier texts the disciple did not often, as in *Mother,*
attain such complete revolutionary consciousness that he could
then play mentor for others. In *Mother* the disciple advances so far
because this enables her life to provide an allegorical account of one
stage in the working-through of history's great dialectic toward its
ultimate resolution in Communism.

The plot formula Gorky worked out for *Mother* (i.e., the disciple
acquires the likeness of the mentor and hence acquires "consciousness") proved so efficient for structuring any novel as a parable of
historical progress that it became the basis for Socialist Realism's
master plot. Or, at any rate, it was a beginning: most fully fledged
Socialist Realist novels have a dual plot, combining a version of
Mother's plot—what I call the "road to consciousness" (or to
greater "consciousness") plot—plus an account of how some
state-assigned task was fulfilled.

After *Mother* emerged from comparative obscurity to be reinstated as an exemplar in the early thirties, many of the patterns
used in it became hallmarks of Socialist Realist fiction. These in-

clude the "road to consciousness" plot formula and the positive-hero character type. Additionally, almost the same set of attributes that indicate "consciousness" in *Mother* became the icon of "consciousness" in the Stalinist novel. The formulaic epithets for the positive hero constitute the core of the Socialist Realist novel's "system of signs," consisting in part of code words ("calm") and in part of symbolic traits and gestures (the hero's pinched face or his picking-up the banner of a fallen comrade).

The post horses that *Mother* provided for Bolshevik literature were to take it a long way, but they could not deliver it to Socialist Realism in its most developed form. When Gorky wrote the novel in 1906, he could not have been expected to anticipate all the changes Bolshevik culture and ideology would undergo in the almost thirty years intervening between *Mother* and the time the canon was instituted. By comparison with Socialist Realist novels of the Stalin period, therefore, *Mother* seems much purer, simpler, and even quainter.

A striking example of change would be the various transformations that Gorky's plot formula had to undergo. They occurred partly because, heartwarming though the tale of a simple old mother rising to consciousness might be, it was not very usable or appropriate for a Soviet literature that had become the repository of official myths about the status quo. Most commonly in Soviet fiction it was an aspiring member of the vanguard who displaced the mother as "disciple"; humility and ignorance were not appropriate traits for him.

The greatest difference between the master plot as it began in *Mother* and its later expression in a Soviet Socialist Realist classic derives from Gorky's narrow sense of revolution and "consciousness." For him revolutionary "consciousness" is almost synonymous with enlightenment (as was the original German word for "consciousness," *Bewusstsein*). In fact, in several sections of the novel, Gorky effectively warns his readers of the dangers of uprisings by ill-educated peasants and of the urgency of educating them, to avert disaster.[30] For many, however, the primary attraction of revolution had been energy and action rather than "light." In Marxism, action is regarded as a greater ingredient in historical change than ideas.

Therefore, the static, icon-like image of the revolutionary in

Mother was, in later Socialist Realist novels, complemented with a
dynamic hero who had a different literary pedigree and who gave the
novel color and suspense. It was he who supplanted the little old
mother of Gorky's novel as "disciple," and the main official model
for him was Gleb Chumalov, the hero of Gladkov's novel *Cement*.

Socialist Realist Classics of the Twenties

When the Revolution occurred in 1917, it was followed by several crisis years. Between the Civil War and foreign intervention, the new regime was in danger of falling to any number of enemy forces, both within and without. The government was threatened by incredible chaos, epidemics, and shortages of basic supplies. Only the most decisive measures could save the day, and great willpower was needed to carry them out.

These extreme times gave rise to a new kind of hero. The static revolutionary martyr was replaced by a dynamic man of action. The new hero appeared not just in Party rhetoric and fiction. Those authors of non-Party, highbrow literature who were not completely alienated generated variants as well.

Times were hard, but for many intellectuals they were not without their own *frisson*. The lure of action and excitement attracted a large number of them to the Revolution, some to act in it, others to gaze in fascination. To such people the Revolution was such a shattering event that traditional language could not express it. All writers, whatever their persuasion, struggled to find ways of describing it. Mandelstam conveys the atmosphere well in a section of his poem "The Horse-Shoe Finder" (1923):

> Where to begin?
> Everything cracks and rocks.
> The air trembles with similes.
> No word is better than another;
> The earth hums with metaphor.
>
> .   .   .   .
> Thrice-blessed is he who puts a name on a song![1]

Many sought to "put a name on the song" or find a metaphor that might resound above the others and live on. It was a time that gave rise to inflated rhetoric and bombastic claims as writers struggled to pin down the quintessential revolution while "everything cracked and rocked."

Few of their epithets for the Revolution and its agents have survived beyond the initial post-Revolutionary years, when they were coined. Yet the hero image to which the age gave rise, and which writers tried to "name," endured in Soviet lore for decades to come. While the epithets of this fiction were highly symbolic, they were still somewhat descriptive and individualized, drawn uniquely for a particular hero. In consequence, one cannot take any single, isolated novel of the 1920s and discuss it as prototypical for the period as easily as one might a Socialist Realist novel from the 1930s or 1940s.

The Socialist Realist novels of the 1920s were no exception in the use of imagery unique to a particular character in a particular novel. But, beneath this surface variety, most of them have much in common. This is because virtually all were written by Party members who took upon themselves the task of popularizing Party policies, and, in doing so, most of them drew on the same source, *Pravda*. Generally speaking, the concerns and imagery characteristic of *Pravda* in any particular year prefigure the trends in Bolshevik fiction published slightly later. Indeed, one can sometimes even pin down the single article that seems to provide the theme for a specific work of fiction.

Of course, even Party rhetoric of the twenties expressed a greater variety of points of view than was possible under Stalin. *Pravda*-inspired fiction was also less homogeneous than it later became. Two major trends in Bolshevik fiction that proved highly productive emerged during the twenties; they generated further paradigms in the thirties and beyond. F. Gladkov's *Cement* and D. Furmanov's *Chapaev* are the most seminal examples of these two broad trends.

Gladkov's *Cement*

In many ways F. Gladkov's *Cement* most comprehensively exemplifies the prototypical Soviet novel. This is largely due to the fact that the plot and positive heroes of *Cement* were imitated more than any other in Soviet fiction, especially in the forties, when Gladkov was director of the Literary Institute, which trains writers. In addition, many of *Cement*'s basic values became hallmarks of the distinctive Stalinist ethos, which emerged in the thirties and forties. And yet, in many ways, it is wrong to see *Cement* as a fully fledged, completely achieved, Socialist Realist novel. It should rather be seen as an embryonic example of such novels, a relic of that stage when the "cement" had not yet hardened. It is much more novelistic than the later, truly Socialist Realist novels, which tend to an abstractness more characteristic of myth.

Of the various official progenitors of Socialist Realism, *Cement* provides the most striking example of the complex evolution of Socialist Realism and the dialectic of the literary and extraliterary forces that accompanied it. *Cement* drew heavily on *Pravda* rhetoric and themes, yet it also used the language and imagery of several nonpartisan, highbrow literary schools and made gestures toward folklore as well. Later, during the thirties, many of *Cement*'s characteristic tropes became clichés of political rhetoric. It is, then, a text that can help us perceive that Stalinist culture was put together from a variety of preexisting elements, not something that sprang full blown from the Moustache.[2]

Pravda *Influences in* Cement

When reduced to its thematic essence, *Cement* seems very typical of "proletarian" novels for the years when it was written (1922–24).[3] It even had a thematic near-identical twin in N. N. Lyashko's production novel *The Blast Furnace,* which was likewise published in 1925 (much as *Mother* had a twin in *In the Fire*).

Cement and *The Blast Furnace* both have an air of having been written with the express purpose of amplifying political rhetoric. They elaborate not just the general ideas of Marxism-Leninism but also the preoccupations of *Pravda* during the years when the action of *Cement* was set (1920–21),[4] especially the central theme that the battle for communist survival must now be fought on the economic rather than the military front.

Both novels emphasize this by providing heroes who have distinguished themselves in Civil War battles but are now redirecting their energies to the tasks of reconstruction. The novels open as their hero, a former factory worker (Gleb Chumalov in *Cement* and Korotkov in *The Blast Furnace*), returns home triumphant from the Civil War only to be dismayed at the state of his home town.

The two plots run fairly parallel from then on. The cement factory/blast furnace is covered with rust and weeds; the local proletariat, betraying their class identity, have begun to raise goats and make cigarette lighters for sale (both goats and lighters being common symbols at this time for petty bourgeois enterprise).[5] When Gleb/Korotkov tries to shame local officials for having allowed the factory/blast furnace to remain idle after the Civil War, they claim that they have applied to the appropriate organs for permission to reopen it but that permission has not yet come through. The hero will not rest with this masked indifference on the part of the bureaucrats; calling a general meeting of the factory workers, he has himself appointed as their representative, and, to try to get things moving, he goes to "the center" (i.e., the local town where agencies of the various government bodies he has to deal with are located). Both within the factory and at the center, Gleb/Korotkov is constantly running up against red tape and indifference from bourgeois experts and bureaucrats, most of whom advise him that it is both technically and economically unfeasible to reopen the factory at this time and that he is naïve and insubordinate to insist on doing so. But eventually, by mobilizing worker enthusiasm for mass voluntary labor—and with a little help from the men in leather jackets (i.e., the Cheka, or security police)—the factory/blast furnace is opened. This event is marked by a mass meeting of workers at which Gleb/Korotkov is praised highly and asked to speak. He feels deeply moved but also inarticulate because, as a true son of the working classes, he operates essentially from the heart. However, he finally manages to summon up some words, and, as the novel closes, he points to the wonderful vistas that await future generations.

There are, to be sure, some differences between the two novels (especially in their love plots). But the main difference is in the style and tone of the narration. Lyashko's narration is very spare and is presented in straightforward, colloquial speech, such as an ordinary worker might have used in recounting his experiences to fellow workers.

Where Lyashko is terse, Gladkov seems to err in the other direction, pulling out all the stops. His prose, highly rhetorical and hyperbolic, often reads like the purple passages of a cheap romance. All this was toned down in later Socialist Realist novels, where the prevailing sense of literary decorum ruled out linguistic excess. But, although the canon required restraint in language, it called for hyperbole in characterization. Thus, while the lush prose of *Cement* was so often attacked that Gladkov rewrote the novel several times,[6] the hero image he projected in Gleb was to become a convention of Socialist Realism. The very matter-of-factness of Korotkov, Lyashko's hero in *The Blast Furnace,* consigned him to relative oblivion, while his more colorful twin, Gleb Chumalov, went on to become one of the best-known positive heroes.

One reason why *The Blast Furnace* was doomed to this fate was because, even though Lyashko was assiduous in covering the main economic issues taken up in *Pravda,* he failed to pattern his hero on the new image it presented. Gladkov picked up the new image, and, as a result, his novel's appearance was hailed by most major Party critics, who, though finding it compositionally flawed, welcomed the book as the first to present a "monumental" or "romantic" image of the proletarian hero.[7] Lunacharsky, the Commissar of Culture, declared in a May Day *Pravda* article of 1926, "Achievements of Our Art": "On this cement foundation we can build farther."

The new iconic image of the revolutionary hero had been used in *Pravda* articles for some time. A good example is found in Bukharin's obituary of Yakov Sverdlov (the head of the Soviet government), published in March 1919. Sverdlov, we are told, died "at his post" from pneumonia, continuing to work selflessly for the Revolution until the very moment of his collapse. Thus his death realized the biographical metaphors for the life and death of the true revolutionary of Russian radical myth, where the proper finale is prison or death from tuberculosis (exacerbated by work)—in either case an end the hero could have avoided had he not been so unswervingly dedicated to the cause.

But Sverdlov, in Bukharin's *Pravda* obituary, does not appear as the typical martyr prince of prerevolutionary radical hagiography. He is not the stern, calm, serious but caring and gentle icon-like figure, all simplicity and shining eyes. The image is different, not simply because Bukharin refrained from using the *same* epithets for Bolshevik virtue as Gorky used in *Mother.* Bukharin's "prince" is not a *static* incarnation of virtue, but a *dynamic* figure, a veritable *perpetuum mobile* or, as Bukharin puts it, a "vessel of inexhaustible

revolutionary energy." Sverdlov's "surging nature," the reader is
told, was never still. One saw this clearly before the Revolution,
when no exile could keep him out of action: he always managed to
escape, crossing the iciest of rivers.

The Sverdlov of the *Pravda* obituary is a man of resolution and
sangfroid, an "exceptional, metallic person." He knows "everyone
and everything," and "all the threads of the administration pass
through him." If one were to sum up the essential Sverdlov in a few
words, Bukharin contends, they would be "energy, will, courage."[8]

Although this obituary was written in 1919, readers will readily
recognize in its characterization of Sverdlov the thirties image of
Bukharin's own victorious rival of those years, Stalin himself, the
"man of steel," of tireless energy and unflinching determination,
who likewise knew "everyone and everything" and had all the
"threads" of the Soviet administration in his hands. This connection has broader ramifications. It is not just that Bukharin's 1919
portrait of Sverdlov prefigures Stalin's iconic image (right down to
the stress laid on his many escapes from tsarist exile through
hazardous icy conditions). Rather, the catch phrases and com-
monplaces of "nonfictional" Bolshevik rhetoric from the Civil War
years (the Sverdlov obituary is a good example) were reechoed in
the political culture of the thirties, when the formulaic biography of
Stalin functioned as a sort of example of examples for the life of the
true Bolshevik leader.

Not just Stalin, but all heroes of the Stalinist thirties portray this
new image, set in the early twenties: they are all "struggle," "vigilance," heroic achievement, energy, and another cluster of qualities
rather like the "true grit" of the American frontier: "stickability"
(*vyderžka*), "hard as flint" (*kremen'*), and "will" (*volja*).

The new man of action was not likened to a frontiersman, however, but to the mythical knight of the Russian oral epic or *bylina,*
the *bogatyr'*. The epithet *bogatyr',* which in tsarist times had been
used as a standard term of commendation for military distinction
and had since lost most of its original connotations of "fantastic,"
recaptured some of its old aura when *Pravda* used it to sing the
praises of truly extraordinary "warriors," the heroes of the reconstruction effort. They were likened to the *bogatyr'* because of
the doctrine that the economy was now a sort of "second front" on
which the battle for communist survival was to be fought. Fiction

followed suit, and *bogatyr'* heroes abound in mid-twenties novels.[9] But of all the *bogatyri* who charged over the pages of twenties fiction, Gleb Chumalov was to live longest in Soviet culture. Heroes cast in his mold were to appear in fiction of the thirties and forties, where the call to perpetual "struggle" was to sound again and again.

Gladkov may have been influenced by one particular *Pravda* article in portraying Gleb Chumalov. This was a front-page piece by the Bolshevik leader G. Zinoviev, called "Yustin Zhuk." It reads like a capsule version of *Cement,* minus the love plot and a few other extras. Zinoviev's article is a tribute to Zhuk, a son of the working classes. Like Gleb, he led his comrades to restore a factory in his home town of Schlusselburg. Invoking a biblical reference to the just men who enable the city to stand, Zinoviev proclaims: "It is through such people that the proletarian state stands. Such people are the cement of the worker and peasant government,"[10] a claim that was echoed in *Cement,*[11] alluded to cryptically in its title, and intoned again in Lunacharsky's eulogy of the novel ("On this cement foundation we can build farther"). As if providing a clue to *Cement*'s connection with Zinoviev's article, Gladkov even uses Zhuk as the name of one of his main characters (not a particularly positive one, probably because "zhuk" [*žuk*], meaning "bug," is not the most felicitous of names for a positive hero).

We will not speculate on whether Gladkov had this article consciously or subconsciously in mind when he wrote *Cement.* "Yustin Zhuk" was just one sample of the clichés of *Pravda* rhetoric of that time, but it provides excellent examples for catching both the interplay between newspaper rhetoric and novelistic practice and the changes the dominant Bolshevik hero image had undergone since *Mother.* Whereas Pavel of *Mother* was like the martyr-prince who "stands firm" for his faith and does not seek to avoid his oppressors' blows, both Gleb and Zhuk are warriors who seek out combat and battle to the end. Both *volunteered* to fight for the Reds in the Civil War. Zhuk died a hero's death in battle. Gleb, before returning to his home town, allegedly "died and rose again" in one particularly vicious battle, and it was his military prowess that gave him his mandate to lead the workers on his return.

Zinoviev's capsule description of Zhuk is not of a wasting, dedicated revolutionary but of a robust figure: "giant Zhuk, a man

with the physique of a *bogatyr'*." Zhuk is said to "perform miracles...in his strong, capable hands everything moved." For the
local workers he was "everything," and they were completely captivated by him. In restoring the factory, Zhuk "overcame millions
of obstacles and reached his goal." The image of Zhuk visibly
converges with the image of Sverdlov, in Bukharin's obituary, as a
"vessel of inexhaustible revolutionary energy." Sverdlov, reduced
as he was by pneumonia, clearly lacked the *"bogatyr"*'s physique,"
yet he could perform prodigies as if he were a *bogatyr'*.

This new hero of Party rhetoric and literature, then, was most
remarkable, not for his political virtue (like Pavel of *Mother*) or
even for his economic achievements (like Korotkov of *The Blast
Furnace*), but for his fantastic feats. And Gleb was a *bogatyr'* par
excellence.

Ostensibly, *Cement* is a novel about postwar reconstruction and
has as its subject problems of supply, administration, labor relations, technology, and guerrilla insurgency on the part of counterrevolutionaries. But Gleb is not merely a concerned worker-cum-
Party-official who devotes his energies to mobilizing the masses,
bourgeois professionals, and bureaucrats for the task of reconstruction. Such a description would more or less exhaust the
role of Korotkov in *The Blast Furnace,* but not of this *bogatyr'*. He
charges over the novel's world with the greatest of ease, taking on
all manner of fierce, unremitting obstacles, each one of which he
manages to overcome with amazing dispatch. Even though Gleb is
ostensibly the workers' deputy on a number of committees and
head of the Party cell at the cement factory, he rarely sits, does
paper work, makes official reports, or reads proposals. Like
Sverdlov, Gleb knows "everyone and everything," and "all the
threads of the administration are in his hands." One admiring on-
looker remarks, as he watches Gleb set every corner of the economy
in motion with his incredible energy: "Dammit, Chumalov old
man! Harness yourself to the factory instead of the dynamos, and
you'll be able to make it work all by yourself."[12]

As Gleb tears around at a frenzied pace, he is constantly engaging
in combat. Bureaucratic organizations "stand in his path like a huge
boulder." His efforts to obtain lumber for fuel are sabotaged by
counterrevolutionaries who have "hidden in the crevasses like a
wild beast...they are charging here like hordes, gnashing their

teeth, whooping, giving off smoke and glinting with blood."[13]

Like the traditional *bogatyr'*, Gleb copes with obstacles that seem beyond him, often without any real struggle taking place. He cuts through red tape and gains entry to officials very much as, in the *bylina*, the hero would, for instance, force his way into a feast to which he was not bidden; thus Gleb "Straightened up, puffed out his chest . . . hit out with his fist and strode forth with great strides . . . burst open the door" and spoke "with a voice like a metal trumpet."[14] Like the *bylina* hero, too, Gleb is full of humor and zest for life, often succumbs to great passion or anger, likes to flaunt his own prowess and intimidate others with threats of violence. He is no saint and no gentleman, and yet, like the *bylina* hero, he has his own code of honor: he is always true to his faith, to his "prince" (i.e., the central leadership), and to his people, the working classes.

The signal motifs for Gleb all identify him as a warrior hero: his military decoration of the order of the Red Banner and his military helmet, tilted back on his head. This iconic motif for Gleb facilitates his identification with the *bogatyr'* because the pointed helmet of the Civil War soldier was very like the helmet worn by the *bogatyr'* in paintings. Gleb's appearances in the narrative are also usually accompanied by refrains that remind the reader of the hero's fighting past: "dead but alive," "gone through fire," "gone through blood," etc. The various bureaucrats in the novel are given individualized iconic attributes too, but mostly of metal and stone (stone, steel, cast iron, anthracite), symbolizing their intransigence and their function as obstacles in Gleb's path.

Thus *Cement* is an allegory of how the "fire" of battle was brought into the stolid, impassive environment of bureaucracy. In giving an almost literal illustration of the *Pravda* figure of speech, the industrial manager or activist as *"bogatyr',"* Gladkov gave his hero-*bogatyr'* more fantastic capabilities than were really envisaged even in *Pravda*. This can be seen in the following words Gleb addresses to his wife, which prefigure a notion generally considered to be characteristically Stalinist. Gleb ends his speech by asserting that anything is possible if only one asserts one's will:

> Even here on the work front you have to have heroism. Here that's pretty hard; you find devastation, decrepitude and starvation. . . . That's right. The mountain has come crashing down and

has crushed man like a frog. You have to make a mighty effort, get on all fours, and heave that mountain back up again. That's impossible? That's just it ... heroism is doing what's impossible.[15]

This claim, made in the early twenties, shows that at this time there were individual writers whose views were more "Stalinist" than those of the current leadership, in which Stalin himself played a prominent role. *Cement*'s faith in the great possibilities of the will form part of the prehistory of that singular political culture that makes the "Stalin" of Stalinism possible.

Literary Sources for Cement

In the twenties the pundits of the literary world rejected *Cement* as modern literature and described it either as crude pamphletry or as a pseudo-epic and therefore hopelessly anachronistic in the twentieth century.[16] Yet in many respects the novel's problem is not that it is out of step with the times but rather that Gladkov made *excessive* use of contemporary literary models. *Cement* is not just a subfunction of *Pravda*. It has literary sources totally unrelated to Party rhetoric, though these sources are mostly from the written tradition rather than the oral. Gladkov showed great zeal and enthusiasm in making Gleb into a *bylina*-like hero, but actually Gleb is no *bogatyr'*, and *Cement* is no extended or updated folk narrative but a novel.

In truth, Gladkov was too ambitious as a writer to be content with just following a simple folk form. He wanted his novel to be not a mere *narodnoe izdanie,* not a sort of folksied-up political pamphlet, but a work of literature. *Cement* was one of those attempts to convey the essence of those incredible times, to "name the song," as Mandelstam had put it. Gladkov did not rest with one single "name"—*"bogatyr'"*; he tried many. Like most novels, *Cement* is generically very eclectic: it contains snatches of mass-labor pastoral, biblical motifs, neoclassicist hymns of praise, and even echoes of that "last moment before the gallows" motif that was a favorite of Dostoevsky's.

There is a biographical reason for *Cement*'s excessive literariness. When the provincial Gladkov, having moved to Moscow after the Civil War with the idea of continuing his prerevolutionary literary

career, read his revolutionary works to a sophisticated literary audience, he was booed off the stage and was subsequently told that
his writing was twenty-five years out of date.[17] Gladkov told a
literary friend of this humiliation, and the friend advised him to
update himself by reading Bely and Remizov, masters of the highly
self-conscious and stylized "ornamental prose" then in vogue in
highbrow circles.[18] Gladkov was so crushed that he didn't write for
another year, but when he did return to writing in 1922, *Cement*
was the first major work he undertook. Not surprisingly, Bely's
influence looms large in *Cement,* especially the influence of his most
famous novel, *St. Petersburg* (1913–14).

   Gorky objected to the "ornamentalism" he detected in *Cement's*
prose, and Gladkov toned it down when he rewrote it successively
in 1934 and 1941. The influence of *St. Petersburg* in *Cement* was by
no means confined to style, for it can be sensed in much of Gladkov's imagery. *Cement* is full of passages about "the abyss" and
"the flight into eternity" and about the sensation of the self suddenly exploding into tiny pieces. Even the metaphoric use of metal
and stone in *Cement* to suggest the power and impassivity of bureaucrats cannot be considered exclusively Bolshevik in origin. In
these years the Bolsheviks certainly did not have a monopoly over
such imagery, and in *Cement* Gladkov's specific ordering of his
stone and metal metaphors is actually highly reminiscent of the
patterns in *St. Petersburg.*

   The novel *St. Petersburg* is perhaps best remembered for its motif
of the bronze horseman (the St. Petersburg equestrian statue of
Peter the Great) as a symbol of "inexorable" autocratic power and
of the suppression of native Russian traditions in the Westerniza-
tion and bureaucratization of Russia. Starting from at least
Pushkin's long poem of the same name, the bronze horseman had
become the key image for the "myth of St. Petersburg," for debates
about Russia's destiny that begin with the premise that its natural
course was changed under Peter when he Westernized Russia, symbolized in the founding of St. Petersburg.

   In *Cement* one senses the spectral presence of the bronze horseman of Bely's novel in many of the scenes involving Badin, Gleb's
most powerful bureaucrat-antagonist. Especially reminiscent is the
scene in which Badin rapes the young communist activist, Polya:

Badin approaches her bed "inexorably" and places his "heavy body on hers."[19]

The imprint of Bely's bronze horseman is even stronger in a scene where Gleb himself, in his capacity as incarnation of Bolshevik power, plays "bronze horseman" (supreme autocrat) to the bourgeois engineer Kleist, who has thus far refused to work for the new regime. Their encounter seems to be patterned on one in *St. Petersburg*, when the statue of the bronze horseman appears before an overwrought intelligentsia terrorist, Alexander Ivanovich, on whose collarbone it places its "ponderous hand" and pours molten metal into him.[20] In *St. Petersburg* the bronze horseman pours metal into Alexander Ivanovich to infuse him with the courage to murder his double-crossing fellow conspirator, Lippanchenko. In *Cement* Gleb pours his "iron" into Kleist so that the engineer will reorient himself from the values of bourgeois society to those of the "iron age"; Kleist becomes a changed man and begins to work for the factory reconstruction effort as Gleb had commanded him to. Still, despite the many parallels, this scene in *Cement* is in some respects an inversion of the exchange in *St. Petersburg*: it is the representative of the oppressed classes (Gleb) who pours "iron" into someone representing the autocratic regime and Westernism. As Kleist's name not so subtly suggests ("German Germanovich Kleist"), Kleist stands for the classic Westernist values in the "myth of St. Petersburg": empty formalism; sterile, abstract, logical thought; a rigidly hierarchical sense; a condescending attitude toward native Russian endeavor; and the bureaucratic cast of mind.

At the same time, some elements from revolutionary fiction have been written into this reworking of the St. Petersburg myth. For instance, those iconic adjectives for "consciousness"—"calm," "simple," and "stern"—are attributed to Gleb. Also, if the exchange between him and Kleist parallels that between the bronze horseman and Alexander Ivanovich in *St. Petersburg*, it also hearkens back to the mentor / disciple pattern of nineteenth-century radical fiction (in his encounter with the more "conscious" Gleb, Kleist sees the light).

Gladkov sees as the essence of Bolshevik power not a new form of autocracy but rather a purifying force that will finally liberate Russia from the wrong done her by Peter and his successors. In literature of the early twenties this was a common interpretation of the Revolution's role. It was, for instance, at the heart of one current highbrow vogue, Scythianism, whose leading writer, Boris Pilnyak, was the most popular writer in the Soviet Union in 1922, the year Gladkov began *Cement*.[21]

These many interrelationships between Gladkov's *Cement* and texts from diverse traditions illustrate two important points. First, the extent to which the basic images and ideas of Stalinist culture should not be regarded as alien to and entirely separate from those of rival intellectual traditions; second, the dual origin of the twenties exemplars both in the language of the Party journalism of the time and in the language of highbrow—and to some extent folk—literary traditions.

Cement's Plot as a Scrambled Version of the Master Plot

Cement's plot presents something of a paradox: *Cement* is *the* source for the plot of the most common type of Soviet novel, the production novel (see Appendix A); yet, when it was written, the master plot had not yet fully evolved. Consequently, *Cement* contains most of the elements that later were to be more systematically articulated in the full-blown Socialist Realist novel.

By comparison with those rigidly coded Stalinist novels, *Cement* is more open-ended structurally, less teleological, and more prodigal in its use of symbolic forms. The phases of the plot have not yet become "functions," to use Propp's terms. The protagonists are still characters in their own right rather than mere subfunctions of their roles as in the master plot. Indeed, the various events in *Cement* that were to become "functions" in Stalinist novels are scattered through the plot in what seems, ex post facto, to be a somewhat haphazard fashion. Many functions that in later novels were conventionally performed only by the hero or his "mentor" are, in *Cement*, distributed among several protagonists—notably those performed by Sergey, a Party member who is purged toward the end of the novel and whose place on the positive / negative spectrum is difficult to pinpoint. The functions Sergey performs include the pivotal one: "the hero transcends his selfish impulses and acquires an extrapersonal identity."[22]

In *Cement* the unsystematic distribution of the hero's functions

does not undermine the political moral to be drawn from the novel
as much as it would in a later Socialist Realist work because Gladkov has not divided his characters into "positive" and "negative."
Badin is a good example of this. He is the very incarnation of power
and effectiveness, and Dasha, Gleb's wife, admires him for this. Yet
he is also Gleb's antagonist, and even a rapist. Later redactions made
Badin more nefarious, yet he still does not emerge as a true "negative
character."

This diffuseness in *Cement* is not due entirely to its being an early,
rudimentary example of the Socialist Realist tradition. *Mother,* the
"founder" of that tradition, has an extremely coherent plot, with
none of *Cement*'s ambiguity in placing its heroes on the positive/
negative spectrum: Pavel is always positive, while his mother becomes consistently more positive. Gleb, by contrast, appears
weaker or even less positive than other protagonists in some scenes,
including not only meetings with his wife, Dasha, but even in encounters with Badin.

It is largely at the end of *Cement* that it begins to differ un-
mistakably from the patterns of the standard Stalinist novel. It
seems to lack a mechanism for closure, for rounding off the plot.
Gladkov merely packs certain protagonists off in a major administrative reshuffle, declares the factory reconstruction to be at an end,
and used this as the sole motive for Gleb's transcendence of self-
interest and being reconciled to the loss of his wife. But Gleb has not
yet mastered his violent antagonism to Badin, and the reader does
not doubt that the old conflicts and contradictions will resurface
after the ceremony that opens the factory. The novel's lack of resolution derives from Gladkov's lingering attachments to novelistic
conventions and his failure to fully mythicize his text. Gladkov
leaves Gleb as an individual to the end and therefore does not use
the ready-made, Marxist-Leninist formulas for historical resolution.

One of the most problematical aspects of the novel for Soviet
critics was Gleb's anarchic, willful tendencies. Gleb actually revels
in his lack of control! The later production novels were able to use a
bogatyr'-like positive hero without permitting his colorful postur-
ing to undermine the novel's pervasive organization ethos and
respect for hierarchy, but Gladkov, in *Cement,* comes close to
celebrating grass-roots initiative without integrating it into a hierarchical structure.

Not completely, however. Like the *bogatyr'* of the *bylina,* who always pays his ritual respects to God and the prince as he enters the prince's quarters, Gleb somehow remains on the right side of due process throughout: as head of the factory Party committee, he is himself part of the local hierarchy; he always takes his plans to the appropriate government bodies for approval; and while it is true that two government organs oppose the restoration of the factory (Glavcement and Sovnarkhoz), Gleb does manage to secure approval from another (Promburo).

The problem is not so much that Gleb stands outside the hierarchical structure and its practices but that his initiative from below is not matched (as it was in later production novels) by any *prominent* guiding force from above. In other words, Gladkov has dispensed with the convention of the mentor / disciple pattern: Gleb has no mentors to temper his willfullness and teach him self-control. Several protagonists assume this function at times (his wife, Dasha; the Cheka head, Chibis; even Badin!), but not consistently or with palpable effect.

Cement not only appears to celebrate willfulness, but, when it actually deals with agents of authority and control, the reader encounters ambiguity, sketchy development, and fuzziness. Symptomatically, the meaning of *the* crucial epithet of the Soviet novel, *spokojnyj* ("calm, confident"), is not fixed. As we saw in *Mother, spokojnyj* is conventionally used as a sign of complete self-control and firmness in the revolutionary faith. In *Cement,* however, this sign is used not only with great ambivalence but primarily to indicate a *negative* quality: bureaucratic indifference and smugness.[23] This fluctuation is a surface indicator of the changing times in which the novel was written. In twenties fiction, *spokojnyj* did not have a fixed meaning because, at the time, interpretations of the Marxist-Leninist opposition spontaneity / consciousness were highly controversial and fluid.

The Spontaneity / Consciousness Dialectic and Bolshevik Novels of the Twenties

For most of the twenties the Party position on the respective roles of "spontaneity" and "consciousness" in bringing progress to Soviet society was not fixed. In part, this reflects disagreements within the Party itself. Also, during the crisis months of the Civil War,

Bolshevik rhetoric gave "spontaneous" forces a much more positive role in history than had been the case before: the Party was
confronted by a series of economic, political, and military crises in
all of which peasant support was a key factor in pulling through.

As the Civil War came to an end, however, and the Bolsheviks
began to gain the upper hand, their concern was less sheer survival
than to regularize the economy and their own administration.
These new concerns necessitated a shift in values—to efficiency
rather than sheer bravery, consistency and control rather than
popularity, etc. The union between the highbrow cult of "spontaneity" (as sheer, elemental energy) and Bolshevik interest in
"spontaneity" (as peasant support) began to come apart.

One can detect the changes in official attitudes from the end of
1919 (in March 1919 the Sverdlov obituary was published in
Pravda). In a *Pravda* article of November 25 entitled "Two Types,"
the author, N. Kostelevskaya, contrasts two kinds of military
leader. The first is daring, energetic, and popular, yet the author
compares him unfavorably to what she calls the "vigilant
helmsman," the solid, knowledgeable bureaucrat who can run an
efficient operation, has a strong sense of the way forward, and,
although he may not captivate his soldiers' imaginations, can earn
their respect and guide them to the right end.[24] In other words,
while the daring folk hero might captivate the masses, his useful-
ness, unless he was "conscious," would be doubtful and very
short-lived; that is, judged by prevailing attitudes in *Pravda*, *Cement* was very dated by the time it was published in 1925.

In Soviet literary histories it is a cliché that during the 1920s
literature went from the cult of "spontaneity" to one of "consciousness."[25] In fact, however, this happened quite early. No
sooner had the Bolshevik press begun to temper its enthusiasm for
"spontaneous" heroes than many committed writers began to sing
the praises of the "conscious" heroes and to disparage the "spontaneous." Predominantly, these writers were themselves Party
members with some experience in writing for the Party press, men
such as S. Serafimovich with *The Iron Flood* (1924), Y. Libedinsky
with *A Week* (1922) and *The Commissars* (1925), D. Furmanov
with *Chapaev* (1923) and *The Revolt* (1924), and A. Fadeev with
"Against the Current" (1923), "The Flood" (1924), and *The Rout*
(1927). It will be noted that all these books were published in or

before 1927—in other words, before Stalin was absolutely in power and before the Party as such had made much effort to guide writers in their choice of themes. In other words, these writers decided to celebrate "consciousness" in their fiction on their own initiative. Most of these works were written because the author felt annoyed at the influence of some popular book that idealized "spontaneity" (especially those written by Pilnyak) and hoped to counteract its influence.[26]

Three of the works cited above were adopted in the thirties as official models of Socialist Realism—D. Furmanov's *Chapaev*, A. Serafimovich's *The Iron Flood*, and A. Fadeev's *The Rout*. Whether as a cause or effect of their adoption, they became important in shaping the master plot as a parable of the triumph of "consciousness" over "spontaneity." Of the three, *Chapaev* will be discussed here because it provides both a more explicitly articulated example of this type of twenties prose than the other two and because, thanks largely to the enormous success of the 1934 film based on it, *Chapaev* played an especially formative role in Soviet culture of the thirties.

Furmanov's Chapaev

Chapaev is based on historical fact. It tells of a legendary peasant Red Army commander, Chapaev, who commanded regiments in Siberia and the Urals during the Civil War. Furmanov had worked as a commissar, or head of political affairs, in Chapaev's regiment for part of the Civil War, and the book describes his own experiences in dealing with Chapaev. It is narrated in the first person by Chapaev's commissar, who, although he goes by the name of Klychkov, pretty much represents Furmanov himself. Most of the other protagonists are either fictional or given fictitious names, but both Chapaev and Frunze (his senior commander) are given their real names and assume much the same roles in the book as they did in historical reality.

Thus, potentially, *Chapaev* provides an interesting example of the tension in Socialist Realist fiction between showing "what is" (or, in this case, what was) and showing "what ought to be" (ought to have been). Furmanov intended his book to make a contribution to Party history rather than to literature, and it first came out with

the publishing house History of the Party;[27] but its ultimate role
was to survive as a *model* work of Soviet fiction. This change of
identity was not as radical as might first appear, for, once the
perception of reality is guided by the Marxist-Leninist world view,
one can invent extra or synthetic figures and events to fit into that
reality without distorting its basic veracity (in Marxist-Leninist
terms).

Chapaev represents a variety of creative journalism. It illustrates
the points made in the *Pravda* article cited above, N. Kostelevskaya's "Two Types." Chapaev and Klychkov are presented in
much the same terms as the two contrasting types in the article.
Klychkov, an educated, selfless working-class Party official, is the
more solid, "conscious," and efficient leader, less dashing than
Chapaev but more reliable and, ultimately, more valuable.
Chapaev, by contrast, is a semiliterate peasant leader and is quite
explicitly identified as an example of the traditional "spontaneity"
of the peasant rebel, the *buntar'*.[28] He is a Party member but is
very confused about its ideology and policies, is anarchic, self-
seeking, and impetuous as a commander, and is a mob orator who
can only speak illogically, "from the heart." As with the "two
types" of the *Pravda* article, Chapaev is daring and commands the
unflinching loyalty of his men as he takes them from victory to
victory, whereas Klychkov, less popular and less spectacular in his
achievements, is a better administrator.

Throughout the book Klychkov muses on the strengths and limitations of Chapaev as a prime example of the "spontaneous" hero.
In Klychkov's view, the risk in giving authority to a Chapaev is very
high because "the spontaneous and elemental [*stixija*] . . . God only
knows what direction it will take."[29] He concludes that, given
Chapaev's fame, his enormous power to sway the peasant masses,
and his great military gifts, every effort should be made to "take
him in hand" and "make him into a spiritual captive."[30]

Klychkov begins the task of "enlightening" Chapaev in a series of
comradely, low-key talks about politics, knowledge, etc. Chapaev is
at first resistant, but Klychkov is soon able to report, using a biblical metaphor from *What Is to Be Done?*, that "the seed is falling on
fertile ground."[31] Soon the proud, gruff folk hero has become tremendously close to his mentor, Klychkov. Chapaev is very upset
when Klychkov is promoted and posted away from the regiment.

By then he is showing promise of maturing into a relatively "conscious" and reliable Party cadre. This hope is never realized, for he is killed shortly afterward. The book closes as his men return to the place where he was killed and swear oaths over his grave before moving on to further battles.

The plot of *Chapaev* sounds rather like that of Gorky's *Mother:* the tale of how an ignorant, superstitious peasant progresses in "consciousness" and knowledge under the tutelage of a formed and "conscious" mentor. But there is a crucial difference in that Chapaev is far from being a humble, modest disciple, like his counterpart in Gorky's novel (the mother herself); he in fact far excels his mentor, Klychkov, in courage, vigor, fame, and even military strategy.

In these respects Chapaev is comparable with that other popular and dashing hero, Gleb Chumalov, of Gladkov's *Cement.* Thus, effectively, *Chapaev* has two types of hero, one (Chapaev) the incarnation of a very positive and vital form of "spontaneity," as was Gleb in *Cement,* the other (Klychkov) the incarnation of "consciousness," as was Pavel in *Mother.* But Chapaev did not retain the same identity (as "spontaneity" incarnate) to the end. The plot charts his progress from a state where he primarily exemplified "spontaneity" to one where he exemplified greater "consciousness." Chapaev did not complete this progression and attain true "consciousness," but his martyr-like death in revolutionary battle conferred on him something like the "grace" (to use a religious metaphor) of true "consciousness."

Thus in *Chapaev* we find a plot that provides a formula for combining the different hero types of *Mother* and *Cement* and also for resolving some of the fuzziness and open-endedness we saw at the end of *Cement,* where the hero is still prey to "spontaneity" and has not yet really resolved the dialectic within himself. In effect, the Socialist Realist master plot involves combining elements from *Mother* and *Cement* by means of a formula one can derive from *Chapaev.* This does not mean that, in writing *Chapaev,* Furmanov deliberately sought a way of amalgamating the other two novels. In point of fact the publication of *Cement* postdates that of *Chapaev* (1925 as compared with 1923); but even if that had not been the case, each of the novels is far from unique in its plot structure and represents general trends in committed fiction. The synthesizing of these trends occurred not in the twenties but in the thirties.

When Furmanov wrote his "historical" account of Chapaev and himself into the Marxist-Leninist pattern of the spontaneity/consciousness dialectic, he was not so much distorting reality as refracting it through the prism of his own deeply felt world view. The novel is less a "fictionalized" or inaccurate account of reality than it is generically somewhat like the Old Russian genre of the chronicle: events are narrated to confirm and embellish the historical position of that power—the Party—which Furmanov serves as scribe. Crucial aspects of writing such a narrative are selection and ordering of historical material and the adjustment of facts to provide a more economical and cogent illustration of that higher-order reality, History.

In his diaries Furmanov discussed his dilemmas in writing *Chapaev* and how he tried to negotiate a course somewhere between actual events and invention. He favored presenting his hero "as he really was" rather than as a "fantastic figure." At the same time, he explicitly rejected a purely "photographic" approach in favor of submitting the petty detail of reality to a "strict selection process" in order to allow his narrative to express something "more enduring, more momentous, and deeper" by means of what he called "symbols."[32]

Many of the "symbols" Furmanov uses come from the common pool of nineteenth-century revolutionary lore, and they provide good examples of the way much of that old lore was being coopted. For instance, the novel's end, with the death of Chapaev and the graveside oaths of his remaining comrades, was a basic motif of the old *narodnye izdanija* and other nineteenth-century texts. In the twenties you can find graveside oaths in much Bolshevik fiction, rhetoric, and even public ritual (consider Stalin's celebrated oath after Lenin's death in 1924), and this convention continued into the thirties and beyond as a major symbol of Stalinist culture.

The key element in Furmanov's "strict selection process" consisted not in his choice of symbols but in his ordering of the material according to the Bolshevik account of history. Both Klychkov and Chapaev appear as eminently human and even vaguely idiosyncratic, each with his own foibles and fears. Yet, at the same time, each has an extrapersonal identity, each fulfills a role shaped for him by History. This aspect of the novel comes out in different ways. For instance, Chapaev, at thirty-five, is in fact no younger than Klychkov, but, because he is politically immature (in Marxist-Leninist terms), he is frequently described as "childlike."[33] Also, since Chapaev's conversion to "consciousness" is motivated by History, it does not have to be accounted for by means of plot and character and occurs almost as effortlessly as Gleb (in *Cement*) clears the many hurdles standing between him and his goal. In other words, the plot of *Chapaev* is mythologized.

Ironically, one of Klychkov/Furmanov's greatest concerns in *Chapaev* was to *demythologize* his hero. At every opportunity Klychkov points out how, in the given instance, the Chapaev of legend is greater than the Chapaev of reality, whose heroism and military feats were really no greater (and perhaps even less) than those of many other Red Army commanders who never became as famous. Klychkov concludes that Chapaev's achievement was not due to any enduring superhuman qualities. Rather, his particular traits *happened* to coincide with the needs of the Revolution at that particular time; at another time, in another place, and in other circumstances, a rather different type of leader would have been necessary.[34]

Furmanov's cool skepticism about Chapaev reflects his opposition to the then commonly held view that Soviet writers should "romanticize" their subjects. Furmanov does not so much *de*mythologize, however, as *counter*mythologize: he sets himself/Klychkov up (impersonally) as a counterexample to that of the then popular hero type, the "spontaneous" folk leader.

With works like *Chapaev*, then, the trend in Soviet fiction that was later to be known as Socialist Realism made what can be seen ex post facto as a major step toward its final place in the tradition of the Stalinist novel. Although the plot of *Chapaev* was similar to that of later Socialist Realist classics, its mode of narration was not. For instance, *Chapaev* has a highly conscious first-person narrator, a form that is extremely rare in later Soviet literature. *Chapaev*, with its direct or semidirect representation of the spontaneity/consciousness dialectic and its relatively motivated plot, is in stark contrast to the more symbolic and ritualized modes of later novels.

Thus, in Bolshevik fiction of the twenties, both literary and extra-literary forces were closely implicated. In *Cement*, for instance, a determining role was played both by Symbolist rhetoric (Bely) and by journalistic rhetoric from *Pravda*. During the thirties the intertwining of the literary and the extraliterary became even more marked. It is obvious that after the "homogenization" of literature between 1932 and 1934, political mythology was more consistently reflected in literary structures than before. However, in the ensuing chapters, I hope to document what is less obvious but equally important: the degree to which political mythology was itself in turn affected by literature, even by ideas and imagery that were present in earlier, non-Bolshevik texts.

High Stalinist Culture

Introduction

When Stalin came to power around 1927, the revolution was already a decade old. It was to pass its second decade during the height of the thirties purges, 1936–37. To have sustained the original revolutionary *élan* for so long would have been an incredible achievement, yet, during the thirties, the leadership did maintain some sort of an *élan,* partly by fiat and partly by creating a fantastic age. That is, whether the achievements were fantastic or not, the ethos was charged with fantastic symbols.

Although consistent in its extremism, Stalinist culture was not in fact a single entity. During the period between Stalin's accession and World War II the culture generated two antithetical myth systems. These could be described in terms of the two somewhat contrary aspects of a socialist or communist revolution. Such a revolution involves bringing about a more rational, egalitarian, and harmonious society, but, in order to achieve that result, it requires extraordinary events and radical change. After Stalin came to power, the leadership, with typical Russian literalism and extremism, separated these two aspects of revolution and tried each in turn, benefiting from the resultant lack of ambiguity by being able to take each to an extreme.

The first phase in this sequence corresponds roughly to the years of the First Five-Year Plan, 1928–31, when the Soviet government launched its campaign for industrialization and for the collectivization of peasant farms. These two programs were accompanied by a very specific ethos and by specific cultural myths. It was an age of radical utopianism, of egalitarian extremism: all of Soviet society was to be submitted to a compulsory leveling until there were virtually no tall trees other than Stalin. There was a cult of the "little man," of the everyday, the prosaic, the practical task. People

looked to a well-regulated, smooth-running social order, to a modernized society in which the technological level was high and enlightenment was spread evenly over the land.

Around 1931 a wave of reaction set in against the Five-Year Plan
ethos. It was as if everyone had tired of the "little man," of sober
reality and efficiency; they looked for something "higher." This
wave of reaction peaked in the mid-thirties in an age of truly fantastic superheroes (and dramatic purges). The culture of this period,
High Stalinism, will be analyzed in the chapters of Part Two.

4

The Machine and the
Garden: Literature and
Metaphors for the
New Society

In December, 1920, the Civil War was drawing to a close and the Soviet government was turning its attention to building up the economy. Lenin addressed the Eighth Party Congress and introduced a slogan for the way forward: "Communism equals Soviet power plus the electrification of the entire country." Lenin maintained that without electrifying all sections of the economy—agriculture, industry, and transport—the Soviet state would be doomed to remain a backward realm of "small peasant holdings." But as he elaborated the theme further, it became clear that Enlightenment values colored his vision: electrification would bring an end to the "dark" of the villages, bring them "enlightenment," and put an end to the nation's scourge of "illiteracy."[1]

Lenin's enthusiasm for electricity had its precedent in Marx, who gave that recently discovered wonder a central role in his materialist theory of science. Marx declared that the "age of steam," in which the capitalist world had been living, was rapidly being superseded by a more revolutionary "age of electricity." He contended that the political revolution he sought would follow this technological revolution.[2] Thus, for both Lenin and Marx, electricity was a symbol of technological progress, of knowledge, and of society organized on a rational, scientific basis.

Stalin always took care to identify his policies as Leninist, and in one of his key Five-Year Plan addresses (at the Central Committee Plenum of November, 1928), he invoked Lenin's slogan in justifying his policy for large-scale collectivization of agriculture: by "electrification," Stalin said, Lenin meant industrialization in general, and the time was now ripe for industrializing the entire country, including agriculture, which would be "industrialized" in the sense that the rural sector would be converted from one based on small holdings to large-scale operation, highly mechanized and subject to central planning and control.[3] And so began the drive to collectivize Soviet farms.

As this statement by Stalin suggests, during the Five-Year Plan period he, and large sections of Soviet society along with him, were infatuated with a vision of industrial utopia. They wanted to convert all the diverse workings of their society to the one model of industrialization: everything should be scientifically planned, mechanized, and large-scale. Indeed, so obsessed were they with the benefits of industrialization that they subsumed under the one ritualized myth of industrialization not only the economic but the political and social revolutions as well. They even believed that social ills could be cured by industrialization. Indeed, it was often claimed, especially in fiction, that human psychology could be changed by putting people to work at machines: inexorably, the machine's regular, controlled, rational rhythms would impress themselves on the "anarchic" and "primitive" psyches of those who worked them.[4]

The machine stood for harmony, progress, control, while that which was not integrated with the machine was condemned as "chaos, hard labor, primordial, and lacking rhythm."[5] It was even pointed out (taking a cue from Stalin)[6] that the traditional revolutionary values of enthusiasm and sacrifice, while laudable in their own way, could never achieve as much as that which was planned and controlled and that utilized the latest technology. Standard pieces in literature of this period show the contrast between what a single machine can do as compared to many men or horses.[7]

In this atmosphere of fervid industrial utopianism, the machine became the dominant cultural symbol for Soviet society. Society was a "train," rushing forth into space to shorten the distances in that vast land, to collapse time and advance Soviet society rapidly over the hundred years it lagged behind the West, so that it could catch up in "ten years," as Stalin had promised in a speech of 1928.[8] It was a "planned city," in which everything was scientifically coordinated and the latest technology used; it was a tractor, purring contentedly; a crane, a dirigible, an airplane, and so on. The machine metaphor was even used for pre-Soviet Russia. In L. Sobolev's novel *Complete Overhaul* (1932), tsarist society is likened to a naval ship, taking part in the Russo-Japanese war, which needed a "complete overhaul."[9]

The modern technological age also provided figurative models

for the relationships between the various elements in society. The
individual was conceived as a "part" of that greater whole, the
machine, and the relationship between him and his society was seen
as mechanical and regulative. Man was a "bolt" or a "whistle" in
the great train of society, a ball-bearing in the tractor, etc. *Pravda*
rhetoric of these years commonly called Party bodies "levers," and
the Party itself was, to use the titles of two novels of the period, like
the society/train's *Driving Axle*, or the society/factory's *Great
Conveyor Belt*. Leaders were also to epitomize machine-age values:
they were to be tireless, disciplined, efficient, and relentless—
subfunctions of the great "machine" they worked for.

It would seem, then, that the industrial nightmare that Charlie
Chaplin portrayed in his film *Modern Times* was the dream of
Soviet society in those years. Alternatively, the machine could be
seen as a vindicating symbol used by a regime bent on imposing
totalitarian order. I believe the machine became a cultural symbol
more out of utopian enthusiasm than a sinister design to manipu-
late. During the First Five-Year Plan, many were affected with millennial enthusiasm. They held that man and his society could be
changed virtually overnight.

In a sense the first Five-Year Plan represents a daring, utopian
attempt at an instant solution to Russia's nagging dilemmas: the
gulf between the illiterate masses and the educated classes, between
rich and poor, between city and country, and so on. The government and large sections of the population truly hoped to resolve
these dilemmas by bringing "the city" (electricity, technology, education, planning) to the entire countryside. The plan's aims can be
compared with those of Peter the Great when he tried to Westernize
Russia and built a new model city, St. Petersburg, as a beacon to
guide Russia out of darkness into the modern era. Just as Peter
imported know-how from Europe to achieve his goals, the Soviet
Russians studied and imported American expertise (especially from
Detroit) to start them on the right road. In spite of the xenophobia
of these years, analogies were often drawn between Stalin and Peter
(the "Westernizer").[10]

The goals of the Five-Year Plan also had some specifically Marxist
coloring. The leadership aimed not merely to modernize but to
eliminate conflict between the bourgeoisie and the proletariat, between mental and physical labor, and so on. For both the age-old
Russian and the specifically Marxist problems, the general solutions

were the same: a compulsory "leveling," so that the privileged
would dissolve in the masses and everyone and everything would be
harnessed to the immediate tasks of the industrial effort.
Bringing the "city" to the "country" was the prevailing but not
the only scheme proposed for attaining this harmony. A significant
minority sought, with some official backing, to achieve it not by
bringing the city to the countryside but by abandoning the big cities
and resettling their population in smaller urban communities. The
entire country was to be filled with a network of small-scale
"socialist" or "green" towns. An explicit aim of many planners of
these towns was to free citizens from the oppressive authority exercised on them in the cities. Many antiurban planners wanted the
buildings in their towns not to be set out on a grid but to "meander,"
to be scattered haphazardly over the terrain.[11]

The antiurban planners, however, shared many of the "enlightenment" values, including a reliance on advanced technology, egali-
tarianism, and the belief that man could be changed by his environment. For both urbanists and antiurbanists, the crucial element in
planning the town of the future was Lenin's symbolic panacea,
electricity, and especially electric trains.

This urbanist / antiurbanist dichotomy among Five-Year Plan
visionaries provides a good illustration of a very basic division
among Soviet enthusiasts in interpreting the Revolution. This split
is dramatized in the contrasting interpretations Five-Year planners
had of the meaning of that seemingly straightforward material
phenomenon, "electricity." For the urbanists electricity meant,
above all, "light" (order, progress, knowledge, technology); for the
antiurbanists it meant, above all, energy—the force that would
drive trains at such speeds that the distances between settlements
could be broken down and the country deurbanized and de-
centralized.

These contrasting concepts of electricity correspond roughly to
the different twenties interpretations of the Revolution. For Bolshevik intellectuals of the twenties, taking their cue from Lenin, the
Revolution meant *primarily* bringing "light" to the country—
"consciousness," a regulated, rational order, an end to all prejudice
and superstition, and modernization. But for many others it meant
primarily some release of energy. There were several different for-
mulations of this sense of the Revolution as bringing a release of

"energy." For the Scythians, the Revolution was the expression of a
native Russian force or "energy" that had burst forth to rend asun-
der the corrupt, artificial, autocratic, and Western tsarist order; it
was something natural, anarchic, and instinctive to the Russian
people. But for many intellectuals—and here E. Zamyatin was a
prime and seminal representative—the Revolution represented a
release of energy in a more philosophical sense. To Zamyatin, revolution was an "explosion," a setting "afire" of the planet to
"thrust it off the smooth highway of evolution." In revolutions,
received truths and dogmas are overturned; what seems certain and
predictable is confounded. Revolution is, in other words, the opposite of bringing "light" and "truth." Zamyatin admired heretics, the
arbitrary, and the contingent. For him no "truth" could be immu-
table; it must be something both Promethean and protean, and only
the heretic-artist could perceive it.[12]

The Five-Year Plan aimed to bring not only "light" to Russia (as
order and knowledge) but also technology. In this the Plan was
flying in the face of the intelligentsia's traditional ambivalence on
modernization. While most Party intellectuals and proletarian writers were enthusiastic about the machine, among non-Party intellectuals there was a fear of the technological age and of
mechanized, regulated society generally. The avant-garde Futurists
and Constructivists were something of an exception, but even in
their case (and for their leader, Mayakovsky, especially) the
exuberance with which they sang of the machine in the early twenties was tempered by doubts by the end of the decade.

So, while for many Soviet writers the Five-Year Plan goal of
eliminating the gap between the educated and the masses was most
laudable, the Plan's central goal of ushering Russia into the
technological age with all possible speed was more problematical.
These writers were able to wear the mantle of a sort of "repentant
nobleman" and dissolve themselves in the masses of "the people"
more readily than they could sing the praises of industrial utopia.
Many were caught up by the age's millennial pathos and overcame
their traditional attitudes, although often their hymns of praise to
the machine seemed a trifle stilted. The nonmachine world, that
which is natural and visceral, came creeping into panegyrics to
technology.

How long Soviet writers could maintain the stance required of

them by "the age" was a real question. But the incipient conflicts
did not come to a head because, in 1931, the radical utopian tide of
the Five-Year Plan reached its high point and then began to retreat.
The retreat itself was sounded from the highest quarters. In a speech
of July, 1931, to Soviet managers, Stalin proposed a highly differentiated system of wage payment, which discriminated against the
unskilled worker, and a change of policy toward the old professional intelligentsia—a change from a policy of "rout" to one of
"encouragement and concern."[13] The immediate reasons for Stalin's signal speech were no doubt largely economic (the hour of
reckoning for the Five-Year Plan—1932—was drawing near, and
production targets had not been met). But it provided a pretext for
putting the entire ensemble of Five-Year Plan values up for review.
Among other things, authoritative voices began to lament the fact
that the age's obsession with technology, statistics, and immediate
practical needs had crowded out that higher and more enduring
value, ideology.

Although Soviet society continued to give industrialization highest priority—and has done so to this day—the machine was quickly
jettisoned as the root metaphor of the new society. It provided a
cogent image of a society where all were to be united as brothers for
an all-out industrial effort, but it had serious limitations as an
illustrative figure for Marxist-Leninist-Stalinist ideology, with its
heavy voluntarist coloring. A machine is too impersonal, a sort of
perpetuum mobile. It does not provide for the guiding role of the
Party and its leaders (even the "driving axle" of the "train" is
locked into the same inexorable rhythm as its minor parts); it cannot
encompass change and historical development, establish legitimacy,
or "show heroes"—all increasingly important tasks of Soviet
rhetoric. Nor, above all, can it express that key notion of the
Stalinist vocabulary, "struggle."

For literature, this reaction against Five-Year Plan values was
especially crucial because it coincided with momentous changes in
Soviet literary life in the early thirties. Stalin's speech to the Soviet
managers came just a month after Gorky's triumphant return to
Russia. Less than a year later, all Soviet writers were organized into
a single Writers' Union, and required to follow the one literary
method, Socialist Realism. Moreover, Socialist Realism itself was

not yet fully formulated at the time it was adopted as *the* method
for Soviet literature. Thus, the guidelines for Socialist Realism were
thought out during a wave of reaction against machine-age values.

When, after 1931, the literary world was able to join the rest of
Soviet society in a reaction against the cult of the machine, it was no
longer able to go back to some of the popular alternative cults of
the twenties, such as the celebration of mass upheaval or the cult of
the artist-heretic as a "seer" of the way forward. When Western
writers react against machine-age urban society, they usually look
nostalgically to the preindustrial environment, to nature. In Soviet
literature the natural world began to supplant the machine too,
although without the nostalgia or sense of refuge from the urban
world that one finds in Western literature. Metaphors from nature
began to supplant machine metaphors in the press and in official
speeches as well.

In literature the cult of the machine was even shorter-lived than
in official rhetoric, lasting for only a year or so at most. Increasingly, novels sang the praises of nature and billed their heroes
as adventurers in the physical world who were engaged in some epic
struggle against brute, elemental forces. When the ostensible subject
of the novel was some factory or construction project, writers
nevertheless contrived to bring nature into the world of the machine. Trees growing in the factory yard became important symbols in the everyday lives of the workers. Machinery was an-
thropomorphized so that, instead of impressing its inexorable
rhythms on human psyches, it took on natural rhythms or even
anarchic rhythms. Natural disasters in the very stronghold of
technology were staged so that the *essential* drama took place in the
natural world, with the machine as mere cardboard backdrop.[14]
When situations proved intractable to the introduction of nature
herself, novelists nevertheless usually used nature as the source of
their novels' controlling metaphors. In other words, to reverse the
title of Leo Marx's study of American pastoral, if, in American
literature, the new Adam was dismayed to find "the machine in the
garden," Soviet writers strove to put "the garden in the machine."[15]

Once the machine was supplanted by the garden, it became
essential that all heroes be shown to have a strong affinity for
nature. In many novels the child of the city would be taken out into

nature by his parents, and its impact on his development into *the* positive hero would have the same formulaic status as the miraculous signs of sainthood which, in *vitae,* conventionally occurred before the saint's adulthood.[16] That this practice represents a change from Five-Year Plan fiction can be seen in Panferov's classic of collectivization, *Brusski,* which came out between 1929 and 1933 and therefore straddles the age of the machine and the age of nature. Its central hero, Kirill Zhdarkin, is, in the sections which appeared between 1929 and 1930, shown to have been formed for collective-farm leadership by his exposure to the city and the machine, but for the sections appearing in 1933 the account of Kirill is virtually redone. The machine is deprecated, and Kirill's leadership qualities are imputed to his childhood among wild horses.[17]

One is tempted to account for this trend by pointing to the fact that most Soviet Russians were peasants or of peasant origin but were being rapidly propelled into the industrial and urban age. It might be said that, by finding signs of nature in the machine world, Soviet authors were both "mediating" the transition from rural to urban life that so many of their readers had to make, and reflecting the world as sensed in a predominantly peasant or recently peasant society. While there is some truth in this, it is not the whole story. One should not forget that, in this period, writers were being officially urged not to concern themselves so much with the practical tasks of the economy but to provide what amounted to ideological parables; and, for these, "nature" was a rich metaphorical source.

Whatever its incarnation in a given Soviet novel, "nature" is essentially an abstraction. Whether present actually or only metaphorically, it is not ultimately self-valuable but stands in for concepts to be dramatized in novel form. The main sources of "nature" must be sought in the world of ideas, in ideology and literature, rather than in the life of the masses.

The Struggle with Nature as a Central Stalinist Image

One important catchphrase of the Five-Year Plan was "The Struggle with Nature." Many of the famous construction projects of the Plan years were launched under this rubric. The great hydroelectric stations, which were the pride of all, were built to tame the arbitrary and destructive powers of the rivers. Collectivized, modernized agriculture would not be slave to the whims of climate. Drought was to be combated with dams, shallow waterways with canals, and so on. The machine would triumph over elemental forces.

One aspect of the wave of reaction against Five-Year Plan values was that in rhetoric the aura of the god-machine was eclipsed by the aura of the god-man. In consequence, the "struggle with nature" scenario was revised somewhat. In fiction the theme of socialist construction was soon transformed from a discourse on geography, technology, statistics, and the virtues of the socialist system (as in M. Shaginyan's Five-Year Plan classic *Hydrocentral,* of 1932) to an epic struggle between man and the elements in which the machine often played no greater role than that of the trusty steed in a *bylina.*

As the thirties continued, the "struggle with nature" theme in both literature and rhetoric become less tied to socialist construction and more and more an autonomous route to heroic status. Soviet man proved himself superior to all men who had existed before by combating the natural phenomena of greatest symbolic resonance in traditional Russian oral and written literature: water and ice (floods, disasters as the ice breaks up, snowstorms, etc.). Of the two, the struggle between man and ice held the highest place: Soviet man was said to triumph over the cold as no other people could—and especially not the Americans.[18] This triumph was to be found above all in authority figures: a standard moment in the mid-thirties biography of a Soviet leader is how he withstood exile or imprisonment in frozen Siberia before eventually escaping. The leader of leaders, Stalin, truly excelled here: after repeated escapes from Siberia, he was finally tested by a stint of exile in the Arctic Circle, with which he coped very well.[19]

Literature was given a fairly explicit injunction to use the theme of Soviet triumph in the snowy wastes. In 1935, when a welcome was organized in Leningrad for the leaders of the famous Chelyuskin expedition to the Arctic, N. Tikhonov, a Writers' Union official, declared in his speech: "our legendary [Chelyuskin] camp was a true Bolshevik fortress which repulsed all onslaughts of the Arctic elements.... Thus it is a living example of the sort of Socialist Realism which our literature is striving to attain."[20] And in fact the potentially dissident writer V. Kaverin, like Zamyatin a champion of the artist as heretic-seer, found a way to enter mainstream Stalinist fiction by taking up the theme of Arctic exploration. By doing so he was advanced from the author of such dubious books as *Artist Unknown* (1931) to the author of a Socialist Realist exemplar (in which he nevertheless managed to champion intellectual values), *The Two Captains* (1939).

The Arctic theme in literature had earlier, and politically very acceptable, precedents. The Soviet Union had virtually coopted as its own that popular American author Jack London, best remembered for his tales of the Alaskan wilds. This source for Soviet writers was especially hallowed by the fact that London had been a favorite author of Lenin's; he had a Jack London story read to him just before his death in 1924.

Krupskaya reports in her memoirs that Lenin's favorite Jack London story was "Love of Life":

> In a wilderness of ice, where no human being had set foot, a sick man, dying of hunger, is making for the harbor of a big river. His strength is giving out, he cannot walk but keeps slipping, and beside him there slides a wolf—also dying of hunger. There is a fight between them: the man wins. Half-clad, half-demented, he reaches his goal. The tale greatly pleased Ilyich.[21]

One aspect of this story that no doubt pleased Lenin was the fact that "man" triumphed over "beast" and "elements" not by virtue of superior physical strength but partly by native intelligence (though he was "half-demented" toward the end) and, above all, by willpower. This interpretation of who survives the cold and why (through will, determination, and sometimes cunning) is typical of London, but it was to become a motif of Stalinist fiction.

Perhaps the clearest example of direct influence from London would be Boris Polevoy's classic of the postwar years, *A Story about a Real Man* (1946). Polevoy's "story" is about a pilot who is shot down by the Germans behind enemy lines in a primeval forest and in bitter winter. The first part of the novel describes how the pilot, Meresev, gets himself back to Soviet territory, and it follows London's "Love of Life" in many ways (Polevoy uses a bear in place of London's wolf). The second half of the novel is taken up with another struggle against overwhelming odds: Meresev (now legless) fights the red tape of Soviet bureaucracy in his bid to be allowed to

fly again. Thus Polevoy gives what was first done against the romantic backdrop of snow and dense forest a more prosaic rerun in the
world of Soviet institutions. Usually the situation is reversed: in a
given novel, what was first treated at a prosaic level is taken for the
climax to a more dramatic setting in the world of the elements.
Either way, the typical Soviet novel is able through this parallelism
to encompass, as required, "the most matter-of-fact, everyday reality and the most heroic prospects."

Man alone, unprovisioned, in conditions of extreme cold and in
constant danger of attack from wild beasts, is in a sense a model for
testing human will and ingenuity against the limits set by "nature"
and historical necessity. In conditions of extreme cold, scientists
say, man must die. But these stories suggest that an exceptional man
can defy that inevitability, and such notions were well embedded in
Stalinist culture. A well-known obsession of Stalin's, which became
much stronger over the thirties, was the notion that *anything* can be
accomplished if only one tries hard enough: the laws of science are
only "blinkers" imposed on man to prevent him from reaching his
full potential. Hence mastery over ice became a major symbol of
antiscientific, Stalinist voluntarism. The snowy wastes provided the
ideal arena for acting out those favorite catchwords of Stalinism:
"stickability," "hard as flint," "will": true grit.

These words had sounded before, during the Civil War. They
appeared again in the thirties rhetoric in a conscious attempt to
identify the leadership's "struggle" against the many enemies
within and without that Golden Age of the Civil War years.
Much of the fiction, biography, and memoirs that came out in these
years was about the Civil War. Indeed *the* Socialist Realist classic of
the thirties, N. Ostrovsky's *How the Steel Was Tempered*
(1932–34), was written largely about the Revolution and the Civil
War. Ostrovsky's novel provides a kind of link between the Civil
War years and the thirties; in the novel's second part, which appeared in 1934, the author takes his hero's struggles into the world
of ice and floods.

The drama of man pitted against the elements, a common theme
of thirties fiction and rhetoric, functioned as a symbolic saga of
struggle that stood in for and enhanced that other "struggle" then
taking place all over the land. Several Party writers depicted the
"struggle" with internal and external enemies directly (e.g., M.

Sholokhov's *Virgin Soil Upturned* and P. Pavlenko's *In the East*), but most writers preferred to engage this theme through a variant on the struggle with nature. This was not only because the grim reality of the purges was thus distanced, but also because battling the elements had its own attraction for them. In the rhetoric of these years, menacing elemental forces had become a key metaphor of struggle as something challenging and dangerously willful that could be tamed only if it met its match in willpower; and writers could relate to that because it came close to the sense of nature that had been popular with Russian writers since the height of Byronism and the Romantic influence (consider Lermontov, Tyutchev, Appollon Grigoriev, and Blok). During the thirties the prevailing ethos made it possible for the Soviet novelist to indulge in the Romantic sense of the fatal attraction of storms, wild passions, darkness, and even that romantic concept, the ineffable. This was not the first time such elements had found their way into revolutionary literature: nineteenth-century texts like *Andrey Kozhukhov* and even early twenties issues of *Pravda* abound in them.

In the thirties, however, there was this difference: novels could naturally not praise willfulness or anarchy, so they were written as adventure novels in which order triumphs in the end. There is an irony here. During the early twenties, Western adventure fiction became very popular with the Soviet reader (especially E. Burroughs' *Tarzan*, translated in 1922).[22] Many avant-garde theorists, such as Zamyatin, Shklovsky, Lunts, and Kaverin, then declared that Soviet literature needed to be more exciting and might learn from Western adventure stories.[23] Under the rubric "a communist Pinkerton," writers set out to write Soviet adventure novels in the style of Tarzan and Pierre Benois.[24] This trend was viewed with alarm in many quarters of the literary community in the twenties because it was Westernist and seemed to be advocating a frivolous bourgeois literature for the new society, but in the thirties and forties one again caught glimpses of the Tarzans and Pinkertons who had been frightened off by late-twenties criticism.

A good example of a thirties Socialist Realist classic with an adventure-novel tinge (other than Kaverin's *Two Captains*) would be V. Kataev's *A Lonely White Sail Gleams* (1936). The title in fact comes from that well-known poem by Lermontov, "A Sail" (1832),

which closes with the lines "And he, rebellious, seeks out a
storm / As if in storms he will find peace."

Kataev's novel is set in Odessa at the time of the 1905 Revolution
and is in many respects a rerun of Gorky's *Mother*. Its counterpart
of Gorky's simple old mother who travels the road to "consciousness" is a middle-class boy, Gavrik. Like Pavel's mother, Gavrik has
no political awareness and must overcome the prejudices of his
background. He does so because, like Pavel's mother, he is attracted
to someone more "conscious" than he, an older, working-class
playmate, and is gradually converted to the side of the revolution
until he comes to play a part in it (distributing arms clandestinely
and assisting in the prison escape of a sailor from the *Potemkin*).
However, Gavrik is attracted to work for the revolutionaries not so
much by their example and the "light" he detects in their eyes (as
Gorky's mother was) as by the "*frisson* of danger" in the work they
do.[25]

Thus, in much thirties fiction, it is not so much reason and order
that are celebrated as danger and adventure. This is largely because
of the informing sense of reality as "struggle"; Stalinist rhetoric
itself often reads like a script for an action serial in which adven-
tures and herculean tasks waited around the corner in every Soviet
enterprise.

If the Stalinist sense of reality is of "struggle," is this then really
encompassed by the term "garden"? In the Stalinist context, can
"garden" be said to provide the most appropriate contrast to "machine," as it did in Leo Marx's book? One does not have to take
one's terms from Leo Marx. One could, for instance, take Ray-
mond Williams' terms, which he uses for the title of the book, *The
Country and the City*. For Stalinist Russia, the best formulation for
the opposition described in this chapter would be not machine /
garden or country / city but the most traditional and general opposition: nature versus culture (the latter representing machine, city,
and enlightenment all in one). In this opposition, however, "nature" too does not have one meaning or even a single group of
meanings. There were two contrasting general senses of nature
dominant in Stalinist culture: first, there was nature as the garden of
harmony; second, there was nature as the arena for struggle with
elemental forces in which the will was tested.

Thus "nature" in Stalinist culture is one of those multivalent signs like "electricity," but of course much richer in associations. In literature, "nature" became that point at which the non-Party intelligentsia, the Bolsheviks, and even the specifically Stalinist writers could converge. "Nature" plays a crucial role in the typical Socialist Realist novel's plot, but at the same time it is a potential source of variety, a place where some of the traditional intelligentsia attitudes can shine through in a Stalinist world. The traditional intelligentsia response to that ensemble of experiences that is called "nature" is usually marked by ambivalence. Not surprisingly, throughout the Stalin era and even in the present day, the nature / culture opposition has been a kind of dialectic in Soviet intellectual life. At times, machine-age values hold sway (order, efficiency, technology, planning, education), at other times values from one or the other of the two aspects of nature—nature as garden of harmony or as arena of "struggle" with elemental forces. And who could doubt that this dialectic is a very basic one and has not yet run its course?

The Stalinist Novel as Pastoral

By the forties, the paradigms of the Soviet novel had become somewhat worn and tired. The conventional patterns for using "nature" were now so hackneyed and outmoded that many forties novels read like incongruous idylls. One example would be S. Babaevsky's *Cavalier of the Gold Star,* winner of the Stalin Prize in 1947. In this novel a soldier-hero, Sergey, returns from the horrors of World War II to an isolated and backward farming region. He is bent on advancing it into the technological age—on electrifying it, even. Ostensibly, he would bring the machine into the garden. And he does: at the end his dream of a power station is realized. Yet somehow it never really affects the landscape or the pastoral tone, which can be sensed the moment he sets foot in his "garden" and espies a "swarthy shepherdess" tending her oxen. She becomes his bride, to stand by his side at the novel's end and survey the "velvet green fields" lit by the "dawn" of the Soviet-given light.[26]

William Empson has said that "good proletarian art is usually covert Pastoral,"[27] and, after reading a few Stalinist novels of this ilk, one might begin to suspect that the assertion is true. However, though the Stalinist novel makes heavy use of nature, it is not "pastoral" in the old conventional sense. But there is a modern "version of pastoral" that Empson himself uses, and in this there is no necessary connection with a setting in nature, let alone with shepherdesses and Arcadian fields. Rather, literature is called "pastoral" if, as P. Marinelli puts it, it

> deals with the complexities of human life against a background of simplicity. All that is necessary is that memory and imagination should conspire to render a not too distant past of comparative innocence as more pleasurable than a harsh present.[28]

A way out of the "harsh present" is also an important underlying motive of the Stalinist novel, but it situates it in the future instead of looking nostalgically to the past.

In the early thirties, when authoritative voices began to tell Soviet writers what Socialist Realism was to be, they recommended that literary works be set in present-day Soviet reality but insisted at the same time that they should include "future prospects," that they should show how Marxism-Leninism leads out of present-day problems and on into Communism.

In order to collapse time as instructed and put "intimations" of the future in the present, novelists had to simplify. This is the motive behind much that is "pastoral" in the Soviet novel. However, the pastoral impulse also derives from the novel's informing ideology, from Marxism-Leninism's own account of history.

A very important moment in the Marxist account of history came with the division of labor. Thereafter, the working man was "alienated" from the means of production and his life became oppressive. In many respects this account is but a variant of the change from a *Gemeinschaft* society to a *Gesellschaft* society, to use Tönnies' terms[29]—the change, in other words, from a simple, unified society to the more complex, pluralistic society of the industrial and urban age. The aim of Marxism was to restore the wholeness that had been lost with the division of labor, to bring back the *Gemeinschaft* world. Marx discussed this in terms of the worker's ability to change jobs and diversify his work experience. However, a major goal of Marxism in trying to reverse the division of labor was to restore the lost harmony between the individual good and the collective good.

During the thirties, writers were enjoined *explicitly* to show how, in the new society, the division of labor would be abolished and all conflict between individual and collective good eradicated.[30] In meeting these requirements, writers gravitated toward nature or nature-like settings for their novels because this brought them closer to the *Gemeinschaft* society, where all conflicts were more readily resolved. This use of nature was a way of simplifying a complex reality, of making Soviet life seem closer to the world of traditional Russia. This did not necessarily represent a deceit or ruse. It could be seen as yet another instance of a kind of late-blooming romanticism, one to which many modern intellectual movements have succumbed. Even Marx's account of alienation and the division of labor can be seen as a variant of that megamyth of man's Fall from unity, which began with Adam and Eve's banishment from the Garden of Eden and which became especially popular among intellectuals as they confronted the realities of industrial and urban society. Russian intellectual history provides many variants, such as those nineteenth-century hankerings after the concord of the village commune, or *mir,* and the intelligentsia's obsessive dilemmas about how to resolve Russia's glaring social contradictions and rid it of autocratic repression.

The primary task of the novel was to show Marx's way out of these dilemmas. According to his account, a *Gemeinschaft* world is to be found not merely before the division of labor but also after its abolition in a state of communism. Between this "before" and "after," society is not only cast out from the garden of *Gemeinschaft* but also thrown into a state of turmoil as the dialectical forces of history work themselves through. Thus the Stalinist novel is no pastoral, in the sense that it does not show the protagonist entering, temporarily, a period or place of relative tranquility, a reality simpler than the one in which he normally lives. On the contrary, since the Stalinist narrative must duplicate the sequence of history à la Marx, it is framed by periods of *Gemeinschaft* harmony and order, but the bulk of the novel shows the period *after* the fall. Unlike the pastoral that is set in one place or state but has built into it an implied contrast with the more complex reality of the present from which the protagonist has come, the Stalinist novel comprises a sequence of contrasting states, A^1, B, A^2, with the motivation for this progression coming from the informing ideology, Marxism-Leninism.

The master plot that took all Stalinist novels through these three stages was not based on Marxism alone, but on Marxism-Leninism—or, rather, Marxism-Leninism-Stalinism. According to the Leninist version of Marxism, the way forward to the resolution of all conflict between individual and collective good lay through a series of ever-higher resolutions of the spontaneity/consciousness dialectic. In effect, Soviet novels were expected to provide an example of the resolution of this dialectic in modern society. To do so in the world of Stalinist Russia was somewhat problematical because of a certain resistance on the part of the state to its scheduled withering-away. In truth, during the thirties, the Soviet state was daily becoming more powerful, bureaucratized, and centralized, more punitive and more hierarchical. But Soviet novels had to be "optimistic." They had to show the resolution of these contradictions and of all those other enduring Russian social problems for which Marxism-Leninism claimed to be a panacea, such as the conflict between the ill-educated and the elite, between urban Russia and the countryside, between the individual and the state.

In writing these problematical aspects of Soviet reality into the Marxist-Leninist master plot, which required some account of their resolution, writers eschewed the mimetic mode in favor of the mythic. Stalinist novels project a less complex, more idealized world, one in which these contradictions can be more readily resolved. These novels are pastorals in the sense that they create an ideological ecosystem, one that artificially pares reality down and rids it of all pollutants so that the "garden" may flourish.

From the thirties on, most novels of the Stalin period were set not in the complex modern cities of Moscow or Leningrad but in a model provincial microcosm—a town, factory, kolkhoz, construction site, or army unit far removed from the advanced urban centers. In such an environment "nature" could play a greater role in the lives of the protagonists. But above all, reality could be "simplified." Some of its harsher aspects, such as the oppressive, hierarchical state bureaucracy, could be made to seem more benign in a setting where the officials would be few and the gap between their status and that of the ordinary people less. The impersonal, all-powerful bureaucrat could become a sort of village elder. *Gemeinschaft* could prevail.

Even within such a simplified ecosystem, the problem of resolving the old social conflicts is merely reduced, not removed. The Marxist model for resolving all social conflicts was the dialectic, with its three-stage progression of thesis, antithesis, and synthesis, which coincides with the Stalinist novel's overall scheme of harmony / discord / reintegration. In the Stalinist novel's attempt to make lived reality mythical, it more often than not reduces itself to a simple, overriding dialectical pattern. It charts a movement between dialectical forces symbolizing order, on the one hand, and disorder, on the other. This dialectic is resolved at the novel's conclusion in a higher—*Gemeinschaft*—order. Social conflicts become, as it were, not so much grim realities, important in themselves, as fodder for the homogenizing narrative dialectic. Moreover, the conflicts are often not directly depicted. They are present only in symbolic oppositions which are, *a fortiori*, metaphorical in their resolution.

It is in this master narrative of the Stalinist novel that nature plays its most crucial role. There is a certain logic in this, since the Russian word for "spontaneity," *stixijnost'*, is formed from the root *stixija*, meaning "the elements." As the abstract substantive formed from "the elements," the Marxist-Leninist term "spontaneity" does not mean merely something unconscious and uncontrolled; it can also mean something either natural or willful and *out of control*.

Even this does not exhaust the very broad range of meanings "spontaneity" could have in thirties fiction and rhetoric. Let us take just one specific source, Gladkov's Five-Year Plan novel *Energy*, of 1932. "Spontaneity" is used in it a number of times to refer to menacing, elemental forces of nature, but elsewhere it refers to recalcitrant workers, human passions, and petty-bourgeois self-centeredness.[31] Gorky himself commonly used "spontaneity" to refer to social deviants and class enemies.[32] This list does not exhaust the range of meanings commonly found for "spontaneity" in thirties texts. Others include the advancing enemy and even technological breakdowns. In other words, all willful things that threatened the common good (the interests of the state) were labeled "spontaneous." This identification having been made, it became possible to use "spontaneity" in its primary meaning of elemental, natural forces to stand in for any of the other secondary meanings of political significance. In this way the account of historical development in terms of the spontaneity / consciousness dialectic, which had been presented quite explicitly in a twenties novel like Furmanov's *Chapaev*, could be represented symbolically

in a thirties novel by the actions of forces that were literally or
metaphorically "elemental."

Since the spontaneity / consciousness dialectic is conventionally
translated into the Soviet novel in parable form as a struggle between elemental forces and those who seek to control them, the
novel typically has as its core the time-honored opposition of
pastoral literature—that between nature and culture. In Marxism
itself this opposition is, in a sense, resolved in favor of culture. For
Marx, *Gemeinschaft* would prevail in a better regulated, more
efficient and streamlined kind of *Gesellschaft*. Lenin was largely in
agreement with Marx on this. And in a way it was precisely this
kind of rationalization that was attempted during the Five-Year
Plan years. But most Soviet intellectuals were at heart deeply ambivalent about industrialization. To them, nature was more whole-
some and pure, more vital and captivating; and yet, to their very
considerable chagrin, nature was more retrograde. Thus nature
both helps and hinders the bringing of harmony to man and his
society.

It is perhaps because of Soviet writers' lingering affection for the
wild, spontaneous, and unregulated that the age of the machine was
so short-lived in Stalinist literature. The seductive hold of nature
over the writers' imaginations also colored their retelling of
Marxist-Leninist doctrine in novel form.

The writers' ambivalent attitude toward nature is built into the
very structure of the Stalinist novel. Nature symbolizes both the
path to *Gemeinschaft* and the enemy that obstructs it. It provides
both the novel's setting and the chief antagonist for the hero. When,
at the novel's conclusion, peace and harmony come to its little
world, this is usually described in terms of the harmony of nature.
Yet it is also nature that provides the controlling metaphor linking
all the various forces that threaten harmony. These forces are wild
and elemental, they are either literally or metaphorically of nature.
But although their objective status is negative, they are also a given
novel's source of excitement and color.

Thus the Soviet novelist has conventionally constructed an
ideological ecosystem for his novel's world even in the literal sense
that he has given its protagonists an optimal *natural* environment.
He has transposed an essentially political and contemporary drama
into that epic-tribal world of man and nature. The main symbolic

antagonists for his hero as a crusader for order are floods, storms, ice, fire, attacks by feral enemies, and bestial or uncontrolled human passions. Some of the most problematical social conflicts can be mediated mythically in novel form. Nature itself is nonpersonal and so provides a highly abstract medium for representing real-life phenomena in fiction, one in which they can be manipulated rather more readily than even fictional characters can be.

The setting in nature has other advantages. It takes political conflicts not merely out of the *place* where they really occur—the complex modern world—but also out of the *time* sequence in which it is so difficult to resolve them—contemporary history. The Marxist schema for the progress of history from harmony through discord and back to higher-order harmony is a complete circle, or rather a narrowing gyre as a series of syntheses bring man ever closer to final harmony in communism. The normal reckoning of history is chronological or linear, but nature is cyclical and thus is subject to change yet is outside linear time. So most Stalinist novelists place in the foreground the time of nature and the seasons rather than the time of the modern world.

By the forties it had become common for the action of a novel to last one year. Indeed, for the forties novel, the year is virtually the unity that day was for neoclassical drama. However, this one year is not a calendar year, in the sense of being marked out in days and months. Rather, the action lasts for one complete cycle of the seasons (or sometimes two cycles): it usually begins in the early summer and ends at the point in the cycle where it began.

It is the way of nature that all things must change. Man must be born, must age and finally must die. Floods and storms must abate, fires die down, and ice melt. Thus when the Stalinist novelist sets his novel within the cyclical time of the seasons, he gives himself a way of resolving even the most difficult of conflicts. When disorder is symbolized by a flood that menaces a construction site, that flood—no matter how inexorable its ravaging advance may seem—must, by nature, eventually retreat.

This aspect of the "struggle with the elements" is quite explicit in A. Chakovsky's novel *Here It's Morning Already* (1949). The lives of a fishing crew out on the high seas are imperiled by a sudden storm. The fishermen are such dedicated citizens that they resist all temptation to jettison either their equipment or their precious cargo of fish. Then, suddenly, the storm abates and their lives are out of danger. As if by some miracle? The narrator comments: "It was as if nature had turned the whole storm on merely so that she could test the will of the people on the fishing boat."[33]

Even raging human passions can be reconciled by the course of the natural cycle. A birth, death, or marriage of someone dear to him commonly gives a protagonist the inner harmony he seeks. The prominence given to the life-cycle and the cycles of nature in these essentially political dramas imparts to Soviet order a spurious aura of organicity and sense of continuity with past traditions. When, in a given novel, the balance of nature is restored, then, at a symbolic level, the ideological balance is restored, with all contradictions resolved.

The organization of the typical Stalinist novel fits the schema in Frye's *Anatomy of Criticism* so well that the novel almost seems made to his order. The novel begins in the summer of harmony and plenitude, proceeds through the autumn of increasing doubt and conflict, through the ice of winter and / or the devastating floods and storms of early spring, to come out at last, at the novel's end, into the sun of a higher-order *Gemeinschaft*. In this second, brighter summer is a world of wholeness, faith, and harmony wherein new life is born to the community as a harbinger of those better summers that will come with future revolutions of the gyre.

5   The Stalinist Myth of the "Great Family"

One of the obsessions of thirties rhetoric was the nation's "enemies." Since coming to power, Stalin had always invoked spectral "enemies," both internal and external, in order to justify his extremist policies, but during the thirties the external enemies, at any rate, materialized. To the west, in Europe, the fascists were growing in power and belligerence, while, in the east, Soviet troops had several skirmishes with the Japanese. In literature, themes from military history, such as tsarist or Civil War engagements between Russians and foreign foes (especially the Germans or Japanese), became very common. And in public life a special place was given to the Soviet border guards. On the opening day of the Third Plenum of the Writers' Union in February, 1936, one of their detachments was marched into the hall, eulogized by all the speakers, and then marched solemnly out.[1]

When the Soviet leaders warned of danger from enemies both within and without, it was in part to provide a mandate for the extraordinary degree of social cohesion they demanded and the extreme means they were using against "unmasked enemies." This crisis atmosphere was an important element in forming the key myths of the thirties, which replaced the machine symbols of the Five-Year Plan.

Like Germany and several other countries in this period, the Soviets focused on the primordial attachments of kinship and projected them as the dominant symbol for social allegiance. Soviet society's leaders became "fathers" (with Stalin as the patriarch); the national heroes, model "sons"; the state, a "family" or "tribe." The new root metaphor for society provided the state with a single set of symbols for enhancing its increasingly hierarchical structure by endowing it with a spurious organicity. The metaphor also served the needs of the Stalin faction in its "struggles": it provided formulas for a symbolic legitimization of the actual leadership (the

114

succession of generations in the "family" stands in for the succession of political leaders and for Stalin's accession to power after
Lenin's death in particular), for the way forward (through the evolution of ever greater sons), and for the unquestioning loyalty of
citizens (blood is thicker than water).

This call for greater attachment to the symbolic family of the
state did not entail a demand for weaker attachment to actual kin.
In fact, in the mid-thirties the state actively sought to strengthen the
nuclear family.[2] As was made quite explicit at the time, however,
the nuclear family was to be strengthened because it was regarded
as a microcosmic auxiliary to the state. Indeed, it was considered
valuable only insofar as it served the state.[3] As the educator A.
Makarenko expressed it in 1935, "The family is the primary cell of
society, and its duties in child-rearing derive from its obligations to
produce good citizens."[4]

Thus the state was prior. If there was any conflict between the
state's interests and the nuclear family, citizens were urged to jettison their sense of family, based on blood ties, and replace it with a
higher one, based on political kinship. If need be, they should even
reject members of their own family, as the school-primer hero Pavel
Morozov had done when he denounced his own father to the courts
as a kulak conspirator.[5] Sinister though Pavel's example might
seem, the general principle behind it—rejection of corrupt blood
ties in favor of the higher-order bonds of political community—was
commonly held by many generations of Russian radicals before the
Stalin era. Many nineteenth-century utopian groups, socialists and,
later, communists, sought to tear individuals away from their own
families and regroup them in that higher community of the
phalanstery, artel, or party. Both Chernyshevsky's *What Is to Be
Done?* and Gorky's *Mother* provide object lessons in this process.
Later, Party fiction of the twenties abounded in individuals who
were attracted to the "familial warmth" of the Party and came to
break their blood ties (if nonproletarian) and throw themselves into
work for the Party.[6]

By the Stalin period, society was thought to have made such
progress that the nuclear family would not be in opposition to the
state but would, rather, be its helpmate. In the thirties the press
published poignant examples of actual kin enacting their familial
roles in that greater symbolic family of the nation. When at the

Writers' Plenum of 1936 the speaker Kirshon issued the challenge, "If any border guard dies, someone will become his brother and replace him. Let our enemies know this,"[7] the enemies did not have to wait long. The journal *Bolshevik* of March, 1937, cites two different cases (one on the eastern borders, the other on the west) where a border guard was killed and his actual brother replaced him.[8]

The symbolic patterns for this "family" have precedents not only in earlier revolutionary lore but also in the social organization of the traditional Russian peasant family. The peculiar geographical, economic, and political conditions of tsarist Russia favored extended households as the basic units of peasant society. For practical reasons such households often recruited new members who had no blood ties to the core family but would be accepted in it as what anthropologists call "structural relatives." In describing this phenomenon, both ethnologists and the peasants themselves drew a distinction between the "small family" (*malaja sem'ja,* the nuclear family or slightly extended type) and this artificially extended "great family" (the *bol'šaja sem'ja*).[9] This dichotomy comes close to what was envisaged as an ideal in the mid-thirties. Indeed, by the forties, writers treating the relationship between the nuclear family and Soviet society commonly referred to them as the "little family" and the "great family," respectively.[10]

Most anthropologists classify family organization in two ways, either laterally, along "the horizontal axis" (i.e., in terms of siblings, cousins, etc.), or along the "vertical axis" (in terms of generations). Looking at kinship in terms of the horizontal axis, one finds that Russians considered a wider range of people to be kin than was customary in the West (milk brother by the same wet nurse, adopted brother, coparents-in-law, ritual sibling, etc.). By contrast, the number of people included in the vertical or generational axis of reckoning was smaller in Russia than in the West. The vertical axis marked the lines of authority and descent and was *patrilineal:* the wife always moved into her husband's family on marriage, and the line of male descent running through her husband's family was considered more powerful and authoritative than her own.[11] It is thus perhaps no coincidence that, although the kinship myths of the Stalinist *"bol'šaja sem'ja"* abounded in 'brothers" and "sisters," their authority figures were "fathers," not "mothers."

These alternative possibilities for reckoning kinship in traditional Russia—by the horizontal axis of brothers and sisters, or by the vertical axis of generations of fathers and sons—provide useful heuristic models for describing the changes in political symbolism that occurred during the thirties. During the First Five-Year Plan, the root metaphor for society was a machine, but this was sometimes translated into human terms as a big "family" of brothers. In the machine no part is self-valuable; it is worthy only insofar as it contributes, together with the other parts, to the overall running of the machine. So, likewise, in Soviet society, all citizens were "little men" who worked together with their brother "little men" and were valuable only insofar as they contributed to the harmonious running of the whole of society. The machine-part / little-man analogy and its fraternalist ethos can be sensed in the following passage from V. Ilenkov's 1931 novel *The Driving Axle,* in which one worker reproaches another for his aspirations to outstrip his brother workers:

Let us take the train, for example: it has a furnace, and wheels, and driving gear, and assorted minor bolts—and everything has its own place. And that is how a train manages to carry thousands of tons. But the bolts are important, and the whistle is important, and the smoke stacks—and all equally so. But you like only the driving axle. That's not the right approach.[12]

Of course, the machine analogy for the relationship between part and whole in Soviet society had to be modified to make provision for the Party as the guiding force or vanguard. In Ilenkov's novel, for instance, the Party was "the driving axle." But there was a marked tendency in this period to emphasize the *parts* in their relation to the whole rather than to give a major role to any guiding mechanism. This was the age of the "little men," of "massism" and "proletarianization." In literature, critics were so much in the grip of the anti-elitist ethos that writers were likely to be chastised if they so much as depicted the factory *foremen* rather than its "little men."[13]

This fraternalist zeal was one of the many Five-Year Plan values that were reversed in 1931, when Soviet society abandoned its cult of the machine. Stalin's July, 1931, speech signaled an end to the era of the "little man," because in that speech he emphasized the value of expertise. He also coined the slogan "Technology is the answer to everything."[14] But increasingly, in official rhetoric, emphasis was placed on the need not for mere experts but for good leaders and managers. In 1935 Stalin explicitly replaced the slogan of the 1931 speech with a new slogan, "Cadres are the answer to everything."[15]

The literary world kept pace with these changes; before long the writer was urged to abandon such follies of the Plan years as the worship of statistics and the machine. Above all, it was said, readers need to be given human subjects they can emulate. In the symbolic landscapes of Soviet models man was no longer to be dwarfed by the machine or to be admired as a reliable "bolt" or "whistle" in the great train of society. Even the stock hero of the Plan years, the shock worker, was rejected as being too "small" to be an appropriate protagonist for Soviet fiction.[16] It was time to give the "driving axle" its due, to show the people their "fathers," as the leaders were now called.[17] And so the thirties saw not merely the end of the machine as the dominant social symbol but also a change in the axis of kinship metaphors from the horizontal to the vertical.

A second fundamental change occurred in the prevailing time perspective. When the ideal was one of infinite brotherhood, no distinction between generations was implied and therefore no before and after—only the NOW. During the First Five-Year Plan, only the immediate practical needs of the Plan were considered worthy of attention; but as the vision of society acquired generational layers, a new concern arose for the past and for origins.

Gorky was a prime mover in introducing the historical perspective in literature. On his initiative several series of collectively written histories were launched: *The History of the Factories* (1931), *The History of the Civil War* (1931), *The History of Young Men in the Nineteenth Century* (1932). Now that MAN had elbowed technology and statistics out of the limelight, he (man) became the focus of most of these histories, which were largely biographical. For instance, the factory histories contained either chronicles of entire dynasties of working-class families, elaborated to several removes, or biographies of individual workers.

This transitional period from 1931 to late 1935 also saw the rise, largely under Gorky's aegis, of a second kind of biographical anthology, giving accounts of assorted social aliens' "rebirth" in Communist society.[18] As the Five-Year Plan ideal of the homogeneous, "proletarian" society was sloughed off, it was stated quite explicitly—by Stalin no less—that the bourgeois *could* potentially be integrated into society.[19] His reintegration would be achieved in much the same way as, during the Five-Year Plan, it was believed that the antisocial worker or homeless hooligan could be socialized—through labor in the factories, camps, and colonies for vagrant youths.

By the mid-thirties the theme of the misfit being socialized to become an adopted member of the great family of the state was losing currency. The main topic of biographies was not the making of reliable citizens but, to use the title of yet another series of biographies founded by Gorky (in 1933), *The Lives of Remarkable People*.

In mid-thirties rhetoric, an entire series of "remarkable people" was singled out as official harbingers of a revolution in human anthropology soon to affect every Soviet man. These new men were not merely "bigger" than that earlier paradigm, the "little man"; they were the "biggest": they represented an order of humanity unlike that of the Ivans. The fantastic age had begun.

Although all official heroes were of a truly extraordinary caliber, they were not all *equally* "big." In rhetoric they were represented as a symbolic family in which the "biggest" were model "fathers," while the less-than-absolutely-extraordinary were model "sons."

The "fathers" were largely the political leaders. The rationale for this role may be found in Stalin's frequent reinvocation of his 1924 claim that Bolsheviks (by which he meant primarily the leadership) were people of superior mettle. In a speech to the Red Army Academy of May, 1935, for instance, he declared:"We Bolsheviks are people of a special cut. We were forged by the great Lenin, our leader, our teacher, our father."[20] It is the leaders' link with the founder of the dynasty, Lenin, that makes them exceptional, and they can, in turn, bestow this exceptional nature on their "sons."

The "sons" were not, as one might expect, the "fathers'" successors. They were not promising Party officers who would furnish the next generation of leaders; rather, they were successors to the "little man"—"little men" grown "big." The clearest case of this would be the Stakhanovite movement, which began in late 1935. The Stakhanovites were production heroes who were honored because they outdid the norms of production many times over. The original

Stakhanovite, Aleksey Stakhanov, was a coal miner, but there were others in fields like cotton and sugar-beet harvesting, textiles, and factory piece-work.

The Stakhanovites would seem to be successors to the "Shock Workers of Socialist Labor" and other production heroes who came before them, but the rhetoric of the times insisted that there was no comparison. Their feats bore witness to a *qualitative* change in human anthropology. A local revolution had occurred, and a select few men had become radically different from all those who had gone before.

The Stakhanovites were not the only model "sons" singled out in public rituals. The list of those feted includes border guards, long-distance skiers, violinists, mountain climbers, parachutists, and, above all, aviation heroes. Few of these categories (except the Stakhanovites) distinguished themselves in any way that might be said to have much connection with "building communism." The official heroes also did not really have any status in the crucial spheres of politics and management. The Stakhanovites, for instance, were mostly unskilled or semiskilled workers, with the most rudimentary education and no claim to political rank or "consciousness." They were, in other words, precisely Soviet society's "little men." Many of the aviation heroes were exceptions to the general rule and were actually Party members,[21] but they did not play a political role of national significance.

How was it that such a radical change, of great political significance, could come about in such otherwise unprepossessing or relatively inconsequential people? An initial answer would be that the change was radical only insofar as it was claimed to be so. After Soviet society had striven so hard during the Plan years to bring about a kingdom of the ordinary, it had now reset its goals and begun work toward creating a society of the *extra*ordinary. Individual feats, such as climbing mountains and breaking international records for long-distance airplane flights, were among the more readily available examples of out-of-the-ordinariness. However, even the Stakhanovites' feats are dubious indicators of major human change toward a higher-order, communist man. Aleksey Stakhanov himself obtained incredible production figures for mining coal largely because an auxiliary crew was set up to do many of

the tasks a miner would otherwise do by himself.[22] Stakhanov had
merely to wield his pick furiously for one shift.

The public conferral of the status "new man" on the Stakhanovite, aviation, and sporting heroes, etc., may be seen as a sort of
ritual elevation of structurally inferior (Stakhanovite) and/or extra-
systemic figures (aviation and sporting heroes). While such "supermen" certainly could claim real achievements, their function was
largely symbolic. They will be referred to as "symbolic heroes."

There were also "symbolic villains." They were exposed during
that other major public ritual of the mid-thirties, the great purge
trials. Indeed, the Kremlin meeting held in November, 1935, to
celebrate the Stakanovites' achievement occurred virtually on the
eve of the worst Stalinist purges (1936–37). The celebration of the
"sons'"feats provided, on the one hand, a necessary positive counterpoint to the purges (revolution achieves radical change by extreme means, which are in turn justified by its results). It also provided the occasion for ritual denunciation of the villains. So, while
public announcements extolled the achievements of the Stakhanovites, the managers and engineers at their enterprises who
(allegedly) tried to block the Stakhanovites' initiative were at the
same time reproached.[23] There were also signs of this pattern in the
case of the aviation heroes.[24]

Both the lionization of the age's symbolic heroes and the large-
scale application of extreme measures to its "villains" represent
expressions of a thirst for radical change and *renewal*—for revolution. This same thirst had led to the ritual "leveling" of the non-
lowly (the bourgeois specialists, etc.) during the earlier, compul-
sively fraternalist phase of the First Five-Year Plan.

At the same time, both the symbolic heroes and the "villains"
must be seen as integral parts of the power struggle that the Stalinist
faction waged during the thirties against real or alleged supporters
and leaders of rival factions within the Party (such as Trotskyites).
As compared to the twenties, the power struggle was on a different
plane both in scale and in means (e.g., physical elimination or in-
carceration of Party rivals rather than politicking and polemics); it
too was "big."

The age's heroes had to undertake an epic struggle against
enemies both within and without, and it was necessary to find titans

as guarantees that the struggle itself was of epic proportions. There were constant reiterations of the claim that Bolsheviks are exceptional people. In Stalin's "We Bolsheviks" speech, quoted above, he asserted that others had tried to deflect the Bolsheviks from the true Leninist path, but they had stood firm. The official champions or mascots of the Stalinist faction, the symbolic heroes, had, therefore, to be "mighty" as well.

The Bolshevik leadership tried to document their extravagent claims to preeminence. Along with the renewed interest in history they and their supporters began to produce self-justificatory writings that not only involved immediate polemics with rival factions but gave an entire *coherent* account of Bolshevik history. They established their legitimacy both by merit (in terms of outstanding achievements) and by lines of continuity stretching into the past. This development culminated in 1937 in the publication of the Stalinist "little red book," *The Short Course,* a comprehensive account of Bolshevik history that was allegedly produced under the close supervision of Stalin.

In this context the "lives of remarkable people" were written in the thirties. It was an age when it seemed that virtually everyone who put pen to paper was writing a heroic biography of one of the official heroes (a member of the Stalinist leadership, a Civil War hero, a leader figure from the national past, like Emelian Pugachev, or a symbolic hero). Whichever of the standard subjects was chosen for a biography, an important function of the book would be to rationalize the status quo and legitimize the current leadership (with a pre-Stalin subject, this could be done allegorically).

Biographies have commonly been a medium of political legitimization. In ancient Rome, emperors often had their biographies rewritten to demonstrate their genealogical links with the gods. In the Soviet context the corresponding privileged origin was an association with Lenin. This was established for Stalin in countless ways. For two other categories of thirties official hero—other members of the Bolshevik leadership and the Civil War heroes—the link was to be with Stalin rather than Lenin; biographies of them invariably highlighted their role in at least one of the following moments, which are crucial in Stalin's self-justificatory record: prerevolutionary exile and prison (which Stalin also underwent—his suffering provides one of his many mandates); the Civil War, and especially the rout of the White Army at Tsaritsyn (allegedly directed by Stalin and therefore *the* moment of the Civil War); the Lenin/Stalin succession; and Kirov's murder in 1934 (a point of reference in justifying the purges).

With the period's new sense of the need for comprehensiveness, coherence, and continuity in all its official chronicles, it was no longer considered sufficient for establishing a subject's worth to point to a link with the great "father" and to some heroic deeds. As in traditional hagiography, the moral status of the subject and his actions had to derive from an entire biography, including his childhood. Moreover, as was already the tradition in Bolshevik fiction, the claim to political legitimacy and to human superiority was expressed, primarily, not in terms of deeds but in terms of character. Stalin set a precedent for this when, after Lenin's death in 1924, he gave an address to the Kremlin Military School. This opened with the words, "I do not think there is any need for me to deliver a set speech on Lenin's activities. It would be better, I think, to confine myself to a few facts to bring out certain of Lenin's characteristics as a man and leader."[25] In thirties and forties rhetoric and literature the "Leninist" characteristics that Stalin listed in that speech (such as modesty and the ability to communicate with the common man) became *the* iconic traits of "father" figures, together with those formulaic epithets (such as "calm" and "serious") that in Bolshevik literature were already conventional signs of the positive hero.

In the thirties the distinction between fiction and nonfiction, between a factual biography and a fictionalized one, became fainter than ever before. One did not just find, as in earlier Bolshevik biographical writing (such as Furmanov's *Chapaev*), a definite ordering and selection of the real-life material to fit the patterns of Marxist-Leninist historiography. All biographies were now standardized so that every subject's life, in both fiction and nonfiction, fit mythicized patterns. A case in point would be Vs. Ivanov's *Parkhomenko* (1938–39), an account of the Civil War commander of that name. This work was called a novel, and it was published in the literary journal *Molodaya gvardiua,* but, by the conventions of the time, it could equally well have been published elsewhere as biography. Whether classified as fiction or nonfiction, all biographies were now fantastic: the Gleb Chumalovs of fiction now dominated nonfiction, too.

These biographies were of two types. One gave the formulaic life of a "father," the other the life of a "son." The two formulas were

related in that both were derived from a common source; but they
were also distinct. The best-represented category among biographies
was that of "father," and especially of the Party leader. This was
so even in fiction: in a 1937 list of works in progress by Leningrad writers, for instance, the majority were about Stalin, Kirov,
Voroshilov, or Ordzhonnikidze.[26] There were, of course, especially
copious biographies and memoirs of Stalin, including a major biography by the Frenchman Henri Barbusse (1936).

What is most striking about the accounts of Stalin's life is that
they follow pretty much the same pattern as those of the other
Bolshevik leaders, such as Kirov and Voroshilov. Biographers emphasized the poverty of Stalin's family in his childhood; they cited
vivid incidents when he was discriminated against on account of
this and had trouble getting himself an education. But Stalin (Kirov,
Ordzhonnikidze, and so on) overcame all these handicaps, and
more besides, to emerge as a national leader. He did so largely
because of certain essential character traits that were strikingly evident even in childhood: energy, daring, antiauthoritarianism, a
strong will, and love of life and freedom.[27] He also showed, quite
early, definite signs of a sort of embryonic "consciousness," just as,
in childhood, the saint showed some sign of his saintly qualities.

The lives of the Stalinist leaders were meant to inspire the
populace, but the lives of the "sons" were meant to provide models
for the populace to emulate.[28] Earlier biographies of citizens had
informed working-class readers of their pasts and had instilled in
them a dynastic pride or had demonstrated the transforming power
of socialism. Beginning in the mid-thirties, the hagiographic or
icon-like function was paramount, and the biographies that best
filled it were set up as exemplars for writers to imitate.

The formulaic course of the early life of a "son," though very
similar to that of a "father," was not entirely identical, for a "son"
was bound to be more childish and irresponsible. Since the biographies of all the symbolic heroes (or "sons") follow much the
same pattern, only one type will be analyzed here.

The Aviation Hero as the Paradigmatic New Man

In many countries aviation feats were a matter of national prestige
during the thirties, and there was an ongoing rivalry between the

U.S. and the U.S.S.R. in long-distance flights. Accounts in the Soviet
press of various record-breaking Soviet flights reveal how important the aviation hero was, not merely as a prestige symbol but as a
chosen "son," a fine example of new-order man. With each
achievement the newspaper writers made claims for the superiority
of Soviet aviation, but the main thrust of their claims was in terms
of *human* superiority.

There were two standard arguments. First, it was said that Stalin
felt a genuine concern for the well-being of his fliers, which was
impossible in a "capitalist" head of state. The Western flier had no
"close fellows";[29] he was a "lone hero," and his country did not
value human life.[30] Stalin, by contrast, in an oft-recounted conversation with one aviation hero, insisted that when there was some
danger that the plane would crash, the pilot should make every
effort to save his own life rather than the plane.[31] And in this cosy
group comprising the fliers and their "caring" leader the pilots used
to refer to each other as "brothers" and to Stalin as "father."

The second argument was in terms of Russian superiority in
combating the onslaughts of the elements. Each aviator's flight became, as it were, his ritual trial by the elements to prove his worth
as a "son." Each "trial," while not directly political in significance,
did have broad symbolic resonance of a political nature. This link
was set up when Stalin originally made the claim that "We
Bosheviks are of a special makeup." He continued: "It is not given
to every man to be a member of such a party. Not every man could
withstand the storms and tempests connected with membership in
such a party."[32]

It was "given" to most of the aviation heroes to be Party members, however. So, when they returned triumphant from one of
those many flights to the frozen regions, they in a sense realized the
Stalinist metaphor. This is suggested in a *Literary Gazette* editorial
celebrating the return of the Chkalov expedition in August, 1936:
"The steel bird, driven by the Soviet heroes, forged its way through
cyclones and storms; the crew with Bolshevik tenacity, will, and
mastery triumphed over all obstacles and completed a flight without precedent in the history of aviation."[33]

The various accounts of the feats of the Arctic fliers not only
established to whom it was "given" to be a member in the family
but also articulated the family members' ritual roles. The stories of

the pilots' lives and works rationalized the "family"'s hierarchical structure in terms that in literature have conventionally stood in for ideological categories. These two aims—to write ideological parables and to write myths of maintenance of the status quo—are linked, since a single system of signs performs both functions.

The iconic attributes of the aviation hero represent a positive but childish brand of "spontaneity." He was presented in both fiction and nonfiction as a man of impatience, high spirits, reckless daring, and indefatigability. He was, as the following typical description (of Chkalov, in this case) ran, all "energy which brooked no obstacles," "will," and "determination." The description continues: "Chkalov was full of great elemental [*stixijnaja*] strength. He was constantly testing it, playing with his muscles, will, and powers of endurance."[34] Several other salient traits contributed to the symbolic heroes' outstanding success: they were poor and educationally deprived but in childhood showed an especial affinity for nature.[35] They came from the people, were defiant, powerful, unswervable.

The "fathers" had likewise from early childhood been marked as "energetic," "bold," and "freedom-loving."[36] However, even in childhood one could discern an important difference between those who later assumed the role of "father" and those who were to become "sons": the fathers were not capable of the sort of gratuitous irresponsibility and bumptiousness that marked the sons.

From the very beginning these gifted but high-spirited children needed greater discipline and self-control ("consciousness"), which the "fathers" never lacked, not even in childhood. Inexorably, the "sons" derive most of their "consciousness" from the "fathers." In biographies of the symbolic heroes one finds an echo of the stock pattern from prerevolutionary radical texts and Bolshevik fiction: a "disciple" (son) acquires "consciousness" under the tutelage of a "mentor" (father).

It was Stalin who most often performed the ritual role of "father" or "teacher" and taught the fliers greater self-control. After all, the conventional epithets for Stalin were "father" and "teacher." He proved himself worthy of those titles by exuding "fatherly warmth" whenever he met pilots.[37] It was even suggested that Stalin's "warmth" was so powerful that it could protect his fliers against the Arctic cold.[38]

The father's care was especially expressed in a series of public

rituals. Stalin usually bade the pilots farewell on their departure to
attempt a record, communicated with them en route, and was there
at the airport to welcome them on their return. Whenever a prominent airman fell ill, Stalin would intervene to supervise his medi-
cal treatment.[39] If he was killed in some disaster, Stalin would act as
pallbearer at his funeral.[40]

Together with the father's care came his authority. A pilot's attempt at a record-breaking flight was usually made on direct orders
from Stalin. Indeed, the entire operation was fairly closely directed
by Stalin, including selection of the crew and equipment. On the eve
of Chkalov's historic Arctic flight of 1936, the crew visited Stalin in
the Kremlin, where he proposed changing their entire flight route.
They readily agreed.[41] Later this route was named the Stalin Route.

These various meetings between Stalin and the fliers amounted to
more than post facto celebrations or briefing sessions. They were
ritual exchanges between "mentor" and "disciple," between
"father" and "son," which conferred greater "consciousness" on
the fliers. Since such encounters were necessarily few in number and
elevated in atmostphere, they were so highly charged that they
became kairotic moments. All the pilots testified to this in their
memoirs. Chkalov, for instance, reported: "After my meeting with
the great leader . . . the content of my life became richer; I began to
fly with greater self-discipline than before."[42] And his biographers
claimed that after that "turning point in his life . . . a new life
began."[43]

For the "fledgling children of Stalin" (*Stalinskie pitomcy*) as the
fliers were often called,[44] he was not merely a nurturing father but
also their mentor. He tempered their "spontaneity" and resolved in
them that problematical dialectic between "spontaneity" and "consciousness." Stalin played the same role for almost every one of the
various categories of symbolic hero advanced at that time. In many
biographies of Civil War heroes, like Parkhomenko, the meetings
with Stalin took place at Tsaritsyn.[45] For the Stakhanovites they
occurred initially by proxy, for it was a speech by Stalin that led
them to perform their great feats; later, at Kremlin receptions, they
met with the "leader" himself.[46]

Despite the transformations that took place in the symbolic
heroes during these encounters with their "father," they did not go
on to become "fathers," too. This is most surprising in the case of

the fliers, since most of them were Bolsheviks and professionally trained. The fliers' encounters with Stalin, like their battles with the elements, are often said to make them "older,"[47] yet they never acquire the epithet "father." The distance between them and the father of fathers is so great that the acme of self-realization for them is to become his model sons.[48]

Besides Stalin there were others who enjoyed the status of a father. While there was no question that Stalin was the greatest living father of them all, "father" was essentially a symbolic title. The role of father within the "great family" was a function rather than a fixed identity and so could be conferred on others— conferred but certainly not assumed. In reality the role was always filled by the great leader, but in rhetoric others were sometimes elevated to this status. Many of those so elevated were already dead (Kirov), but those still alive fell generally into two categories: either selected members of the top political leadership who supported Stalin (Voroshilov, Ordzhonnikidze, etc.) or authority figures in specialized areas whose authority was largely limited to that area, people like Makarenko (education), Gorky (literature and culture), and Marr (linguistics). These authority figures had, to chosen sons within their area of specialization, an analogous relationship to the one Stalin had to the aviation heroes, Stakhanovites, etc. As "fathers," their lives tended to be written to the same pattern as that of the political-leader "fathers": they were poor and under-privileged in childhood, "bold, energetic, and freedom-loving," etc. In their later lives the pattern tended to diverge; to be manifestly without peer and advanced in one's field was sufficient mandate for the more limited authority figure.

What was it in the biography of the "father" that gave him his mandate to lead, and why were model "sons" not destined to acquire it even after their meeting with Stalin? One reason, to judge from a common focus of the Bolshevik leaders' biographies, is that the sons had not undergone the incredible suffering and sacrifice that their fathers endured in exile and prison in tsarist Russia.[49] In the specific case of Stalin, a legend was also cultivated in the thirties to the effect that Lenin, before his death, had summoned Stalin and passed the Bolshevik leadership to him.[50] This legend was discredited after Stalin's death, when Khrushchev published Lenin's

Last Testament, in which Lenin expressed doubts about Stalin as a possible successor.

The father-son relationship illustrated in the case of the flier was a basic paradigm of thirties political culture. It was not applied exclusively to such dramatic cases as the fliers and their leader but could be translated, *mutatis mutandis,* into any number of lesser situations, in which any authoritative figure could play "father" to a subordinate or assume some other paternalistic role. For instance, Chkalov called his flying instructor "dad," while Stalin he called "father."[51] Similarly, Aleksey Stakhanov had an "elder" mentor at the mine, the Party head Dyukanov, but only Stalin played "father" for him.[52] In other words, because the primary model for determining one's role in the "great family" was binary and simple (father / son), it could be adapted to all levels of the Soviet hierarchy.

Thus the rhetoric of the mid-thirties provided for a new utopian kinship model projected on the basis of the few examples of the "biggest" human being extant in Soviet society at that time. The model posited an ongoing hierarchy of fathers and sons, the model sons being found in the various superlative examples of positive "spontaneity" (such as the Stakhanovites and Arctic fliers), and the fathers in Stalin and anyone else accorded vaguely comparable "wisdom," "care," and "sternness" to guide the chosen sons to "consciousness." The father-and-sons paradigm replaced the Five-Year Plan ideal of infinite fraternity and provided a new pattern for determining status within the "family" in terms of a hierarchy of maturity and care. But, despite the many gradations of maturity, society's sons were not to grow into fathers; rather, they were to be perfected as model sons. The burden of paternity was to fall on the very few.

The Novel of the Thirties

What happened to the novel when the "great family" emerged as the master trope of Soviet rhetoric? Not only did authors stop writing about little men and technology to write of big men and their amazing feats; novels also adopted from rhetoric the conventional pattern of fathers and sons. The myth of the great family

gave the Socialist Realist novel its final shape or master plot.
In the mid-thirties, authoritative critics began for the first time to
demand that novels be tightly organized. This demand impelled
writers to adopt the master plot. The pressures can be sensed in
criticism. A case in point is P. Pavlenko's novel of 1936, *In the East.*
This novel seems in every respect to be the sort of writing called for
in the thirties (and critics acknowledged that fact).[53] It is about
guarding the Soviet borders in the Far East against the Japanese and
White Guardists, and it appears to have all the ingredients necessary for approval: a collection of former Civil War heroes who bear
familial affection for each other; a mentor from among them
(Schlegel) who is now a senior official in the security organs; a
young and energetic heroine (Olga) who yearns to perform great
feats but must be brought to greater political maturity (since her
father has died, his old Civil War comrades form a family of surrogate fathers to guide Olga); the *taiga,* nature, aviation, new construction, battle, parachuting, border guards—all this and much
more (including Olga's seeing Stalin).

Yet critics all fasten on one particular flaw, which they deem
fatal: the novel's "fragmented composition,"[54] a quality that had
often been noticed, in passing, in earlier reviews of novels but was
not considered tremendously important until now.[55] In the case of
In the East the problem was that, as the authoritative Fadeev remarked in one review, "it is poorly constructed, and many of the
characters are not sustained."[56] "Poorly constructed" has a specific
meaning here, i.e., "not corresponding to the paradigm." The
young heroine, Olga, was never "changed" by one of her mentor
figures, nor did Pavlenko ever make proper binary pairs out of his
protagonists, one representing "spontaneity," the other "consciousness." Even in the relationship between Schlegel and Olga
there are elements of sexual attraction on Schlegel's part, which of
course undercut his ritual role. In another article of the same period
Fadeev said: "It is high time it was realized that in creative writing
even the most 'correct' political views will not ring true unless they
find their own living, model, artistic incarnation."[57] In effect, then,
by the mid-thirties the mandatory quality "party-mindedness" did
not merely entail using politically correct attitudes or themes; it
required of the novel a "lifelike" incarnation of political values,

organized "correctly". In other words, the novel became a
ritualized biography.

The final adoption of the master plot did not, however, represent
the imposition on literature of patterns taken over wholesale from
rhetoric. There was a complex pattern of cross-fertilization between
the two. The myth of the "great family" informs some important
Socialist Realist novels published *before* it became a convention of
Party rhetoric, i.e., novels published before the mid-thirties. An
excellent example of this provided by one of the all-time classics of
Socialist Realism, N. Ostrovsky's *How the Steel Was Tempered*.

Ostrovsky's novel was originally written in the late twenties, and
its plot follows a stock pattern for *minor* committed fiction of those
years.[58] He had trouble getting his novel published in literary journals because of the "unconvincingness" of its characters; but a
former member of the Party underground, who worked on the
Komsomol journal *Molodaya Gvardiya,* defended the novel and
helped get it published there (Part I, 1932; Part II, 1934).[59] However, no one outside the journal paid the book much attention.

In late 1934 the situation changed radically when a *biography* of
Ostrovsky was published in *Pravda*. Before long the army took up
the novel and set it for study circles; it was soon studied by civilian
organizations as well. The novel became enormously popular
(although it is impossible to ascertain whether this popularity preceded public recognition or not). Ostrovsky was already dying of
bone tuberculosis by the time the Order of Lenin came through, but
his last months were gladdened by extravagant public recognition;
the radio and press broadcast daily bulletins on his health, and
thousands came as pilgrims to his Crimean villa (provided by the
state).[60] Incidentally, Ostrovsky was completely untrained as a
writer, and his novel was scorned by the pundits of the literary
world. His lionization could therefore be construed as a further
example of the ritual of status reversal.

It was not just because Ostrovsky was a lowly figure that *How
the Steel Was Tempered* was so extravagantly promoted in the
mid-thirties. His novel provides an ironic instance of latter-day
"social command."[61] Almost every major feature of both the novel
and Ostrovsky's life coincided with a defining aspect of High
Stalinist political culture. The novel sang the praises of the Civil

War ethos, of struggle, heroism, and "Bolshevik will," but, above all, it provided what the age demanded—an entire heroic biography to function as an example for others.

Certain crucial aspects of the life and character of both Ostrovsky and of Pavel Korchagin, the hero of this autobiographical novel, correspond to the iconic attributes of the symbolic hero of the thirties. Korchagin (Ostrovsky) is humble in origins and poorly educated, and in his childhood and early manhood people shake their heads at his pranks, his daredevil feats, his anarchic tendencies and lack of discipline.[62] Even after he matures sufficiently to join the Party, he shows no interest in Party studies and usually fails to do his reading assignments and to obey directives.[63] To counterbalance all this, however, Pavel proves to be a man of unsurpassed energy, will, endurance, and dedication to the cause. He survives—often by dint of sheer will—a long series of encounters with death. This dying and reviving hero comes through one struggle after another only to find himself, at the end, the victim of a terminal disease. Yet, even in the final debilitating months, Pavel is not broken or bitter; his only fear is that he might have to "leave the ranks" before the mighty struggle is won.[64]

Pavel Korchagin, like the mid-thirties symbolic hero, stands for the individual who, though distinguished by his humility and his readiness to give his all for the cause, represents a highly childish brand of positive "spontaneity." The thirties symbolic hero was said to come to "consciousness" in a momentous meeting with Stalin, but the great leader did not play so crucial a role in the life of Pavel Korchagin. As became a convention of Stalinist fiction, the novel's hero has, as his mentor, not Stalin himself but a sort of Stalin-to-scale, a figure with Stalin's significance but proportionate to the small world in which the action takes place.

Most thirties novels have a single mentor as their positive hero. *How the Steel Was Tempered,* however, is picaresque, and therefore the mentor tends to change with each new "microcosm" Pavel Korchagin visits. But it is a clear example of the tendency to make the "son" of lesser political stature than his mentors. Paradoxically, then, although the mentor figures are unquestionably more positive than Pavel himself, he is *the* hero of the novel. Indeed, from the mid-thirties on, the consensus of Soviet criticism has been that Korchagin is *the* positive hero of Soviet literature, *the* model figure for the Soviet people to emulate.[65] The reason why the positive hero is, in political terms, of lesser stature than some other protagonists (his mentors) is because it is his role to resolve symbolically that problematical dialectic between the forces of "spontaneity" and those of "consciousness." Like his counterpart in the real world, the symbolic hero, such as the Stakhanovite or Arctic flier, he is an actor in a ritual mediation of political contradictions (people vis-à-vis leaders, etc.). Reality's contradictions, and the disparities between Marxist-Leninist-Stalinist theory and practice, are all mediated in myth.

In fiction the issue of legitimate Leninist succession was also written into the father-sons pattern. In most novels this issue was not engaged directly, only symbolically (included in the list of conventionalized signs for the hero's mentor is some association with Lenin). Except for Stalin's guest appearances, the senior stateman was usually a major protagonist only in that happily removed setting of an earlier historical period (the Civil War, at most recent). Even in such cases, however, it was common for the author to have his hero leader pass through an initial period of childish exuberance and impulsiveness before donning the austere cloak of supreme responsibility.[66]

In one historical novel of governance, A. Tolstoy's *Peter the First* (published in installments from 1929 to 1945), the author does appear to be working the issue of legitimate Leninist succession into the symbolic pattern of the passage of the generations from father to son. Moreover, the relevant section, once again, was published before the mid-thirties. In Part II, which appeared in 1933 (and was authoritatively described as a marked improvement on Part I),[67] A. Tolstoy treats the theme of the death of Peter's mentor, Lefort, in such a way as to suggest that his real point of reference is that crucial moment of Soviet history when Lenin died and Stalin succeeded him as the only true successor.

Lefort had been Peter's chief advisor in his plans for modernizing Russia. He had also (according to A. Tolstoy's account) encouraged Peter to be wary and tougher with his political enemies. When Lefort falls unexpectedly ill and dies, Moscow is secretly overjoyed, but the courtiers all fake grief over his coffin. Only Peter is truly grief-stricken. He says farewell to his mentor, touching the edge of his coffin as he does so (a gesture symbolic of clasping the baton from his mentor), and declares: "I shall not find another friend like him. Together we shared our joys and our sorrows; in our thoughts we were of one mind." Then, suddenly, Peter pulls away from the coffin, dries his eyes, and assumes an august, aloof pose to the rest of the world. He is changed and will henceforth be tougher in his dealings (the spirited and impulsive tsar will be more "conscious"). Indeed, his conclusion, on seeing the behavior of the hypocrites around him, is "We should not have started at Azov [i.e., with a military campaign against external enemies] but with Moscow!" (vindication of the purges?). Only to his mistress, Anna Mops, can Peter express his grief. To her he says, "We have been orphaned. . . . Death has taken the wrong person."[68]

The symbolic pattern of the passage of generations is, in the Stalinist novel, rarely as clearly linked to that crucial moment when Stalin succeeded Lenin. But Lenin's death in 1924 and the "oath" Stalin delivered to mark the occasion cast their semantic shadows over all the many scenes in later Socialist Realist novels when the positive hero stands by the deathbed or bier of his mentor.

A. Tolstoy's stress on orphanhood is of interest because of the major role orphanhood plays in the political myths of fathers and sons. It is surely no accident that a very high proportion of all thirties heroes, both fictional and real, were either fatherless at birth or lost their father in early childhood. The term orphan was even used to describe children who had one parent still alive.[69] The list here extends through such political leaders as Kirov, cultural authority figures like Gorky and Marr, Civil War heroes like Schors, to Aleksey Stakhanov himself and a virtual majority of novel heroes. And let us not forget the enormous attention paid in the thirties to the *besprizorniki*, the actual or de facto orphans of the streets.

This trend could be ascribed to the fact that both Lenin and Stalin lost their fathers at an early age or perhaps simply to the high death rate among underprivileged Russians during those hard times under the Old Regime. But such explanations are inadequate and a bit simplistic. It should be remembered that from at least Oedipus to David Copperfield and beyond there has been a marked tendency for literary heroes to be orphans. This is because the child without a father is to that extent a child without an identity. And in the great tale of Soviet society, whether told within fiction or without, all are orphans until they find their identity in the "great family."

6 The Sense of Reality in the Heroic Age

The official abandonment, after 1931, of the "little man" as the cornerstone of the new society was not an isolated change; it was part of a sweeping reevaluation of basic ideals encompassing most aspects of reality. One way of synthesizing the changes that took place during the first half of the thirties is to see them as representing a reorientation from a horizontal, undifferentiated ordering of reality to a vertical, hierarchical ordering. Citizens were encouraged to look not alongside, to their "brothers," but upward to the "fathers." The sense of time shifted from a temporality that was homogenized (everything is NOW), to a new sense of the importance of history and genealogy.

An alternative way of synthesizing these value changes is to see them not in terms of a swing in the axis of value orientation from the horizontal to the vertical but as a basic philosophical reorientation with repercussions in most aspects of Soviet life. During the thirties the Soviet Union de facto abandoned its faith in positivism in favor of a variety of idealism verging on mysticism.

During the Plan years, positivism had reigned. Facts and statistics had a charisma unequaled before or since. Positivism matched not only the age's concern for practical matters and technological progress, but also Marxism's self-image as a form of "scientific socialism" grounded in "the materialist world view." Moreover, positivism was in keeping with the the Plan years' militant anti-elitism; it was a democratic, undifferentiated way of knowing: no fact was manifestly superior to any other, the only ground for value being verifiability.

After 1931 the positivist craze was quickly sloughed off, along with the other extreme enthusiasms defining the Plan years. The official platform was soon to become even antipositivist. Many articles appeared in the thirties attacking positivism as "objectivism" or "pseudo-objectivism." When rhetoric alluded to this departure from positivism, it commonly invoked the Marxist distinction between quantitative and qualitative change.[1] "A positivist," it was claimed, "is the person for whom science is a form of accurate accounting done with facts of 'medium dimensions' which are reckoned by *quantity* and not quality," and this leads to "indifference to everything great, significant—a tendency to reduce these to the dimensions of banal phenomena."[2]

This distinction between quantitative and qualitative change was also stressed in the authoritative *Short Course of Party History* (1938) in the crucial fourth chapter on dialectical materialism, attributed to Stalin.[3] In this chapter Engels is quoted on the distinction between qualitative and quantitative change. Engels draws a comparison with physical processes, pointing out that, when water boils, there are at first progressive, quantitative changes as the water gets hotter. But when the boiling (or freezing) point is reached, a *qualitative* change occurs, a change in the water's actual physical structure.[4] By analogy with these changes in water, there are so-called "qualitative leaps forward" (*kačestvennye skački*) in history. A revolution is precisely one such qualitative leap forward: when the dialectical tensions reach their boiling point, a revolution brings about a qualitative change in society. This formula for evaluating change became a commonplace of theoretical writings in the late thirties.

The formula was found not only in theoretical texts. It was precisely in terms of "qualitative leaps forward" that the Stakhanovites' achievements were described. Their production records were claimed to be immeasurably greater than any previously attained, so much so, it was said, that they could not be measured quantitatively by those mere "facts of medium dimensions." Only by leaping off the mundane ground of the feasible were they able to attain such fantastic heights of production.

Although these leaps were officially grounded in theory, once the leaper took to the air he was already in the realm of the fantastic. The thrust up from prosaic reality to somewhere "higher" became a key image of political culture in the thirties. All those paragons of the new master race, the symbolic heroes, were said to make such a leap, figurative or actual, and thus go "higher." The Arctic fliers, for instance, were described in rhetoric as "reaching out into higher realms,"[5] or "flying higher than anyone else in the world,"[6] and the Arctic itself was called the "highest" point on the globe.[7] "Ever Higher!" (*vsë vyše*) became the cry of the age.

These symbolic supermen seem almost to have anticipated Superman of the American comic book (who entered the scene in 1938, three years after the Stakhanovites). Because of the age's concern for establishing lines of continuity reaching back into the past, its fantastic heroes were not totally new creations, as Superman was, but harked back to the great epic heroes—some real, like Pugachev or the Civil War heroes, others purely legendary, from Russia's past. In rhetoric, virtually every important person or event was named after some counterpart in folklore, revolutionary history, or traditional times.

Every Soviet schoolchild of these years was taught that, in the words of a current slogan, "Fairytale Has Become Reality." In their classrooms they sang songs like "Ever Higher":

> We were born that fairytale might become reality.
> To conquer the vastness of space
> Reason gave us steel wings for arms,
> And in the place of a heart they gave us a fiery motor.

> Ever higher and higher and higher
> We urge on our bird's flight,
> And in every propeller there breathes
> Peace for our borders.[8]

So much of what is quintessentially "mid-thirties" is contained in this song: feats reckoned in spatial terms, conquest, securing the borders, transposition of things pertaining to the modern world of technology into the epic tribal world of nature and the elements, and, finally, the cry "Ever Higher!"

In rhetoric the major analogy given for the symbolic heroes was that figure of folk literature the *bogatyr'*. The heroes' entire image was patterned along the lines of this colorful figure. Like the *bogatyr'* the symbolic hero was not merely a man who performed amazing feats; he was also defiant and high-spirited. The most commonly used adjective for the traditional *bogatyr'* was "daring" (*derznovennyj*); for his modern incarnation it was a variant of the same word, *derzkij*.

Except in relation to Stalin (their "prince"), these modern

bogatyri were, like their antecedents, essentially rebels. The symbolic hero's antiauthoritarianism was directed largely at bureaucrats and scientists, who performed for him a function similar to that of the monsters or obstructions barring the traditional *bogatyr'*'s path on his way to serve his prince. The bureaucrats and technical experts tried with all manner of red tape and "scientific" arguments to prevent the symbolic hero from performing his larger-than-life feats. But the modern *bogatyr'* always persisted and won through. As one panegyric said of the flier, Chkalov, in 1939:

> . . . limited and malicious people tried to force him into the dead-end of old norms [for flying], of limits to the possible, regulations, etc.; nevertheless, he—true Soviet man that he was!—shattered all these impediments with one *bogatyr'*-like thrust from the shoulder.[9]

These thirties *bogatyri* imitate the patterns of Gleb Chumalov. In Gladkov's *Cement* (1925), Gleb, like the Stakhanovites and aviation heroes, strode into Soviet institutions in his seven-league boots and with one *bogatyr'*-like gesture sent flying all the red tape, restrictive orders, and constraining advice from the experts.[10] The "tale" of the twenties had been coopted into rhetoric.

As in *Cement,* in thirties rhetoric the Civil War provided a connecting link between the traditional *bogatyr'* and his Soviet reincarnation. One of the symbols used to link all three was a close relationship to horses. In thirties biographies of Civil War generals, writers stressed that even in childhood the hero had had a way with horses, an early sign of his heroic mettle.[11] Before long not only Civil War heroes were said to form early bonds with horses, but other thirties heroes as well.[12] In short, this became another sign of a hero's positive "spontaneity."

If the hero missed out on spending time with horses in childhood, alternatively, as an adult, he would perform feats with some metaphorical "horse." The aviator was often said to drive not a plane but a bird, which can be compared with the firebird on which the prince often rode in folklore. The aviator and the bird were usually so close that they were as one, as is implied in the line from the song "Ever Higher," quoted above ("Reason gave us steel wings for arms").

The close relationship was usually with a wild horse. In fact, the hero's childhood affinity with wild horses seems to have been an early sign of the "surging initiative" that will lead him in adulthood to abjure the tame and make his leap forward. It is perhaps significant that in Russian the word for "leap forward" is *skačok*, or a leap on horseback.

The thirties symbolic hero is somewhat like the wild mustangs of cowboy romance, which prove themselves superior to tame horses. The Stalinist hero is the "Thunderbird Son of Flicka" of those vast Soviet expanses. But one does not have to go as far afield as the American cowboy to find comparisons for the function of the horse in the life of the thirties symbolic hero. Native Russian literary traditions are rich in horse symbolism. In Gogol's *Deal Souls,* three horses drive the troika, which is Russia, unremittingly on to her future destiny. In Bely's *St. Petersburg,* the horse bearing the autocrat is about to take a great leap into the unknown. In Soviet fiction of the twenties, the "Scythian," that wild horseman of Russia's past, charges over the steppes, at one with his steed, symbol of that which is natively Russian, instinctive, antirational, and elemental.

In all three images the horse's leap or ride is inexorable, iconoclastic, not born of reason but of innate powers. The horse's place in high Stalinist myth had its rationalization as a motif for the Civil War hero, but it also reinforced those defining traits of the symbolic hero—defiance and iconoclasm—contained in that common capsule description of him as the one who "breaks established norms" (*lomajuščij uzakonënnuju rutinu*).[13]

The thirties hero-*bogatyr'* as a figure who "dares," who "breaks" established norms of science or conventional bureaucratic practice, seems strangely at odds with the authoritarian, dogmabound society in which he works. There is an incipient paradox between his "daring," "freedom-loving" nature and his ritual role as a model son.

To some extent this paradox is resolved because the model "son" is not rebelling against the "father" but, on the contrary, is like him in nature. The "father" had, in early childhood, also defied authorities (i.e., the tsarist and church authorities) as his "sons" are now doing. Also, while the symbolic hero does indeed defy, he also relishes an opportunity to pay tribute to a truly luminous authority figure, a "father." It is only those false authority figures, the stultifying, restrictive bureaucrats, whom the hero's "surging" nature leads him instinctively to defy. Thus his "revolt" is more a matter of joining the father in his struggles against those bureaucrats and their ilk. Stalin is in many respects the greatest *bogatyr'* of them all. As Barbusse describes him in the 1936 biography: "The story of his life is an unending series of victories over countless monster-like obstacles."[14] If the model sons have seven-league boots, their father must have seventy-league boots, for it is said that, with his stride, Stalin covers ten times the distance anyone else covers.[15] Stalin also "dares" to break through established norms for the attainable. One metallurgical engineer remarked ecstatically, after meeting Stalin: "For Stalin there are no limits, no canons, and no traditions that he will not break."[16]

Stalin is capable of the greatest leaps forward of all. His powers are often represented in *bogatyr'*-like terms, but the father is a more protean figure than the sons, and his essential nature is not as easily exhausted by a single analogy.

The Neo-Platonist Element in High Stalinist Epistemology

The thirties reaction against the earlier cult of positivism and mundane materialism reached an extreme in a cult of higher-order knowledge. In a sense the thirties cry "Ever higher!" embodies its own mysticism. It reflects the general tendency in language of this period to draw away from its directly referential function into the associational or merely allusive one. The language of these years could almost be called incantatory. It was the medium of a system whose beliefs were ultimately inexpressible. They could only be alluded to.

In many respects the system of knowing had by the mid-thirties developed into a variety of Neo-Platonism. Many of the attacks on "objectivism" implied that empirical knowledge represents mere "appearance," something as insubstantial (when compared to the real truth) as the shadows to which, in Plato's myth of the cave, most mortals are limited in their perceptions.[17] Besides merely "seeing appearances," it was possible to "know" a higher reality, but this reality was accessible only to the fathers.

The symbols and myths of High Stalinist culture suggest an entire new cosmology, organized vertically. At the lower, "ground" level are ordinary mortals, who form a shadow world. The Kremlin, which by the mid-thirties had already acquired enormous symbolic value, stands above them as a link, a Jacob's ladder, between the terrestrial and that which is "higher." Above, at a great height, stand those supraterrestrial beings, Lenin and Stalin.

That Lenin had access to higher-order truth was axiomatic in this period. That Stalin had it also was implicit in the various descriptions of him given in biographies and memoirs. He is described by Barbusse as a man of few words—"like an ancient prophet."[18] He is to knowledge what his son is to action: a "titanic sage" able to take "ten paces" to his *bogatyr'*'s one because he "sees far ahead" and has access to "mystery."[19] One contemporary remarked that to listen to Stalin was like seeing a work by an artist of genius whom you don't understand at first; only years later do you begin to grasp what he is trying to express.[20]

Ironically, one is reminded here of the artist-seer who became for certain twenties intellectuals an important symbol for the anti-dogmatic. Examples of idealization of the artist-seer can be found in Zamyatin's works and in Tynyanov's description of Khlebnikov in his introduction to the collected works of Khlebnikov, published in 1929 (on which Kaverin based his portrait of the artist-hero Arkhimedov in his novel, *Artist Unknown*, of 1931). For Tynyanov, Khlebnikov was an artist in the sense that he was a man who had a new "vision," a figure who had the "courage" to ignore the norms and taboos of conventional art. Anyone who cared to follow such an artist, Tynyanov maintained, would "see" differently from the way he had seen before; or, rather, since the artist-seer would be so far ahead of his times as to be able to "predict the future," anyone who sought to grasp what the artist had "seen" could do so only hazily.[21] Thus the notion that Stalin was a seer who sees far ahead and, like his "sons," breaks established norms provides a further example of the extent to which thirties political culture shared many of the ideas and images of earlier, non-Party (or even dissident) intellectual movements.

This cult of the artist-seer among certain groups of twenties intellectuals was an implicitly aristocratic cult. High Stalinism democratized the notion by giving access to higher truth to the model sons as well. However, while the father had complete access to the "forms" of higher-level knowledge, the sons could grasp them only intuitively, inchoately, and with their father's guidance. This aspect was especially stressed in accounts of the Stakhanovites. At the October, 1935, meeting held to celebrate the Stakhanovite movement, Stalin said: "The thing that strikes us above all is the fact that this movement began, as it were, of its own accord, spontaneously [*stixijno*]; it was a movement from below, not born of any pressure whatsoever on the part of the administration of our enterprises."[22]

The Stakhanovite was humble in origins and education, yet his achievement in raising production norms was quite explicitly not due to sheer physical strength.[23] The secret of his success lay in his *daring* to discount scientifically established norms. Any man who had the courage to go beyond that threshold, it was claimed, could outdo production quotas by "ten to one hundred times."[24] Thus the Stakhanovite stood as an emblem not only in daring and achievement but in epistemology as well. Among the many extravagant epithets coined for him, "Prometheus unbound" suggests precisely that.[25]

But whence came his knowledge if not from science, education, or direction? Actually he was directed; but the official answer is "spontaneously," on the one hand, and "from Stalin" on the other. The Stakhanovites in their various autobiographical writings always stressed that it was some speech by Stalin that had inspired them originally to perform their feats.

The main source of all the thirties symbolic heroes' "knowledge" came ex post facto (after their feats), in encounters with Stalin at the Kremlin. In the many published accounts of these meetings, one gets a vivid sense of the striking parallels between High Stalinist myth and Plato's myth of the cave. When bidden to meet Stalin, the symbolic heroes typically approach the Kremlin with trepidation and nervous confusion; they feel all churned up inside and unable to express themselves.[26] When they enter the Great Hall of the Kremlin, where they are to see Stalin, they are dazzled at first by a "blinding" light.[27] But once they look at Stalin, they find the courage to speak, to put in words what they "know" within about their feats.[28] After such a meeting, everyone detects a radical change in the heroes. One participant in a Kremlin ceremony reports, for instance, that, ever after, he "saw differently than ever before."[29]

In such meetings with Stalin is the great paradox resolved: out of the surging elemental darkness the wild, inchoate "mustang" comes to see the "forms" in the dazzling Kremlin hall in order that henceforth he may have words to express what he has so far grasped only hazily and intuitively. Once he "knows," he changes from rebel to leader and is reintegrated: he commonly starts studying at some institute, and he joins the Party.

These Kremlin rituals provide a striking example of the crossover between fiction and Bolshevik reality. The meeting with Stalin is the ultimate stage in the gradual evolution of the mentor-disciple exchange, a basic pattern of prerevolutionary radical fiction. The exchange has become a more elaborate, ritualized, and elevated occasion, and it now occurs not just between some lower-class everyman and a bearer of consciousness but between an upcoming citizen and the head of state. No longer does the mentor figure merely happen, due to circumstances, to be more conscious than his disciple (as in Gorky's *Mother*), who, once enlightened, can go on to play mentor to others in turn. In the later version of the rite, the mentor has privileged access to the mysteries and will impart them only to the chosen and worthy.

In Bolshevik fiction of the twenties one can find embryonic examples of this developing trend in the conventional mentor-disciple pattern. For instance, in Gladkov's first redaction of *Cement* (1925), Gleb at one point goes to visit the Cheka head, Chibis, senses in him "mystery" and "vision," and concludes that Chibis must have seen Lenin in order to have such knowledge.[30] Gladkov thus anticipates the day when the mentor-disciple exchange would involve not simply the occasion for exchange of "consciousness" but also a myth for maintenance of the status quo. "Privileged" access is via the nation's leadership or its official forebears.

In the third redaction, of 1941, the exchange between Gleb and Chibis has been expanded slightly to include the new convention in which anyone privileged enough to speak to one of the great fathers will have "new words":

> You see, I haven't seen him [Lenin], Comrade Chibis, and it seems to me I have missed out on the main thing in life. If only I could see him and hear him, then I would discover myself anew. I can't express this—I am poor in words. . . . But then they would be different. . . . Big and profound. . . .[31]

Lenin passed his "light" and "mystery" on to Stalin. Now Stalin was passing it on to his chosen few. The myth of the "great family" provides not only for a succession of generations but for a chain of kairotic moments akin to the laying-on of hands in a church adhering to the doctrine of apostolic succession. In his meeting with Chibis, Gleb missed out on the laying-on of hands and therefore failed to transcend his state of "spontaneity" and gain an extra-personal identity.

For the time being, however, the chain is not infinite. Not all are able to receive the "mystery" and "light" that the leaders have to give. The number of "sons" chosen to undergo the rite with their "father" is very small. It comprises only the symbolic heroes. Others, though they will grow in "consciousness" by means of a series of lesser mentor-pupil exchanges, are not yet sufficiently "high" to "see" the mysteries.

Thus, in the thirties, the chosen "fathers" and "sons" had a different status in society from that of all other citizens. Although the rationale for their election derives in part from their superior natures, extraordinary service, and sacrifice, the ultimate criterion is epistemological: only if they "know," only if they have "seen" or been given directly the "mystery" and "light" of the other, more real, world (as in Plato's myth of the cave), can they claim the right to lead.

In a sense this division between those who "see" and those who cannot provides a rationale for the elitism of the vanguard. But it is not merely a rationalization. This ontological division is very fundamental to High Stalinist thinking and reaches into most aspects of life. The chosen / not chosen dichotomy is only one of a series. Two other dichotomies of especial importance are the two kinds of time and the two kinds of place.

A striking example of the two orders of time can be found in Aleksey Stakhanov's description of his first Kremlin meeting with "Our Father." During the meeting, Stalin addresses the assembled Stakhanovites, and at the end they respond with the inevitable tumultuous applause. Stalin repeatedly tries to put a halt to this flow of applause, but in vain. As a last resort he takes out his watch and points to the time. But, Stakhanov reports, "We did not acknowledge time." So they continued to applaud, undaunted.[32]

The Stakhanovites did not "acknowledge time" during their

meeting with Stalin because the time of that meeting was of a different order from that of everyday reality, something akin to the "great time" of which Mircea Eliade speaks in his analyses of myth.[33] It was a time that could not, like the quotidian, be reckoned in "facts of medium dimensions"—by measures of progressive, incremental, "quantitative" change (such as how many minutes have elapsed).

There are two orders of place, too: those that are close to the forms, on the one hand, and, on the other, those that embody merely that temporary, present-day stage attained in historical evolution. In general, Moscow (or the Kremlin alone) symbolizes the higher-order place. Like the Stakhanovites, it represents a prefiguration of that which is to come; it is the place from which that Jacob's ladder rises, leading to "higher" reality (one Stakhanovite actually reported that, when he met Stalin at the Kremlin, he felt as if he were on a high tower).[34]

In the mid-thirties the Soviet leadership set out to make Moscow literally higher than other Soviet towns. A decree of 1935 for the transformation of Moscow called for building higher buildings. The press reports of this scheme were colored by rhetoric to the effect that Moscow was in some way more advanced than the rest of the country.[35] The leadership seemed to be trying to create a "myth of Moscow" to supplant the myth of St. Petersburg. As if to confirm that aim, not only was Moscow to be "higher"; it was to be more rationally planned as well, and built largely in granite, the building material associated with Peter's work in St. Petersburg.

In Stalinist culture of the thirties there were, then, two orders of reality, ordinary and extraordinary, and, correspondingly, two orders of human being, of time, of place, and so on. Ordinary reality was considered valuable only as it could be seen to reflect some form, or ideal essence, found in higher-order reality. The distinctions between ordinary reality and fiction lost the crucial importance they have in other philosophical systems.

At this time, as at no other, the boundaries between fiction and fact became blurred. In all areas of public life—in meetings, the press, speeches, ceremonials, in those incredible, carnival-like mass processions where "enemies of the people" were borne in effigy, in the infamous political trials of 1936–38—the difference between fiction and fact, between theater and political event, between liter-

ary plot and factual reporting, all became somewhat hazy.
Not only did literature and life converge in these years, but the
dominant literary modes were affected by the change in the prevailing sense of reality. The more Soviet society came to reject
positivism and that empirical truth of "medium dimensions," the
more the imaginative element came back into literature. In the earlier, prosaic days of the Plan years, positivist zealots, in their effort
to squeeze the last bit of fiction out of all literary works, had left
them almost bone dry. As a result, plot lines embodied mechanical
and transparent motivations for providing readers with statistics,
technological data, and object lessons in the value of mass labor.
The reaction against these trends was gradual, but by the mid-
thirties it had reached the opposite extreme. At first, critics merely
denigrated "industrial fiction" as being dull and lacking in human
interest. They called for a literature about people rather than statistics, but based on "the typical in reality." Soon this catch phrase
began to lose its appeal. In terms of Zhdanov's formulation of
"socialist realism" at the First Writers' Congress of 1934—that
literature should combine "the most matter-of-fact, everyday reality with the most heroic prospects"[36]—it could be said that, up to
that point, "the most matter-of-fact" had tended to dominate in
fiction but that, having been bogged down on the flat plains of
reality for so long, Soviet literature now seemed to anxious to climb to
more heroic heights.

In order to describe *homo extraordinarius,* one needed more
fabulous forms, such as fairytales. In fact, Gorky had for some time
been advocating a sort of marriage between literature and folk
forms, especially since his return from exile in 1931. In his speech to
the First Writers' Congress (1934) Gorky called on literature to
model its heroes on those of "folklore, i.e., the unwritten compositions, of the toiling man."[37] Initially, this admonition resulted
chiefly in the investment of resources in collecting oral folklore:
hundreds of people went scurrying around the countryside record-
ing tales and *byliny,* and a plethora of journals, institutions, conferences, etc., were set up to classify and disseminate the material
thus collected.[38]

Before long, folklore ceased being a sort of cottage industry for
academics and was incorporated into the myths of the "great family." Efforts were even made to establish a connection between the

country's "fathers" and its folklore. In the new biographies of Stalin, Voroshilov, and others that were being published at this time, it
was stressed that in childhood these leaders had been prepared for
heroism by imbibing folklore from their mothers.[39] In his thirties
speeches, Stalin used what he had learned from his mother by often
referring to some folklore figure.[40] And Gorky, in a 1935 article
"On Folktales," gave a touching account of how, in the extended
family in his grandparents' house, they would settle down on winter
evenings to hear his grandmother's fairy stories, and he remarked
that these had had a much more profound effect on him than the
religious tales offered by his austere and authoritarian grandfather.[41]

When the tale-teller was given a place in the "great family," the
marriage between the fable and Socialist Realist literature soon
followed. Heroes became larger than life, their feats ever more
fantastic and epic, and the language of the text ever richer in
epithets and imagery transplanted from the folk tradition. Production heroes were now fed fairy stories and adventure tales rather
than statistical manuals as models to guide them in writing sketches
about their work.[42]

The use of folk genres for didactic pieces, popularizing ideology
and policies, was not new, for it had been a feature of the *narodyne
izdanija* turned out by revolutionaries in the nineteenth century. But
there were two major differences in the thirties revival of folk
forms. First, the Soviet literary establishment attempted to turn
back the clock and create a *genuine* folk literature in praise of the
new age. Second, the primary function of thirties "folk" literature
was to legitimize the Stalinist leadership.

In 1937 the publishing house "Two Five-Year Plans" invited
some genuine singers of *byliny* to venture out of their remote villages and come to Moscow to create *byliny* about the won-
ders of the new age. With the concern for legitimacy and origins
so typical of official bodies in the period, they invited a certain
Marfa Kryukova because she was the granddaughter of the *bylina*
singer used as a source by the great nineteenth-century collector of
folklore, Rybnikov.[43] Indeed the Western scholar C. M. Bowra
includes in his book *Heroic Poetry* not only the family tree of the
impressive Kryukov dynasty of bards but that of another dynasty as
well, the Ryabinins, whose fourth generation was likewise coopted

to sing the valor of the new *bogatyri*.[44]

These were no isolated examples. Starting with the First Writers' Congress in 1934, when the bard Suleyman Stalsky was presented to the Congress and given a special ovation, folk bards (especially representatives of non-Russian peoples, like Stalsky from Dagestan and Dzhambul from Kazakhstan) were assigned major roles in Soviet literature and honored with awards like the Order of Lenin and the Stalin Prize.

The care taken to ensure that these bards had good pedigrees was not a reflection of mere officiousness. The main work done by the *bylina* singers was celebrating the greatness of the dynasty of fathers and sons and, to a lesser extent, the symbolic heroes. A typical list of subjects about which *byliny* were written comprises Lenin, Stalin, Voroshilov, Ordzhonnikidze, Kaganovich, Kirov, Kalinin, Chapaev, Budyonny, Schors, the aviators, the polar explorers, and the Stakhanovites.[45]

The majority of the neo-epics featured Soviet leaders who were prime actors in the official saga of Stalin's life and works. The pervasive obsession was with the legitimacy of the Lenin / Stalin / Trotsky succession. One finds negative epics (such as Dzhambul's "Destroy!," composed for the 1938 trial of Bukharin, Rykov, and Trotsky)[46] and positive epics celebrating the magnificent line of the leadership. A good example would be Kryukova's "Tale of Lenin" (*Skazanie o Lenine*, 1937), whose protagonists are "the red sun Vlademir" (Lenin); the half-fabulous pagan prince of the traditional Russian epic, the "Big Idol" (*idolišče*, Alexander III); the "magic knight" (Klim Voroshilov); Stalin *-svet* ("light"); the "furious viper" (Lenin's would-be assassin, Kaplan); the "villain Trotsky"; and several *bogatyri,* such as Chapaev and Blyukher.

The poem commences in the late nineteenth century with the execution of Lenin's older brother for terrorist activities, and it ends with Lenin's death and Stalin's succession. Its plot follows the general outline of the rewritten Stalinist version of Bolshevik history, but most of the well-known stages in the progess toward Stalin's hegemony are translated into *bylina* clichés. For instance, Lenin makes a revolution in 1917 by gathering all the people around a magic pillar and tugging away at a "magic ring" until Mother Russia is turned away from the landlords and manufacturers. Like the folktale, this poem is also built on a triadic pattern: it is

punctuated by three meetings between Lenin and Stalin, after each
of which Lenin sends Stalin out into the world to do his work.[47]

The heavy use of the oral folk tradition in the written literature,
the rhetoric, and even the public ritual of the thirties did not really
represent a "marriage" between two previously distinct traditions.
Indeed, the list of heroes Gorky presented to the First Writers'
Congress as good models for Socialist Realism—a list compiled, he
said, from "folklore, from the unwritten compositions of the toiling
man"—includes Hercules, Prometheus, and Doctor Faustus.[48] In
other versions of this list Gorky included even Don Quixote, that
pioneer figure in the history of *literary* self-consciousness.[49]
Moreover, the most persistent theme of Gorky's articles on literature published in the thirties was the necessity of purifying the
literary language and *expunging* all regionalism, earthiness, and
folkisms from Soviet prose.[50]

Literature was to provide either occasional pieces written to celebrate the honor and glory of the Bolshevik leaders or models of the
new man. These aims were not particularly well served by reviving
folk genres. Indeed, for all the inspired outpourings of the people's
bards, nowhere were the state's interests better served than in that
old mainstay of literature, the novel. In the "folk" epic or tale, the
crudity of the engrafted folksiness and the transparency of the devices reduced its effectiveness as a repository of myth. When an
actual event, like the Revolution, was translated into a specific
folklore motif—such as tugging at a magic ring and turning it away
from the owning classes—its singular political and ideological
significance was diluted.

The thirties novel was more popular, but it was never very "folk."
In writing a novel, the author would usually invoke parallels or
imagery from folklore merely to embellish the plot.[51] In other
words, folk elements were nonessential features in the Stalinist
novel because the hero's exploits were not self-valuable as "feats,"
as they are in traditional folklore; the novel was, rather, a political
allegory.

It might seem that mid-thirties literature simulated a certain folksiness rather as it simulated organicism and the *Gemeinschaft*
world and that the powers-that-be cultivated the "people's bards"
as court chroniclers because this enhanced their claim to be of and

by the people. The extravagant recognition they gave these largely illiterate singers and tellers of tales who came from outside the literary establishment provides another example of the ritual of status reversal. Just as Stakhanovites did not, in reality, perform their feats without direction but were instructed by local officials (Party officials, primarily),[52] so, too, professional writers were usually assigned to the people's bards to "help" them compose their *byliny* and folktales.[53]

Yet the neo-folk elements did not represent mere clever packaging or embellishment of propagandistic tracts, for they were also a symptom of the convergence of "the real" and "the fictional" in High Stalinist ontology. One cannot discount the possibility that the leaders of the thirties were themselves partly caught up in the age's official myths. Robert Tucker has argued in his *Stalin as Revolutionary,* for instance, that Stalin's self-image as a Bolshevik revolutionary was patterned by the object of his childhood fascination, the Georgian epic hero Koba, whose name he sometimes took as an underground alias in his prerevolutionary days.[54]

The use of folk elements in thirties rhetoric and literature had broader functions than providing patterns for the hero cult. Their primary function was to provide a medium—"words"—to convey the new sense of reality. Thirties values comprised a belief system in which the notion of transcendence was central: going "higher," going beyond the this-worldly and mundane, beyond the realm of mere appearance. It was in effect a neoreligious doctrine of salvation and rebirth. For this belief system a new language was needed. However, the language most often used in the West in such situations—the language of Christian symbolism—was officially proscribed. And so, in a sense, folklore was, in the rhetoric of the thirties, a makeshift, used more as an enabling language, a medium, than anything else. In the postwar forties, this veneer of folkism rubbed off as easily as, in the thirties, it had been laid on.

The natural generic antecedents of thirties literature, therefore, are found not in folktales but in the written tradition of religious literature. The incantatory nature of the rhetoric should not be confused with the characteristic repetitions of folk genres. It could be compared with the highly stylized medieval Russian homiletics (using *pletenie sloves*). In other words, for all Gorky's claim to have been influenced in his own work by the oral tradition and to have rejected the religious texts that were read to him in his early childhood, the works produced by the new literary tradition—Socialist Realism, which he was brought back to guide—were, like his own *Mother,* closer to the tradition he claimed to have jettisoned: the religious texts.

The God-building Heresy as a Subtext of High Stalinist Culture?

In the thirties *the* iconic attribute of all official heroes was "daring." But "daring" (and, especially, "daring" to discount all established norms and constraints) is a central concept in Nietzscheanism. In short, there was a heavy dash of Nietzscheanism in that decade's political culture. Indeed, even the purges could be regarded as an exercise in Nietzschean praxis.

Nietzscheanism and Marxism-Lenism were for the most part antithetical philosophical systems. The element of Nietzscheanism in Stalinism could thus be seized on as evidence corroborating the perennial claim that Stalinism represented a departure from, or perversion of, true Marxism-Leninism.

Actually, it is highly doubtful whether Nietzsche was a *direct* source for the image of the thirties hero as a man who "dares," but he may have left his mark by proxy. Nietzsche's ideas colored the writings of many Russian thinkers of this century, including, in the twenties, Zamyatin, Tynyanov, and Kaverin. Nietzsche even had an influence on some Party intellectuals, an influence reflected in the philosophy of God-building that Gorky himself espoused for a time, early in this century. Lenin denounced God-building as a heresy. And yet the God-builders (Gorky, Lunacharsky, Bogdanov, and others) seem to have had the last laugh, for the language, ideas, and myths of their earlier works, inspired by the ideas of God-building, can almost all be found in the official rhetoric of the thirties.

There are many examples of this in that most curious work of Gorky's neo-Nietzschean phase, his short prose piece of 1903, "Man." "Man" is a conflation of disparate trends in the intellectual history of the eighteenth and nineteenth centuries. At the same time, "Man" contains many of the catchphrases and ideas of High Stalinism; for instance, it was written not as a paean to Everyman but to the man who could go "far ahead of the ordinary man and above life."[55] It praises the man who is not of "medium dimensions" but reaches up "higher." As with the Soviet superhero of the thirties, the pattern of man's progress to true "awareness" (*soznanie;* cf. Marxist-Leninist "consciousness" or *soznatel'nost'*) runs through a series of combat engagements with willful, irrational phenomena which are overcome partly because the hero "dares." The recurring refrain that accompanies man's progress is this: "And so rebellious man proceeds on through that terrible murk of the mysteries of existence. Onward and upward! Forever onward and upward!" This refrain is often shortened to simply "Onward and upward!" Here, it would seem, we have the origin of that defining catchphrase of the thirties, "Ever onward, ever upward!" Indeed, Gorky himself used it in articles he wrote in the thirties.[56]

A later work that Gorky wrote during his God-building phase, *A Confession* (1908)—the work Lenin attacked—basically expounded the same ideas as "Man" but showed less European influence. It drew more from native-grown and Russo-centric intellectual movements, and especially from certain varieties of Slavophilism that idealize the folk rebel and Mother Earth. *A Confession,* like "Man," also contains many ideas and catchphrases that seem to anticipate High Stalinist culture. For instance, one can find parallels with the patriarchal line of the "great family." The narrator/hero is a foundling, abandoned on a noble estate. When he grows to manhood and sets out on a spiritual quest, he becomes convinced that each of the mentor figures he encounters must be his true father.[57]

In *A Confession* Gorky also used particular phrases that were to reecho in the thirties (e.g., "the people are immortal" and "the tribe"). His language, however, was distinctly liturgical (e.g., "*Veliko-mučenik velij, čem vse, cerkov'ju pravoslalennye—sej bo esi bog, tvoraj čudesa*" ["You are a great martyr, greater than all those who have been glorified by the church—for you are god, you perform miracles"]).[58] Gorky undoubtedly chose this language because he quite explicitly wanted God-building to replace the Christian religion, but his use of it goes beyond conscious stylization. For all his emphasis on reason and knowledge in his writings of these years, these are mystical, elusive categories.

All this evidence would suggest that High Stalinist rhetoric and fiction were colored by the ideas, tone, and even the language of God-building—that Marxist heresy deplored by Lenin. Still, it would be wrong to make a direct identification between the symbols, language, and ideas of one social-intellectual context and another. In attempting to assess Gorky's influence on Soviet rhetoric and literature, it must first be recognized that Gorky's own ideas and key symbols did not come to him *in vacuo*. As presented in "Man" and *A Confession*, they represent a mixture of different elements, derived from both Russian and Western European intellectual movements. Thus it is not necessarily the case that Gorky was a kind of intellectual *bogatyr'* who singlehandedly moved the great "boulder" of Soviet culture.

Although much of the symbolism of Gorky's God-building period surfaced again in Stalinist rhetoric, in the new context neither its functions nor its meaning were exactly the same as before. This can be appreciated if one looks at Gorky's 1933 essay bearing the suggestive title "Onward and Upward, Komsomol!" Gorky here urges the komsomol to be zealous in eradicating "two-legged parasites" (people clinging to old, bourgeois, self-centered values) and to keep before him the image of Pavel Morozov, the pioneer hero who denounced his father as a kulak and died a martyr's death for it. In other words, Gorky himself later used, in support of the "vigilance" whipped up for the Stalinist trials, the language and symbols of his original idealistic vision in "Man."

During the First Five-Year Plan Gorky was himself an advocate of values that were implicitly opposed to those he expressed both later and in his earlier, neo-Nietzschean, phase. In an article of 1928, "On Little People and Their Great Work," he expresses a new vision, one of countless little men (rather than the godlike big men) who performed great deeds with small, modest, collective efforts.[59] The ideal that Gorky proposes here involves a long process of gradual, incremental or "quantitative" change and is implicitly opposed to the ideal of radical, "qualitative" change, of "great leaps forward."

Thus it might be said that, when Gorky arrived in Moscow to head up Soviet literature, he stamped the idiosyncratic imprint of the ideas he brought with him not only on Socialist Realist literature but on Stalinist political culture and rhetoric. Yet it could also

be said that Gorky himself was caught up in the major cultural
vogues of Stalinism and that he changed his ideas along with the
swings of the axes of value. For Gorky, as for so many other actors
in the thirties, the questions "Who whom?" (*kto kogo*), "Who
what?," and "What whom?" are ultimately insoluble, for "who,"
"what," and "whom" were all part of the single interacting process
in which fiction, myth, ideology, reality, actors, and historical
figures all were caught.

III

An Analysis of the
Conventional Stalinist
Novel

7

The Prototypical Plot

In some ways the most definitive characteristic of Socialist Realism is not the mode of writing it envisages but its radical reconception of the role of the writer. After 1932 (at least) the Stalinist writer was no longer the creator of original texts; he became the teller of tales already prefigured in Party lore. Consequently, his function is rather like that of the chroniclers of the Middle Ages, as described by Walter Benjamin:

> By basing their historical tales on a divine plan of salvation—an inscrutable one—they have from the very start lifted the burden of demonstrable explanation from their own shoulders. . . . [They are] not concerned with an accurate concatenation of definite events, but with the way these are embedded in the great inscrutable course of the world.[1]

The Stalinist novelist must present a fictionalized account of reality and events, but these "historical tales" must be based on something analogous to the "divine plan of salvation" followed by the medieval chronicler, namely, on the Marxist-Leninist account of history. None of the discrepancies between theory and practice that give such headaches to the theorists (such as the state's resistance to its scheduled withering-away) needs to concern him, for he does not have to *prove* anything. As chronicler he merely *shows* how, in the particular model situation he has chosen, social and political contradictions work themselves out in successive resolutions of the spontaneity / consciousness dialectic.

A corollary of the Soviet novelist's status as mere teller of tales is his lack of autonomy over his own texts. It is the prerogative of his editors, critics, and patrons to see to it that the purity of the tale is preserved in the novelist's work. This prerogative has been demonstrated again and again by evidence that writers have been pressured into rewriting and / or that their works have been altered by editors without their permission. The author's creativity is not completely frustrated, however; for, working within the well-known parameters of the Socialist Realist tradition, he can yet bring his ingenuity and imagination to bear in translating History into symbolic form. Thus one can find a range of literary quality even among works that have preserved the purity of the tale.

A. Fadeev's *The Young Guard* (1951) provides a good example. For reasons of textual history, the purity of the "tale" has been more conscientiously preserved in this novel than is usual even in the classics of Socialist Realism. Thus the novel is virtually a textbook example of the master plot; yet this does not prevent it from being one of the finer examples of Socialist Realism in terms of literary quality. Actually, it is an example of the master plot in its most generalized form. This is not a production novel; hence, many of the functions to be found in that fuller version of the Soviet novel (outlined in Appendix A) are omitted.

In the summer of 1943 the Central Committee of the Komsomol assigned Fadeev the task of writing about Komsomol resistance in the Donbass mining town of Krasnodon during the German occupation of late 1942 and 1943. At that time Fadeev was secretary of the Writers' Union. As captain of the team, he could be expected to obey all the rules. Fadeev prepared himself for this task very conscientiously. He read the diaries of the participants and their families, sifted through documents, and spent a month in Krasnodon taking interviews.[2] The resulting novel was a tribute to Komsomol heroism that singled out as hero the real-life commissar of the Krasnodon Komsomol movement, Oleg Koshevoy.

When Fadeev published *The Young Guard* in 1945 in the Komsomol journal of the same name, it was acclaimed by the critics. In fact, their response suggests that *The Young Guard* had been chosen as *the* paradigm of Socialist Realism for the forties, to be for that decade what N. Ostrovsky's *How the Steel Was Tempered* had been for the thirties. It was in this climate of enthusiasm that *The Young Guard* received a Stalin Prize, First Class, in 1946.

In late 1947 the situation changed. The eulogies came to an abrupt halt as critical reviews of the novel appeared in *Culture and Life, Pravda,* and other authoritative periodicals. All of the attacks on the novel centered on the minor role accorded to the Party in the dramas at Krasnodon. It was suggested that, had Fadeev felt a little less bound by the documents he had read, he would have written the novel differently.[3] To translate these criticisms into the terms I have used in Part Two, Fadeev was too tied to "appearances" and failed to depict the higher reality of the "forms." He extolled the exploits of the "sons"—which would have been admirable, except that he neglected to tell of the pivotal role of the "fathers." In other words, Fadeev did not tell the tale correctly. Several other prominent writers were also attacked for failing to depict the Party's role accurately (e.g., V. Kataev for *For the Power of the Soviets* [1949] and K. Simonov for *Smoke of the Fatherland* [1947]). But Fadeev was the most senior. For all his status as titular head of Soviet literature and author of two Socialist Realist classics (*The Rout* [1927] and *The Last of the Udege* [1930–40]), for all the care he took to research his story, Fadeev was not entitled to autonomy over his own text.

Rather than be judged a poor chronicler, Fadeev met those criticisms and set about rewriting the novel. The second redaction was published in 1951 and was given the official stamp of approval in a *Pravda* editorial of December 23, 1951. This redaction was thereupon reincorporated into the Socialist Realist canon as an exemplar; consequently, the second redaction is the source referred to here.

The main changes Fadeev made in rewriting *The Young Guard* were additions. The number of chapters swelled from fifty-four in the first redaction to sixty-four in the second, and many of the old chapters were expanded. Most additions show the work of the "fathers" in the form of local Party officials and the role of an internal mentor in the Komsomol group, Ivan Turkenich, a wounded Red Army officer who directed the Young Guard's Party-given assignments.

In particular, Fadeev gave a central role to the head of the Party underground, Lyutikov. In the first redaction Lyutikov had been a shadowy figure, having no major role and, in any case, killed in chapter 29. But in the second redaction it is Lyutikov who provides the main guidelines for the Young Guard's work (while Turkenich directs the day-by-day operations). He is *the* mentor figure for the novel's model "son," Oleg. Besides giving Oleg a ritual "father," Fadeev also strove in the second redaction to enhance the "son" quality of Oleg, to make him more of a normal lad and less the pure, heroic martyr.[4]

The second redaction represents a remarkably pure and classical version of History's "divine plan" told in terms of the myth of the "great family." The novel is almost perfectly transparent and lacks the impurities that most other Soviet novels have—e.g., ambiguity, characters who are individualized and not complete subfunctions of their historical roles.

This redaction was published in 1951, only two years before Stalin's death. However, since the first redaction, which provides the bulk of the text for the second, was published in 1945, before the distinctive conventions of the forties had evolved, the novel is (even in its second redaction) closer in imagery, plot, and characterization to fiction of the "heroic age" of the thirties than to typical forties prose.

The Plot of *The Young Guard*

In Socialist Realist fiction, the Soviet "divine plan of salvation," or Marxist-Leninist account of History, is condensed by means of highly codified conventions and told as a tale. This tale is of a questing hero who sets out .in search of "consciousness." En route he encounters obstacles that test his strength and determination, but in the end he attains his goal.

Thus described, the structure of the typical Socialist Realist novel does not appear to be very distinctive. The hero's quest is but a variant of the most common plot type of all. How many heroes of world literature set out to attain a goal, encounter obstacles en route, and so on! The Soviet novel is somewhat distinctive in that the hero's quest typically has a dual goal. On the one hand, he has before him a task from the public sphere. He may, for instance, aim to supervise the construction of a dam or to raise production yields. But his second, and more important, goal is to resolve within himself the tension between "spontaneity" and "consciousness." Since the public and private goals are fused, the hero's personal resolution becomes a historical allegory.

In the following summary of *The Young Guard* one can see how the public and private tasks are fused in a single plot:

> In late 1942 the inhabitants of the Donbass mining town Krasnodon are confronted by an imminent German invasion. Most attempt to flee, but many are forced to return when they en-

counter the advancing Germans. The Party organization and
partisans manage to evacuate, but they do so only after organizing an underground Party organization to stay behind under the
leadership of Fillip Petrovich Lyutikov. Many attempt to flee the
town, including the novel's hero, Oleg Koshevoy. While Oleg is
absent from the town, his role as "son" is temporarily assumed
by a younger lad, Seryozha. But Oleg is turned back, and, together with other members of the Komsomol who did not manage to flee, he organizes a resistance organization called the
Young Guard (which is also the name traditionally used for
the Komsomol movement). The Young Guard is led by Oleg as
commissar and by Ivan Turkenich as commander. Some members of the group establish contact with the Party underground,
and Oleg periodically has secret meetings with Lyutikov, who
gives him advice and instructions for the terroristic and counterpropagandistic work of the Young Guard. The Young Guard
executes a series of daring coups against the German occupiers;
but before the Soviet troops advancing from Stalingrad are able
to liberate the town, the Young Guard organization is uncovered
by the Germans. Most of its members are arrested (together with
Lyutikov and another member of the Party underground), and,
after prolonged torture and interrogation, they are executed.

Oleg's public task is to undermine the Germans' grip on Krasnodon by organizing the Young Guard (under Party guidance) in
terroristic and counterpropagandistic activities. As he sets about
this task, Oleg grows in "consciousness." Through his Komsomol
work Oleg gains greater confidence, experience, and maturity and
an increasing understanding of the need to subordinate his individual initiative and even his sense of what is right to the judgment of
the collective.

In Socialist Realist novels the public task provides content and
specificity (it tells *which* obstacles are to be overcome, etc.) for the
hero's ritual progress toward "consciousness," but it is only periph-
erally a motivating force. The actual motivating structure that enables the hero to attain "consciousness" is closely tied to the various myths of High Stalinist rhetoric.

Nature in *The Young Guard*

It will be recalled that the characteristic tropes used in High
Stalinist rhetoric to describe modern Soviet Russia gave it the air of

an epic, tribal world, where man communed with nature and the elements. This tendency is quite marked in *The Young Guard*, where only occasionally does the reader get a sense that the action is set in a mining town of the mid-twentieth century. One of the specific ways in which Fadeev gives his modern setting a more traditional aura is by using that great classic of early Russian literature *The Igor Tale* as a hidden referent. The theme of *The Young Guard* lends itself to this identification, for both texts are about brave princes who go to fight a foreign foe but are, most of them, slain or captured (Oleg is a "prince" in the sense that he was a Komsomol leader). In *The Igor Tale* these events are meant as a call for national unity, and this was a prevailing motif of forties rhetoric in the Soviet Union, too.

As in the epic (and High Stalinist rhetoric), the hero's main feats and challenges are against foes and nature (or nature-like phenomena). The setting is ostensibly a twentieth-century industrial town complete with rival bureaucracies, modern armies, coal mines, tanks, jeeps, etc. But the metaphorical system for presenting the heroes belongs "mostly to the vocabulary of the hunt, of the domain of agriculture, and to that of meteorological phenomena." This description comes from Nabokov's commentary on *The Igor Tale*,[5] and it is appropriate for a work about twelfth-century Russia. Yet it applies almost equally well to *The Young Guard*.

Nature's role in the novel amounts to considerably more than providing an occasional decorative simile. Closeness to nature seems to be a major criterion for establishing that a protagonist's "spontaneity" is positive. On the surface of things, Oleg could hardly be described as a child of nature. He lives in a mining town and is from a fairly educated family, which has close Party ties. His mother is a schoolteacher, and his late stepfather had had technical training. An uncle who lives with them is a mining engineer. Yet, in a lyrical passage, where Oleg recalls his mother as she was in his childhood, we are given a pastoral idyll composed of brief scenes one would associate with the daily life of a rural peasant.[6]

In Stalinist novels nature usually provides not merely the setting but the antagonist (or the controlling metaphor for the antagonist), i.e., the major obstacle of the hero's path to "consciousness" and task fulfillment. *The Young Guard* is untypical in that a natural disaster does not occur at the novel's climax. The device is not essential to this novel because of the vicious, "elemental" obstacle in the form of the German occupation. As the enemy advances over the plains to take the town, the narrator likens the roar of its tanks to the droning of bumblebees,[7] and he likens the advancing troops first to "a black shadow looming up behind [the people's] backs, with its wings already extending north and south"[8] (here there are also hints of the eclipse which the princely heroes saw as a bad omen as they rode to battle in *The Igor Tale*), and then to "A long, fat, green serpent, with its scales glittering in the sunlight, which, as it wound its way forward, extended farther and farther from the horizon."[9]

The struggle with nature is used mostly as a training ground for the sort of manliness it will take to meet such a foe. For instance, Oleg recalls his stepfather's part in his upbringing as constituting a "training in courage" consisting of "working in the fields, hunting, training to handle horses, canoeing on the Dnieper."[10] And when Oleg emerges from this preparatory period, his first exploit is to rescue a fair maiden from distress by calming the stampeding horses that threaten to harm her.[11]

In the political culture of the thirties, special abilities with horses—especially with wild horses—was, as I have mentioned, a mark of the truly valiant son-*bogatyr'*, the reincarnation of the legendary Red Army cavalryman of the Civil War. The Civil War plays an important role in preparing the "sons" in *The Young Guard*, too. Almost all the "father" figures of this novel had been active in the partisan movement or the Red Army during the Civil War.[12] Oleg's stepfather had been also, and much of the "training" in courage he gave to Oleg consisted of imparting skills that would be useful in partisan life. When Oleg becomes involved in underground work, he takes his stepfather's old code name (Kaschuk) from his partisan days.[13]

Fadeev's use of the distinctive symbols of High Stalinist rhetoric is even more marked in his descriptions of another young hero in the novel, Seryozhka, the young Komsomol who assumes Oleg's function as positive hero in the early sections of the book, when Oleg is absent from the town. Seryozhka is marked from early childhood as one who performs great physical feats. A true example of positive "spontaneity," his hallmark is *extra*ordinary energy and *extra*ordinary ambition for doing something truly great. His energy, however, is accompanied by a childish highspiritedness that is always getting him into scrapes. His models for the "truly great" feat come either from the epic-tribal world or from the roster of thirties official heroes and their achievements. In one section, Seryozhka goes over in his mind the kinds of feats he longs to emulate. He first enumerates wistfully a series of daring deeds involving prowess over nature: swimming deep under water, scaling the loftiest peaks, battling storms and reefs at sea, wrestling with boa constrictors, jaguars, crocodiles, lions, and elephants. He brings his list into the modern period by adding some official heroes of the thirties: "People who are just as simple as you," i.e., "Frunze, Voroshilov, Ordzhonnikidze, Kirov, and Stalin," the Chelyuskin (Arctic) expedition, the most famous aviation heroes (Chkalov, Gromov, and Papanin), and Stakhanovites from Seryozhka's native Donbass.[14] The Party leaders' feats are described solely in terms of fleeing exile, the fliers in terms of triumph over physical obstacles. The Stakhanovites' feats are never made explicit; only their fame is described. In other words, Fadeev has stripped his account of the official Soviet heroes of any material that might make their actions seem incongruous as a *natural* sequel to such exercises in courage as wrestling with jaguars.

This is but one of the many places in the narrative where nature is used to suggest the organic status of the Party and its government in Soviet life. In a passage describing Seryozhka's childhood, for instance, the narrator reveals the device, so to speak, by implicitly identifying the struggle with nature with the preparation of cadres. He observes: "Seryozhka grew up like grass in the steppe. He was toughened [*zakalën*] by all the suns and the winds, and the rains and the frosts, and the skin on his feet grew tough, like a camel's, and no matter what ill or wounds might befall him in life, everything would be healed in an instant, just as with the fantastic *bogatyr'*."[15] Thus, on the one hand, this child of nature is explicitly identified with the *bogatyr'*, while, on the other, his nature-given powers are the "powers" of the incipient bureaucrat or Party executive; the word *zakalën*, which Fadeev uses here, is a standard term of Party rhetoric for "trained" and "tested" cadres.

Zakalën occurs in a context that has no other ostensible connection with political life, but, since *zakalën* is a sign with a very clear referent to any Soviet reader, the political dimension is implicit in the narrator's observation. Through the use of just such signs and other analogous techniques, the subject of Soviet political institutions and leaders is always engaged in a novel, whatever the subject matter. Consequently, whenever a hero attains the end of his quest, whenever he reaches "consciousness," then, symbolically at least, he also resolves any apparent contradictions there may have been between his own inclinations and interests and those of Soviet society.

The Plot as a Rite of Passage

The Stalinist novel usually depicts modern institutions and hierarchies, yet the motivating structure that brings all conflicts to their resolution harks back to the traditional world. This can be seen in the main plot elements of the typical Socialist Realist novel. A hero sets out consciously to achieve his goal, which involves *social integration* and *collective* rather than *individual* identity for himself. He is inspired by the *challenge* of overcoming the obstacles that bar him from realizing those aims: those "spontaneous," i.e., arbitrary and self-willed, aspects of himself and forces in the world around him (predominantly the elements themselves but also other obstacles that have the force or quality of the elements). The hero is assisted in his quest by an older and more "conscious" figure who has made just such a successful quest before him. All these aspects of the typical Soviet novel's plot suggest that the most appropriate analogy to it can be found not in one of the many literary variants on the quest structure but rather in the rite of passage of traditional culture.

The most classic form of this rite is a tribal initiation. A youth undergoes a series of trials and, if successful, is initiated into manhood status and becomes a full-fledged member of the tribe. Anthropologists do not, however, confine their discussions of the rite to traditional or even to preurban societies, for rites of passage are at least metaphorically present in many of our present-day social customs (e.g., graduation ceremonies). However, because society is presented in the Soviet novel *as if* constituting a simple, organic whole, and because the hero is constantly engaged in tussles with elemental forces, it is in fact more appropriate to draw a *structural* (as distinct from a thematic) analogy with the rite of passage in precisely its most classic expression—initiation into a tribe.

In the majority of Stalinist novels the plot runs roughly as follows. In the opening sections the hero is presented with some task in the public sphere, the fulfillment of which will really test his strength and determination. In the middle sections he endeavors to complete the task, against formidable obstacles, and, as he meets each test, he gradually achieves the required degree of self-mastery and impersonality to be initiated. The novel reaches its formal end in a scene where the moment of passage is enacted. A character who has already attained "consciousness" presides and helps the hero shed the last vestiges of his individualistic consciousness and cross over to "there." At that moment the spontaneity / consciousness dialectic is symbolically resolved.

Since the moment of passage is the novel's structural pivot, the character functions of the two who take part in it are absolutely crucial—that is to say, the hero's function and the function of those who officiate at the hero's passage, or, in the present context, the initiate (hero) and the elder (his helper). In order to maintain the exalted "there"-ness of the state reached by the hero at the end, the number of characters who assume either of these functions is limited to the smallest possible number. Usually only two are selected from among all the positive characters—in *The Young Guard,* only Lyutikov as elder and Oleg as initiate. But each is given a whole series of *extra* markings (other than "serious," "calm," etc., for "consciousness,"[16] plus the Leninist traits) that establish and justify his unique ritual role.

Some of the differences between the markings used for an initiate or elder and those used for other positive characters are purely qualitative. In order to be an elder or initiate, for example, a given protagonist must be more "conscious," more committed, and exhibit more leadership qualities than other positive characters.

Two additional sets of criteria must also be taken into account. First, since legitimization of the present leadership is an important function of the Stalinist novel, it is crucial that the initiation rite be enacted in such a way as to proclaim symbolically the purity and perpetuity of the Leninist line. It is essential that the rite occur under the auspices of an elder whose biography and attributes place him in a line of direct Leninist succession. Consequently, the markers for the elder are fuller and more conventionalized than those of the initiate.

The character who assumes the role of elder should be of proletarian origins or at least have been in the Party for some time and hold a fairly high rank in the local administration (there are recognized substitutes for elders of a younger age group or who are not Soviet). He should have been tested by revolutionary or enemy fire, and, as a token of his preparedness for sacrifice, he should bear such scars as physical wounds or personal loss. The elder should also have seen Lenin or have worked for the cause in Lenin's day. As time goes on, it has been harder to meet this last criterion, and several alternative ways of establishing a Leninist connection have evolved.

The initiate's function, which is to aspire to elderhood, predicates change. This function therefore does not have its own criteria, independent of those for an elder. Even the stipulation that the initiate be *less* experienced and *less* self-controlled than the elder is not independent. Consequently, at the beginning of the novel, when the initiate should be farthest from elderhood, there are no rigid specifications for initiate status; but, the more criteria for elderhood that are met by a given character representing the positive form of "spontaneity," the more likely he is to be singled out as the initiate. During the novel the initiate will acquire more and more of the features that would qualify him for elderhood. In a sense, the main purpose of his series of trials is to make up for any deficiencies his *vita* may have at the outset. But he does not have to make them up fully in order to be initiated. They are, as it were, *compensated* for in the act of initiation itself. It is unrealistic, for instance, that a young initiate in a novel of the 1940s should have seen Lenin, but he can acquire this characteristic through ritual; then, in the words of the Soviet slogan, "Lenin lives on" in him.

Fadeev followed most of these conventions in *The Young Guard*, but there are some minor departures from the standard pattern. For instance, almost all of the ten or so local Party officials meet the criteria for elderhood, but Lyutikov is the logical candidate because all the others are either junior to him or are out of town during most of the novel. Likewise, neither Lyutikov nor Oleg bear any "scars" acquired in revolutionary struggle, but they cancel out that deficiency at the end, when *both* make the supreme sacrifice. Finally, since the age gap between initiate and elder is greater than is customary—Oleg being a mere sixteen-year-old, while Lyutikov is over fifty—Oleg lags far behind Lyutikov in meeting the criteria for elderhood; but many of the criteria not met by him *are* met by other members of his family—on his behalf, as it were. For instance, his

grandparents were proletarian, his stepfather had been a partisan in
the Civil War, and several of his relatives had also been active in the
Party.[17]

A final set of markings for elder and initiate derives from their
respective roles in the motivating structure, the rite of passage. The
main formula here is that the elder should be shown to be old and
about to "pass on," while the initiate is young and maturing. Thus,
regardless of the actual age of the elder, he will be described as
being tired, gray, wasted, and stooped. If the author does not see fit
to represent him as aging, he may achieve a similar effect by rendering his elder seriously ill or badly injured (he has given his health
to the cause or has risked his life for it). By contrast, the initiate is
conventionally hale and hearty, and, as the novel progresses, he is
seen to "grow": his back may become straighter and his step more
sprightly and assured.

In *The Young Guard* Fadeev not only adopts this schematic contrast but emphasizes it. His initial description of Lyutikov and Oleg
at their first meeting runs: "a heavily aging man . . . and a youth in
his prime." For all the most elevated moments he consistently prefers to use the epithets "the youth" and "the old man" rather than
their actual names. Furthermore, when Fadeev introduces Lyutikov
into the novel, he begins by describing how Lyutikov is old, over-
weight, constantly short of breath, and has been in ill health for
some time. Only after that does he provide the reader with information about Lyutikov's biography and present position![18] Indeed, it is difficult for Lyutikov to make any appearance in the
narrative without Fadeev's refreshing our memories on these
points.

In most novels the pivotal opposition of elder and initiate is not
immediately apparent to the reader because the elder, being so
hallowed a figure, rarely occupies the center of the stage. In some
novels, indeed, he does not appear any earlier than the initiation
scene. In such cases, the author merely has some local senior put on
the mask of the elder for this scene, or he has some elder figure
appear as if from nowhere, like a *deus ex machina*. Usually, however, the elder is involved for at least one scene prior to the initiation, when he prepares his initiate for the rite.

For this preparatory phase of the rite, the elder's role vis-a-vis the
initiate is like that of a mentor to a disciple, a father to a son. In

other words, it is but a variant of that archetypal binary model for the process of (political) "enlightenment" that Stalinist rhetoric inherited from nineteenth-century Russian literature and further developed in its myth of the "great family." In most Stalinist novels there are several such man-to-man exchanges in which a relatively experienced and politically advanced character helps one less advanced to "progress" by some combination of personal example and persuasion. The initiate and mentor may also be involved in such exchanges with personages other than their ritual partners. In *The Young Guard,* for instance, Oleg is "enlightened" not only by Lyutikov but also by the Young Guard commander, Turkenich, and the list of people his mentor "enlightens" during the course of the novel would be too long to enumerate here. But there is a difference between the ritual exchange of initiate and elder and all other such exchanges in a given novel: the initiate's "progress" is qualitative but for all the others it is quantitative (incremental).

All scenes involving the elder and initiate are customarily more symbol-ridden than those describing the meeting of any other mentor and novice. In *The Young Guard,* for instance, Fadeev stages the meetings between Lyutikov and Oleg in such a way that they seem like mystical rites occurring in a world totally cut off from the everyday. To begin with, the meetings are confined to the magical number of three, and they are spaced out in the text in such a way as to make them into symbolic landmarks dramatizing Oleg's progress toward "consciousness." They do not begin until halfway through the book—not, as it were, until Oleg has made enough progress to be singled out for such an encounter. The second occurs about three-quarters of the way through the book, and the third and final meeting takes place during the closing pages.[19] Additionally, in all three, Fadeev makes heavy use of dark/light symbolism, as if to create a mystery-enhancing chiaroscuro.

The difference between the status of these three encounters and all other mentor/novice exchanges in the novel can be sensed by comparing the way Fadeev stages Lyutikov's second meeting with Oleg and another, somewhat parallel, meeting between Lyutikov and a different novice, the Young Guard member Volodya. In both cases Lyutikov goes to see his novice in order to persuade him to temper his feelings and *appear* to cooperate with the Germans in the interests of the cause. In each case the narrator observes that

Lyutikov "taught" the youth in question for some time, after which the novice was able to see Lyutikov's position. But in closing his account of Lyutikov's second meeting with Oleg, the narrator never actually indicates when it ends; the final paragraph devoted to it is followed by a complete nonsequitur, describing entirely different people and events.[20] It is as if "there" is so remote from "here" that the narrator cannot convey the transition in words. For Lyutikov's meeting with Volodya, by contrast, the narrator reports that, when Lyutikov left, he joked with those in an *adjoining* room, thus establishing the continuity with ordinary life.[21]

The first two encounters between Oleg and Lyutikov represent rites preparatory to initiation; their final meeting embodies the act of initiation itself. To make clear the functions these three meetings perform, some general observations about the initiation rite and its parallels in the plot of the Soviet novel need to be made. In his classic account of the rite of passage, Van Gennep identifies three phases for all such rites—separation, transition, and incorporation. Separation involves taking the subject away from the previous environment he knew and possibly attempting to expunge all memory of it. The transition phase is often marked by "instruction in tribal law and gradual education as the novice witnesses totem ceremonies, recitation of myths, etc. [while the] final act [incorporation] is a religious ceremony."[22]

Detailed parallels between the traditional rite of passage and the ritual in the Soviet novel are few, but the general structure of the rite is nevertheless adhered to. For instance, most Soviet novels open as the hero leaves his "habitual environment" and goes to another place. (In *The Young Guard,* the action takes place in Oleg's home town; but, at the beginning, he leaves the town and, when he comes back, it is already under German occupation and is therefore very different.) This new environment then functions as the testing ground of his manhood and the place of instruction in "tribal law," "myths," etc. In other words, the bulk of the Soviet novel describes the middle phase in the rite of passage, the "transition," in Van Gennep's terms.

The novel culminates in a scene marking the moment of passage itself, the rite of incorporation. The elder presides and confers his own status as a tribal elder on the initiate. Very commonly the elder will give the initiate some advice or "instruction." Since this is a rite of incorporation, the elder also often hands the initiate some object or token that symbolizes belonging to the "tribe"—e.g. a banner, badge, or Party card. Alternatively, the two may be linked temporarily when both touch the same object (as when Peter briefly touches Lefort's coffin in A. Tolstoy's *Peter the First*).[23]

In the initiation scene of *The Young Guard* we find both instruction and the symbolic physical link. The scene takes place when Lyutikov and Oleg have already been captured by the Germans and are led out, *bound together*, to be interrogated. Lyutikov makes a last statement to his captors, in the tradition of the revolutionary's trial speech. His speech is not intended to move his captors, who are essentially *outside* the bounds of the family. When Lyutikov begins, "The words I speak are not for you," Oleg stands by listening, and "his big eyes...have a clear expression, clearer now than ever before."[24] He has made the passage into "consciousness."

Beyond such symbolic gestures, most Stalinist novels contain no action that could be said to constitute the act of initiation. Indeed, in some novels this act amounts to no more than a conversation between the two protagonists. Nevertheless, the conversation has the status of an initiation rite because it changes the life of the hero forever after. Furthermore, if the events themselves do not suggest anything particularly portentous, the deficiency is more than compensated for by the narrator. Not only does he elevate his tone for the occasion, but he often describes the final encounter as one in which the "baton" (*estafeta*) is passed on or as one in which the elder gives his "testament" (*poučenie*).[25]

This final scene represents a passage not just to "elderhood" but to a resolution of the spontaneity / consciousness dialectic, and this is accomplished in no vague allegory; that is, the dialectic is not resolved in an imagined world but in a particular time and place and by very specific people. In other words, although the resolution of the dialectic is symbolic, those who participate in the rite are clearly identified as representing the Soviet leadership of the time in which the novel was written. By implication, then, only they can give access to "there," and thus the rite that serves to mediate a problematical conflict in society simultaneously serves the function of legitimizing the status quo. Both functions—mediation and legitimization—are well served by the enormous prominence given in the Soviet novel to the remaining element cited in Van Gennep's account of the rite of passage: death and rebirth.

The symbolism of death and rebirth lies at the heart of any rite of passage; one self must die so that the other may be born. When the Soviet hero sheds his individualistic self at the moment of passage it could be said that he dies as an individual and is reborn as a function of the collective. This symbolic death enables the initiate to be "born anew" and—like his counterparts, the symbolic heroes of the thirties platform—"see," "know," and "speak of" new things; for in that moment he leaves the everyday world (the kingdom of mere appearance) and goes to that other place, to "there."

The elder and initiate, then, function as bridgers of those huge ontological gaps between History and the here and now. The elder in his ritual role always resides in History. But the initiate (and the elder, too, whenever he puts aside his "mask") can participate in both times. In the fairytale, or any other genre in which the hero goes to a remote time or place, it is normally explained how he got there: on a broomstick, for example, or through Baba Yaga's house, or via a time machine. But in the Soviet novel the mechanics are not explained. Death is sometimes used to smooth over this problem. Nevertheless, there are often rapid, unmotivated transitions, like the one at the end of Oleg's and Lyutikov's second meeting.

The unmotivated element in these transitions is most marked when the hero makes his crossing into History. The mandate to lead is normally acquired by the initiate on two levels. On the first plane, it is established that he is more efficient, energetic, knowledgeable, and dedicated than any other positive protagonist (save the elder). But at times the argument moves to another plane, to myth; and ritual then takes over from reason. In general, the two planes complement each other, *except* that on the plane of "reason" the initiate appears much more mortal than he does in the ritual scenes (in everyday situations, Oleg, for instance, often blushes and feels awkward). Nevertheless there is a disjunction between the two, a "suddenly." The protagonist who on the "reason" plane appears to be most eligible for initiate status receives it by fiat on the second plane.

In some ways this disjunction can be explained as a mere change in mode—i.e., from the mimetic to the symbolic. After all, there is no need to explain how the hero got "there" because, actually, he is still "here": Oleg never leaves the region, and, from the materialist standpoint, he does not do so even in death. Still, even a change in mode has to have some justification. What makes rapid changes possible in the Soviet novel is the fact that the Soviet sense of History enables Great Time, in Eliade's sense, to be present in the everyday—even if only symbolically.

Soviet thinking is millennial. So much emphasis has been placed on dramatic changes that a sense of gradual linear progress is weak. Official spokesmen are constantly trying to recapture the Revolution. A typical example of this is Stalin's famous Five-Year Plan remark, "We are behind the leading countries by fifty to a hundred years. We must make up this distance in ten years."[26] Many great moments have been identified in the past, and many are foreseen for the future; in the interim, a lot of ordinary time has to elapse. This problem is smoothed over by making the future goal and past glories invest the present with their significance. A hierarchy is thus established in which the present moments are not valuable in themselves but represent modest, particular instances of Great Moments.

This sense of History informs the text of *The Young Guard*. No incident there is unique, nor is its significance confined to the action of the novel. Each occurrence either echoes or prefigures a greater event. By being linked to their counterparts in History, those that are essentially mundane and trivial become magnificent, and even the novel's most elevated scenes are further enhanced. One striking instance of the latter is a lyrical passage inserted toward the end, in the midst of successive accounts of the arrest and interrogation of Young Guard members. In this passage an unidentified narrator recalls his sense of loss when his closest friend and Komsomol comrade was killed in the Civil War.[27] The narrator, telling of his great grief, which found expression in an unbearable desire to drink from the boot of his dead comrade, implicitly invokes a recurring pattern in the *Igor Tale*, where Igor dips his helmet in the Don to drink of grief.[28] Thus Fadeev sets up an endless series of similar great moments of patriotic sacrifice, a series begun in Russia's past and continuing into the future.

The hierarchical pattern present in the Soviet account of time is also built into the novels themselves, where events of major import reverberate in parallel but lesser occurrences. In *The Young Guard*, some of the "light" that was caught in Lyutikov's second meeting with Oleg is reflected in his more pedestrian meeting with Volodya. When a minor character loses his life in a novel or is wounded, the incident gains importance by standing in for the greater tragedy that would have occurred had the hero himself died.

Thus, through a mix of symbolic actions and parallel events of more everyday proportions the "broad processes at work" in Soviet society are dignified by their ideational forms. History is more "real" than reality, and the changes back and forth within a novel from the realistic to the symbolic are not as radical as they appear to be to the Western reader. Even the climactic moment of passage is but a shadow of the "form" of the passage into Communism.

Three Auxiliary Patterns of Ritual Sacrifice

Sacrifice was a dominant value in the nineteenth-century intelligentsia's ethos. Revolutionaries strove to become what the populist N. K. Mikhailovsky called "martyrs of history."[1] Prison and exile, death from tuberculosis or some other debilitating disease, brought on by sacrificing one's health to the cause, separation of lovers and families—all became not traumatic limitations but opportunities for election.

The Bolsheviks incorporated this particular strand of general radical lore into their own mythology. *Mother* provided a panoply of variations on the theme of sacrifice, culminating in the ultimate sacrifice made by the mother herself. Later, in the thirties, the ritualized biographies of the Bolshevik elect all stressed their subject's great suffering at the hands of tsarist oppressors. For instance, Pavlik Morozov's martyr's death (so young!) at the hands of the kulaks ensured him the role of *the* exemplar of loyalty to the "great family."

The increasing emphasis on revolutionary sacrifice in Stalinist hagiography more or less coincides with the increasing "sacrifice" in Soviet political practice, i.e., with the instensification of the purges. Indeed, the emphasis laid on the personal price paid by Bolshevik leaders in earlier years can be seen as an indirect vindication of the "price" they were then exacting from their own victims. However, it is also probable (and this is a point that Merleau-Ponty explores in his *Humanism and Terror*)[2] that, during those incredible show trials, executions, etc., both accusers and accused saw the sacrifices impersonally—saw them as the results of History's inexorable onward march.

Sacrifice played a major role in all Stalinist novels. The reasons for this, however, were not limited to Russian revolutionary myth and actual Stalinist practice. They were, at least in part, formal; that is to say, sacrifice is a major element of the traditional rite of passage, both in the preparations for that rite and in the moment of passage itself.

In a traditional rite of passage, the preparation of the initiate is usually classified as a "transitional" or "liminal" phase, liminal because it involves "a symbolic retrogression into Chaos. In order to be created anew, the old . . . must first be annihilated." The initiates "receive protracted instruction from their teachers, witness secret ceremonies, [and usually] undergo a series of ordeals."[3] There is an enormous variety in the types of ordeals; some of those commonly found are "circumcision, long periods of seclusion or food taboos, symbolic or token wounding, and deprival of sleep."[4]

As in traditional expressions of the rite, the Stalinist novel used a wide range of preparatory "ordeals" and sometimes even dispensed with them altogether. The majority of ordeals represented symbolic encounters with "chaos," i.e., with the elements or with elemental forces. "Ordeals" involve not only suffering but the transcendence of suffering. The transcendence theme was not confined to the hero's struggle with elemental forces; it is also represented in three auxiliary narrative patterns, auxiliary because they are structurally subordinate to the central plot, which charts the hero's progress toward "consciousness." These narrative patterns are of death, love, and villainy. Most Socialist Realist novels contain some elements of all three, but love and villainy, being essentially auxiliary to the central plot, are not mandatory. All Stalinist novels include some kind of "death," however, because death is involved not only in the preparatory or liminal phase of the rite but also in the moment of passage itself.

Death

The symbolism of death and rebirth lies at the heart of any rite of passage—the killing of one self to give birth to the other. The majority of initiatory ordeals more or less clearly imply a ritual death—or at least some token mutilation—followed by a resurrection or new birth. In the Stalinist novel, death and token mutilation have a predominantly mythic function. When the hero sheds his individualistic self at the moment of passage, he dies as an individual and is reborn as a function of the collective.

This death also assists that important function of all conventional

Stalinist novels—legitimization. Since the novel seeks to show that members of the present leadership are the only legitimate agents of History, the importance of death-and-rebirth symbolism extends beyond its function of assisting the individual hero's passage from individual to collective status.

Martyrdom has always been a primary mode of vindication. Death as the supreme sacrifice acts as the ultimate sanction. Martyrs leave to the living an obligation to emulate their high moral example. The most obvious case of this is the *imitatio Christi*. But in many civil states there are also martyrs who are held up as examples, and in Soviet rhetoric extremist practices are often justified by citing past sacrifices and the need to anticipate future dangers.

Death also assumes enormous importance in the Soviet sense of history and national identity. Most of their great moments—the 1905 Revolution, the 1917 Revolution, the Civil War, Lenin's death, and World War II—are marked by human sacrifice and loss. Furthermore, these moments seem to be more crucial as points of reference for defining Soviet identity than other great moments that might appear to have more to do with "building communism"—the First Five-Year Plan, for instance.

In the Soviet novel death plays a major part in the rite of passage, which is a rite not merely of maturation but of election: the elder confers on the initiate a mandate to rule as one of the chosen few (i.e., as a member of the vanguard). This crucial difference, which reflects on the status of the hero vis-à-vis all the other positive and "spontaneous" heroes (the "tribe" will not accept all adult males as elders), makes symbolic death all the more important an element in the rite. Death is not only a preliminary to rebirth and the highest point on the Richter scale of sacrifices. So many of the elect (and Lenin in particular) have preceded the initiate in death that, if he is to legitimize his own rule and inherit the past by a rite of "incorporation," he must undergo a symbolic death that will place him momentarily together with "them." A journey to that timeless land beyond the grave also removes the problem of the gap between "their" time and the actual time in which the novel is set.

Death has traditionally been an important element in becoming a hero. In death the Greek hero often achieved semidivine status. Ritual sacrifices were offered at his tomb, to honor and also to appease him, since he continued to be powerful even in death. Heroes were those who had "wrought or suffered in some extraordinary way," especially "in the field of warfare or other strenuous activity."[5]

The "heroic code" or cult of heroism was also important among the Russian intelligentsia in the second half of the nineteenth century. Leopold Haimson has likened it to the ancient cult of heroes: only those who had suffered in revolutionary struggle could be honored as heroes.[6] These values were largely transferred to the Stalinist myths, where they provided ready-made formulas for myths that served to maintain the status quo (those who lead are those who have fought and suffered most).

Since heroic death is a true sign of heroic status, it is a rare Socialist Realist novel that fails to include either death or threat of death for the hero(es). Normally death hovers over the pages of the entire novel and claims many victims—and, even more, near victims—but only symbolically will it claim the hero's own life. Looking death in the face is, of course, an excellent test of the hero's manhood. Usually he *all but* makes the ultimate sacrifice in several variants of two basic incidents: trial by revolutionary (or enemy) fire, and some struggle with forces that are either literally or metaphorically elemental. The most dramatic of these is saved for the climax of the hero's ordeals.

In this final trial the hero comes so close to death that he is often believed dead or dying until he "comes through," an action that both provides proof of his exceptional strength and capacity for life and represents symbolic rebirth. In this catastrophe, one of the hero's subordinates usually dies or is wounded as a surrogate sacrifice (this tokenism bears comparison with the traditional custom of mutilating the initiate as a part of the rite of incorporation). The funeral of the tragic victim becomes an occasion for great pomp and ceremony.

Societies often use funeral orations as occasions for "a public reformulation of the social norms [which] serves as a sanction for behavior."[7] In Russia there was just such a tradition among the revolutionary intelligentsia and Bolsheviks. Both their actual leaders and their fictional heroes were wont to make graveside speeches about History and the need for sacrifice, after which they often swore oaths to affirm their undying revolutionary resolve.

In Socialist Realist fiction the author often does not content himself with a token sacrifice but has the hero die himself. This happens
in *The Young Guard.* The moment of passage occurs, it will be
recalled, when Oleg and Lyutikov are bound together and Lyutikov
gives Oleg his last testament in the form of an address to the German interrogators (of such lofty content that he assumes they will
not understand it). But this final exchange between elder and initiate is enacted not for its traditional sequel, in which the initiate
goes on to assume the status and duties of an elder. Instead, the
two are separated by their captors, and each is later executed. Thus
a ritual of regeneration by succession ends tragically in the death of
the one who is to succeed.

This variant, which is no less representative than symbolic or
token death, does not actually undercut but rather serves to
heighten the theme of regeneration. A leader of great potential dies,
but this does not mean that he has died to History. Even death
cannot deter History's onward march. In *The Young Guard,* for
instance, though Oleg and over sixty other Komsomol and Party
heroes perish at the hands of the Germans, other heroes survive to
carry on.

Moreover, it is not necessary that there be any specific survivor to
mitigate the tragedy. The hero's body may have died, but his spirit
lives on: a death-and-transfiguration situation. In *The Young
Guard* this interpretation of the hero's death is made quite explicit
when, in describing the final tortures Oleg and Lyutikov undergo,
the narrator makes a distinction between their earthly bodies,
which are subject to these tortures, and "their spirit," which
"wafted at an immeasurable height, wafted as only man's creative
spirit can."[8] The same distinction between a revolutionary's earthly
body and his spirit, which lives on after his death, was a cliché of
both Bolshevik and nineteenth-century revolutionary fiction.[9] It is
also implicitly present in the slogan about Lenin: "More alive than
the living" (*žyvee vsex živyx*).

The death-and-transfiguration variant does not represent a different denouement but only, as it were, the other side of the same
coin. In the Soviet novel either the hero actually dies and lives on
symbolically, or he dies symbolically and lives on in actual life. But
the difference between "symbolic" and "actual" here loses its
significance when it is recognized that in both versions the death's

primary importance is symbolic. Any individual death merely imitates the paradigms that are to be found in the great moments of
Soviet history—the Revolution, the Civil War, and so on. In particular, because the hero dies in body but lives on in spirit, this act is
but a reflection of an Idea—Lenin's death in 1924—which in the
Soviet Union represents the highest point of reference for any rite of
legitimization, and also underwrites all death-and-transfiguration
ritual. At the same time, should it happen that the elder dies rather
than the initiate, since his "baton" will be grasped by a young,
"serious," and exceptionally energetic leader, this is essentially
another symbolic reenactment of Lenin's death; it is merely taken
from a different aspect (it shows Lenin as the authority figure rather
than as the one who died too young).

The death of the hero is a mere reflection of a form that is prior
and more essential. This fact contributes to the extraordinary degree of depersonalization in depicting the hero. Whether he lives on
after the moment of death or not is of no great consequence, for the
individual tragedy is not History's tragedy.

Thus, in the novel, History assumes such overwhelming priority
that everything specific to an individual, including his physical self,
is of consequence only if it is assigned a symbolic function. This
makes the Stalinist novel distinctive in modern literature. In the use
of death as a plot element, this dissimilarity of the Soviet novel is
not as noticeable, because death enjoys a symbolic function in literature in general. But the differences become glaring when love enters the plot.

Love

In his book *The Characters of Love,* John Bayley remarks: "It has
become difficult to imagine literature without love. Since the Middle Ages the two have depended on each other more and more, and
their interrelation now is as complex as civilization itself." Bayley
goes on to claim that "It is ... *eros* rather than *agape* with which
literature is most concerned."[10] He has, of course, taken an extreme
position here; nevertheless, the interdependence of love and literature is commonly assumed in the West.

In the Stalinist novel, however, love is an auxiliary ingredient in
the plot. The hero's love life is not valuable in itself; it serves only to

aid him in fulfilling his tasks and in attaining "consciousness." This
is so much the case that in the West the standard Stalinist plot has
been somewhat snidely dismissed as "Boy gets tractor." This quip
could be expanded slightly by the addition of "plus or minus girl."
Whether he "gets girl" or not is of little importance as long as he
gets "tractor," i.e., successfully completes his public task, which is
inextricably tied to his quest for "consciousness." If he gets "girl"
as well, this enhances the general glow of well being at the novel's
end. If he does not, this loss becomes another of his sacrifices, and it
serves to heighten the sense of his achievement in reaching the goal
of his quest.

Love is played down for an additional reason: the well-known
puritanism of Socialist Realism. When the hero does "get the girl,"
he cannot get her as an erotic object; she must be his spiritual
companion and a means of adding to the new generation of the
"family."

This puritanism was not always mandatory in Soviet literature.
Much of the literature of the twenties was highly erotic (including
many scenes in Gladkov's *Cement*). As late as 1930, when the third
installment of *Brusski,* Panferov's classic on collectivization, came
out, it was still possible to treat *eros* in literature fairly explicitly. In
that installment the reader is treated to this sensual scene: the
heroine swims in the river naked and her husband and would-be
lover dive in and try to embrace her in turn.[11]

In 1933–34, when the theory of Socialist Realism was being formulated, those in authority rejected this sort of "naturalism," "zoolo-
gism," and dwelling on the dark side of human nature.[12] A puritanical climate prevailed for most of the thirties and forties, and explicit
sex relations involving positive heroes were virtually taboo in novels.
Instead, one often finds oddly suggestive scenes, such as the following, from Babaevsky's *Cavalier of the Gold Star* (1947–48):
Sergey, the hero, goes to visit a "swarthy shepherdess" and is obliged to stay overnight "because of the rain." He wakes in the
middle of the night to find the shepherdess in his room "in a white
dress." They go off for an idyllic moonlight walk on the steppes.
Break. The action resumes next morning, when Sergey discovers he
feels "unusually good, as if that night had poured new strength into
him."[13]

Soviet puritanism cannot, however, account fully for the modest role that love itself, as distinct from sex, so often plays in the plot. Its modest role becomes more explicable if we view the novel as patterned on the initiation rite. In traditional versions, the rite usually begins when the youth is taken away from the mother- or female-dominated world in which he has lived until then.[14] The "ordeals" he then goes through are not conducted in a world without females, but they are primarily tests of his manliness, and success in love is not considered a criterion of manliness in the context of tribal initiation. The three main variants of the love plots in Soviet novels of the thirties are conditioned by the fact that the hero's prime concern is to prepare himself for initiation.

In the first variant, the hero undergoes trials in a world that is without female attachments. This void may be absolute or merely circumstantial. He may have a loved one, but, because of specific circumstances—the war, their being posted to different stations, illness, etc.—she is not present in his world for the period of the trials. The author may well see fit to reunite the couple for the happy finale. Alternatively, the loved one may *in theory* be close at hand, but in fact they meet very infrequently. It is as if, during the excitement of the ordeals, the love plot tags along behind.

One sees something of this in *The Young Guard*, where Oleg is so engrossed in his struggle against the German occupiers that he really has no time for love. In the second redaction, in order to make Oleg more of an ordinary "lad," Fadeev inserted short passages showing Oleg attracted to local girls, but none of these attachments is followed through.[15]

Another common variant can be related to the fact that in most tribal initiations the initiate is a youth who has just arrived at puberty and is therefore only on the brink of adult sexuality. In this second variant the love object is more mature than the hero. She is often older, but it is not so much her age as her greater political maturity that is important. Hence the hero's somewhat adolescent attachment to her becomes a stage in his progress toward initiation. The love object functions as an example for him and often provides him with "instruction." The attraction may even involve mawkish sexual interest on his part, but the "older" woman responds to this with bemusement, sternness, or all that "care" that *agape* can bring.[16]

In the third variant of the love plot the hero is also assisted in his progress toward "consciousness," but here the function of his love attachment is paradoxical, for the woman is a witch and temptress. It is only in this variant that explicit sexuality is permissible. As in hagiography, the hero must overcome his sexual temptations if he is to achieve "grace" and be initiated. Indeed, for the Soviet hero, his sexual drives (as distinct from the desire to propagate, to found a Soviet family, which is quite different) are but another manifestation of the willful forces of nature that he must transcend.

The woman as witch has been a stock-in-trade of Soviet literature since its very beginnings. Most often the "witch" represents the wrong social class and its interests or else petit-bourgeois individualistic values. Who else would present herself as a sex object, after all! If the hero becomes attached to her, this will undermine his work for the collective good. In such cases, as was said in Kaverin's *Dr. Vlasenkova* (1952), "This is not love [on the hero's part] but a disease of the will."[17]

Besides providing the initiate with trials, his sexual infatuation functions as part of the "liminal" phase, i.e., the period of psychic chaos through which the initiate must pass before he can achieve psychic stasis. Another common sign of his psychic chaos is the temptation to show anger toward his class enemies or pity for them. All such impulses are, like sexual passion, expressions of willfulness and must be mastered: the hero must attain an extrapersonal perspective.

Villainy

The villains and class enemies of Stalinist fiction must be vanquished, purged, or "rehabilitated." The formula varies according to how hard-line the particular novel and/or current platform is. Villains threaten the *Gemeinschaft* world—are interlopers in the "family" and undermine it. Thus the hero can prove his manliness by having the strength and courage to eliminate this threat. The way he does this provides the third of the Socialist Realist novel's auxiliary patterns of ritual sacrifice, the tale of villainy.

It should not be forgotten that much Stalinist fiction was written during one or another of the many purges. Several Western commentators have likened the purge trials themselves and their accompanying ritual (such as the mass demonstrations, at which those to be tried were borne aloft in effigy) to "dramas of victim-age." In the words of Hugh Dalziel Duncan, "the 'bad guy' is transformed into a victim whose suffering and death purges the social order. In art this is called 'catharsis,' in religion 'purifica-tion.'"[18]

To some extent, this dynamic is also present in the Soviet novel. The villain is a symbolic victim who must be purged in order for the microcosm to be purified. But this is not a complete explanation of the function of villainy. The tale of villainy is subordinated primar-ily not to the aim of social cohesion but to the initiation ritual. And, since it is thus subordinate, it is an *optional* extra.

One must distinguish between external enemies (invaders, spy infiltrators, etc.) and internal enemies (Soviet citizens). In Stalinist novels, external enemies are largely faceless or they are caricatures (as in *The Young Guard*). The major exceptions to this rule are the individual foreign agents who penetrate the country and live there in disguise (a good example of this would be the Japanese spy Murusima in Pavlenko's *In the East* [1936]).

A substantial villain plot is normally mounted only for internal enemies. Internal enemies can function as one of the many possible monster-antagonists that block the hero's path to the "tractor," to fulfilling his public task. They may be active saboteurs, or persons seeking to reverse the Revolution and bring back the old regime or in league with or under the spell of foreign powers, or, in their mildest versions, they can be simply misguided bureaucrats. Such villains are often represented as being very formidable, potentially more powerful than the hero; in the end, of course, he vanquishes them finally, irrevocably, and often somewhat *suddenly*—as it were, with one thrust of his *bogatyr'* shoulder.

The villain is routed with despatch because, although he may be useful in fleshing out the plot by providing trials for the hero, it is preordained that he will prove less powerful than the hero: History is incontrovertibly on the side of the positive heroes. Also, the forces of chaos must be dispelled before the hero attains true "con-sciousness." Therefore, the villain is usually eliminated before the hero is initiated by the mentor figure. Alternatively, this rite will give him the strength he needs to stride forth and vanquish his foe.

The depiction of villains in Stalinist novels is quite different in mode from that of positive heroes. There is, for instance, very little trace of a system of signs, used for portraying positive heroes (i.e., "calm," "stern," etc.). In fact, villains commonly receive a fuller psychological portrayal than the heroes do, although they are not very individualized. The clichés for the Stalinist villain were in fact very like those of twenties prose. But their origins can be traced even further back. The depiction of the villain is comparable with the standard ways in which the prince's enemies were portrayed in the chronicles.

To account for how a particular villain could still exist in Soviet society, novelists normally invoked his social origins. But the matter did not rest there. Like the medieval chronicler before them, the novelists typically delved into the villain's psyche for further sources of his nefariousness. Their findings were standard; in fact, the villain's motivations were quite like those attributed to the prince's enemy in the chronicles, namely, pride, envy, vanity, or greed.[19] The result of frustrated pride, envy, vanity or greed was usually malice. Most Soviet villains are quietly seething with it and yearn for an opportunity to take their revenge.

A more important parallel with medieval texts is found in the author's tendency to delve into the *inner* selves of negative protagonists—something they do not often do for the positive heroes.[20] This differing treatment of villains and heroes had its own logic, since both the Soviet Russians and the medieval chroniclers were officially inspired in their writing by a world-historical view that included an image of the ideal man. Model figures had to have "epic" wholeness; the villain was a person who was not whole. Most often, in fact, there was a contrast between his inner and outer selves: he would present one guise to the outside world but have quite another identity in private.

This way of depicting villains added a level of complexity—however rudimentary and conventionalized—to the otherwise largely "simple" narrative found in the Stalinist novel. Irony and a satirical or even jocular tone—elements otherwise unknown in Stalinist novels (unless the novels are explicitly satires)—can come into play in the treatment of villains.

Villains who present one face to the world and another in private also illustrated the rhetorical dictum that the country was full of "masked enemies," pretending to be loyal citizens but, underneath, seething with anti-Soviet sentiment and watching for every opportunity to use it effectively. Thus the villains of fiction served the further function of providing object lessons in the need for "vigilance," the need "to take nothing on trust but examine everything very closely."

IV

Soviet Fiction since World War II

Introduction

Although the Soviet people emerged from the Second World War as victors, they were to face some very hard years in the ensuing decade. The war had been won at an incredible cost. West of the Volga most of the industrial plant had been razed, along with the cities, farm buildings, and bridges. Twenty million people had perished, not to mention livestock slaughtered and crops burned.

The era of postwar reconstruction was inevitably grim. With little equipment and few horses or able-bodied men available, many tasks had to be done with rudimentary tools or bare hands. Shortages were the order of the day. There were several famines, and many died from starvation. The regime gave economic recovery priority over human welfare, and the country was even exporting grain for foreign currency from the very areas in which people were dying of starvation.

The political climate of these years matched the economic in sheer grimness. The forties saw the beginning of the Cold War, a rise in Russian national chauvinism, and a return to large-scale purging. It was a particularly hard time for the Soviet intellectual. Many of them suffered because they did not follow the correct authority figure in their work or were too "cosmopolitan," i.e., pro-Western or Jewish.

The Khrushchev era has been hailed in the West as having saved the day for the Soviet intellectual. Many of the excesses of the Stalin era were attacked. The power of the secret police was weakened. Vast numbers of political prisoners were released. The anti-cosmopolitan campaign ceased. Many of the crazy dogmas and canons of the forties were discredited. Greater freedom was granted to both writers and intellectuals.

At the time, these changes seemed dramatic indeed, yet now the

Khrushchev era seems in many respects (except for those mentioned above) not radically different from the Zhdanovist. Rather, the Khrushchev era was a distinctive part of a definable whole—postwar Soviet Russia. This period began around 1944 (when Soviet society had already begun to think in postwar terms, even though the war was not yet over), and it continues through the present. It comprises three distinct subperiods: the postwar Stalinist years (1944–53), the Khrushchev years (1953–64), and the post-Khrushchev years (1965 to the present).

The three postwar subperiods shared much the same ethos, and it is very different from that of the thirties. The pervasive concern of postwar Soviet society has been not with the heroic and the extraordinary, as in the thirties (although forties rhetoric still celebrated reaching for "higher" or impossible feats), but with the true and the false. The questions asked in this period were not How can a feat be performed? but How should one live? What is artistic truth? Who is the true intellectual, the true leader, the true (or just) human being? Each of the three subperiods in the postwar years posed different questions touching these issues, and each period had its own defining answers, but the same general concerns obtained throughout.

9   The Postwar Stalin Period (1944–53)

In Soviet rhetoric of the forties one finds few new images or myths. Symbols that had been the mainstay of thirties culture continued to be used: the elements, fathers and sons, *bogatyri,* and so on. Many of them had now lost their cogency and so were used rather routinely, less discriminately; for example, elements from "machine-age" and "fathers and sons" rhetoric were often lumped together. It was almost as if the Stalin era, having continued for so long, had exhausted its power to generate new mythic paradigms, as, twice before, it had been able to do.

Whether rhetoric clung to the old because the Stalin era was too tired to come up with anything fresh, or whether this happened through fear of change is hard to say. The effect remains the same: all areas of intellectual life were marked by an imposed conservatism, and in each field the parameters of what was acceptable were even narrower than they had been in the thirties.

This was especially true in literature. In Western literary histories the Soviet forties are often referred to as the "Zhdanov era," so named for the chief Party spokesman on cultural matters, A. A. Zhdanov (also remembered for his speech to the First Writers' Congress in 1934), whose ex cathedra pronouncements set "the line" in most intellectual fields. In 1946 he delivered a "signal" lecture (regarding the journals *Zvezda* and *Leningrad,* which were considered to have transgressed the permissible) that put an end to the relatively liberal literary climate of the war years. In this lecture Zhdanov reaffirmed the tenets of Socialist Realism he had outlined in his 1934 address.

As a consequence of this lecture, the literature of the entire decade of the forties was marked by a zeal for Socialist Realist purism. The zeal was not confined to safeguarding first principles; it was also applied to keeping intact the tradition of the "model novels." Many articles were devoted to praising one or another of them.

In response to such articles, writers in the forties did a lot of homework on the official exemplars, and it shows in their novels. They used the stock symbols of Socialist Realism, the roster of conventional epithets (such as "stern" and "calm"), the old catch-phrases, like "stickability," and the stock plot devices and functions. Almost all of the decade's production novels, for instance, stage a natural disaster for the climax. Also, woven into the fabric of almost every novel there is mention of such favorite topics of the thirties as the Arctic or taiga explorers, aviation heroes, the sufferings of prerevolutionary Bolsheviks in prison and exile, and Stakhanovites.

Many forties classics read like reruns of either *Cement* or *How the Steel Was Tempered,* or of a combination of the two. *Cement* was an especial favorite. In Babaevsky's *Cavalier of the Gold Star,* for instance, it seems to be impossible to put the local economy back on its feet again (in this case by building a power station rather than restoring a cement factory) until the hero (Sergey) points out that all problems can be solved by organizing local volunteers to collect timber. When petty bureaucrats undermine Sergey's visionary plans for the region, he goes to the local "center" to get support, and the progress of the plan slows down while he is away.[1]

Some of the thirties clichés have been modified for the new times. For instance, the use of a special affinity for wild horses as a sign of the hero has been largely supplanted by a closeness to the birch tree or to the forest as a whole. The forest and the birch are both Russian symbols for the native land, and this change reflects the growing nationalism (and the increasingly less anarchic positive hero: the rustling forest is no "mustang"). Also, the Stakhanovite theme and the theme of triumph over the elements are now commonly combined and vested in a Michurinist or Lysenkoist strand in the plot: the hero/heroine is either personally engaged, or impressed by someone else who is engaged, in overcoming the limitations of the environment (usually climate). He/she is developing plants or animals that can flourish in conditions hitherto considered impossible ("Nothing is impossible" and "Man can triumph over nature" echo the thirties slogans). In this context the hero will often encounter the Great Father, who now has "wise gardener" and "knower of nature's secrets" added to his standard epithets.[2]

Besides perpetuating the stock symbols of Socialist Realist fiction, writers were now required as never before to preserve the purity of the "tale." In their anxiety to prove their dedication as "chroniclers," writers tended to overdo their obeisances to the master plot. Most of its standard functions do not occur once, but are proliferated throughout a given novel. For example, a novel typically has not just one mentor figure but many. In consequence, the forties novel often is to its thirties antecedent as baroque is to classical. Functions lost their logic and their ideological purpose in the novel's overall design and became yet another pattern of whorls in some superabundant decoration.

The two functions used with greatest extravagence in forties novels were the mentor's "last testament" and the scene in which he symbolically "passes the baton" to the hero. Most novels did not rest with one such scene but contrived to introduce at least two or three. Perhaps the one that outdoes them all in this respect is the rewritten version of V. Kataev's *For the Power of the Soviets* (1951). The novel's hero is a young boy, Petya, who, together with his father, is stranded by chance in Odessa when the Germans take the town during World War II. He spends most of the occupation with a group of partisans who have hidden in the Odessa catacombs.

Petya receives so many batons in this novel that one begins to suspect that his function is to receive batons. Even on his way to the catacombs he stumbles on a dying sailor, who entrusts him with his banner and Komsomol ticket. Once in the catacombs, Petya first receives a pistol from a partisan who, it transpires, is soon to be captured and killed (when he takes the pistol, Petya looks at him "as if he were the sun").[3] Then, from a dying old worker Bolshevik who has been in the Party since 1908 but whose health had been broken by the struggle (and who takes almost the entire length of the novel to die), Petya receives a cigarette lighter and a candlestick, which the worker had made himself and which, at the end, enable Petya to guide the partisans out of the catacombs (light / darkness, once again). On their way out they of course pass by the grave of the Old Bolshevik for one of those customary scenes by the grave of a fallen comrade. Before leaving the catacombs, Petya has also been given a radio set, and he is thus able to transcribe Stalin's November 7, 1943, speech before the Battle of Stalingrad; in this task his father assists him, and the chief of the partisans, Druzhinin, rests his hand on Petya's shoulder all the while. Finally, after they enter liberated Odessa, Petya reads on the prison wall the last words of this same Druzhinin, written just as his German captors were about to drag him off to his execution.

The effect of such superabundance in forties novels is not to reinforce the master plot but rather to undermine it. The functions become so diffuse that the overarching plot loses much of its inner logic. The result is the main weakness of forties novels—incongruity. Several other literary idiosyncrasies of the decade also contributed to this incongruity. For instance, although life in the Soviet forties was decidedly grim, the response of literature was to become "gayer." With the partial exception of novels about the war, most works exemplified the promise that Stalin made in his November 7 Stalingrad speech, "Even our street will have a feast day [*prazdnik*]." In literature everything was rosy-hued, and a recurring scene was the feast of plenty, especially in kolkhoz novels.

This "glossing-over of reality," or *lakirovka*, as it was called by unsympathetic writers, went hand in hand with another literary doctrine widely held in the forties, "conflictlessness" (*beskonfliktnost'*); according to this, Soviet society was now so advanced in its progress toward communism that it was somewhat unrealistic to depict villains in contemporary settings. Rather than show the clash or "conflict" between the good and the bad, authors should show the tension or dialogue between the good and the as-yet-less-good.

Western critics have held that such doctrines and practices led not to the end of "conflicts" in fiction but to the end of literature itself. The repressive climate of the forties produced hollow literary characters and hollow literary forms.

There is much truth in this observation; but one should not dismiss the forties altogether, for it was, paradoxically, a seminal period. Though the forties were in many respects similar to the thirties (e.g., in the priority given to heavy industry and in the terror and intellectual tyranny), in the matters that are central to my discussion this continuity was superficial, and it obscured fundamental changes. For all the tired, clichéd rhetoric, for all the Zhdanovist repressiveness and cultural conservatism, there was in fact a new spirit abroad in forties culture, a spirit that defines the postwar era.

The Pursuit of "Culture"

In recent years a number of Western scholars have opened up new persepectives on the forties and have called into question the standard Western account. A good example of this is Vera Dunham's book *In Stalin's Time* (1976). Dunham contends that the hallmark of forties culture was not repressiveness and grimness, not shortages and hardship, but acquisitiveness, philistinism, and even naked greed. She is perceptive in seeing the "feast day" tone of postwar fiction as not representing mere falsification, covering up shortages with pictures of plenty, but reflecting the new values and aspirations of the growing middle class. As she says: "In postwar novels, objects, from real estate to perfume, took on a voice of their own. They provide a material inventory of embourgeoisement." Two small details from forties novels that she singles out as signs of the new times are a preference for the color pink (a diluted form of red!) and "scalloped edges" on a student's dormitory bedspread, the sort of touch that would have been scorned in the prewar era of ascetic revolutionaries.[4]

Perhaps one should not go quite so far as Dunham and write off the decade as the heyday of a New Class, characterized by conformism and galloping greed. Although her well-documented account errs in the direction of overstating the case and bringing out the decade's less laudable aspects, she has made an important contribution in jogging Western thinking on the forties out of its rut of seeing those years as dominated by the *same* evils as in the thirties, only in worse form.

In the forties the veneration for "culture" superseded the cult of the heroic. When, in the thirties, rhetoric sang the praises of those many "symbolic heroes" from aviation, production, exploration, etc., their feats were reckoned in terms of quantity (tons of coal, etc.) or physical measures—speed, height attained, prowess, etc. In the rhetoric of the forties, the heroes tended to be scientists, inventors, scholars, and creative people generally.

The Stakhanovite movement was not abandoned. There was, however, a significant shift in its focus: the major arena for "revitalization" changed from the factory, kolkhoz, and bureaucracy to academic and scientific circles. There the Stakhanovites were used as model "sons" to storm "the doors of the temple of science" in the name of "a new science." Many experts were required to revise their textbooks to accommodate the "scientific discoveries" made by Stakhanovites.[5] Also, the doctrines of certain cultural authority figures of humble origins and often rudimentary or belated professional training—"fathers" in their field of specialization (e.g., Marr, Lysenko, Gorky, and Makarenko)—were declared axiomatic for the given field, to the detriment of experts who had attained their status by more traditional routes.

Clearly, much of the attention paid to intellectuals during the forties was repressive. Yet this very repressiveness reflects the increased importance learning and culture had achieved in society. Moreover, not all the state's attentions were oppressive, for the status and material rewards that went with success in intellectual fields offset many of the restrictions and hazards.

Soviet Russia, once interested in rivaling the West in record-breaking flights, mountain climbing, etc., now desperately wanted to establish priority in scientific discoveries. Even the Great Father had ambitions in that area. One of his last works, the essay "Marxism and Questions of Linguistics" (1952), was intended not merely to be a contribution to Marxism-Leninism but also (as Solzhenitsyn suggests in his satiric portrit of Stalin in chapter 19 of *The First Circle*) to establish Stalin's *own* credentials as an intellectual.

In the forties, then, the key terms were "culture," "science," "thought," "art," and "technology." The last term, "technology," had been prominent in thirties rhetoric, too; but with its new penumbra of "culture" and "science," it had a grander ring.

This widespread change in values was soon reflected in literature. Writers were as vehemently enjoined to write of scientists and engineers as, in the thirties, they had been urged to stop writing about them, it having then been said that scientists and engineers were lily-livered intellectuals, probably bourgeois to boot, and therefore less worthy subjects than the rugged Stakhanovite, border guard, or aviation hero.[6] Writers who in the thirties had made a living out of hagiographic biographies of that age's heroes now started churning them out about scientists and engineers. Even Kaverin moved on from the topic of Arctic exploration and aviation (in *Two Captains*) and started a trilogy about biologists (*The Open Book*, 1949, 1952, 1956). Y. Trifonov entered the field to produce a work called *Students* (1950) and, in the same year, M. Slonimsky emerged from the relative obscurity he had enjoyed since the twenties to put out one called *Engineers*. Even when a novel's title or subject matter was not about intellectuals, it was nevertheless mandatory for all of its positive heroes *qua* positive heroes to have some experience of culture or higher education. Even in that great pastoral of the forties, Babevsky's *Cavalier of the Gold Star*, the hero's "swarthy shepherdess" could not bring herself to marry him without first furthering her education.[7]

The new emphasis on "culture" did not mean just higher education, operas, books on the shelf, scholarly research, etc. The Russian word for culture, *kultura*, is broader in its range of associations than the English word. It includes such things as using a handkerchief, saying "Thank you," and having a well-furnished apartment. In other words, the details that Vera Dunham has culled from fiction to support her claim that forties literature was imbued with petit-bourgeois, philistine values are in Russian eyes no less the proper accoutrements of "culture" than creative writing and scholarship, which Western intellectuals might find more praiseworthy.

"Culture" in Russian has traditionally stood for what happens when a peasant moves from his wooden hut and abandons his traditional dress in favor of a more urban and / or Western way of life. The more divans and bedspreads with "scalloped edges" he acquires, the more "cultured" he proves to be. Alternatively, it has stood for the way the aristocrats live as distinct from the masses. "Culture" is modernization (a sewage system, paved roads). "Culture" is politeness. It is in that broad context that culture is also learning and the arts.

As the Soviet Union became an increasingly industrialized and urbanized modern nation, and as more and more people acquired higher education and were employed as white-collar workers or at least as skilled laborers, the aspirations and interests of its citizens were inevitably affected. The Soviet Union developed into what we in the West would call an "organization man" society. Most of its working population achieved, or hoped to achieve, a place within some institutional hierarchy. They sought to rise in the hierarchy of status and enjoy a higher standard of living, and to this end they endeavored to comport themselves as was deemed fit for a person of their standing. The heroic age was at an end.

This change did not come precisely with the end of World War II.

Many of the postwar values had begun to emerge even before the war. This can be sensed in thirties fiction. The hero of *How the Steel Was Tempered* (1934), Korchagin, is an irresponsible, anarchic fellow whose instincts are in the right place but have to be tamed. By contrast, the hero of Y. Krymov's classic *The Tanker Derbent* (1938), Basov (a Stakhanovite leader), is never exuberant or mischievous but always concerned about orders and his duty.

The change in postwar values reflects the increasing confidence that individual Russians felt after World War II, but it was also generated from above. It was an official doctrine that the experience of World War II had brought about a radical change in Soviet man, who was now more sophisticated than he had been before. Ironically, the canonical source for this doctrine was that same *Zvezda* and *Leningrad* lecture by Zhdanov that had turned back the clock in Soviet literature. The claim that Soviet man was now different was presented most strongly in one particular paragraph toward the end of Zhdanov's lecture. That paragraph was to become *the* authoritative source cited whenever anyone wanted to advocate, or make some claim of, any sort of change at all. The passage runs:

> With each day our people attain an ever higher level. Today we are not the people we were yesterday, and tomorrow we will not be as we were today. We are already not the same Russians we were before 1917. Russia is not the same, and our character has changed too.[8]

Even though the role of the war was not explicit in Zhdanov's speech, his rhetorical words had the effect of elevating that event to the status of a second revolution in the Soviet roster of Great Moments—a revolution that had wrought a *qualitative* change in Soviet man. Zhdanov's lecture did not introduce this doctrine (which had been around since 1944), but it canonized it for the entire decade.[9]

In literature it thus became an axiom that the man who had been through the war emerged from it changed. This privileged experience was not confined to soldiers: in many a kolkhoz novel the wife left behind became (in the tradition of Dasha in *Cement*) the finer and more committed person for having been forced to cope with the hardships of the war years without the support of a husband.[10] In general, however, it was at the front that man was changed. The heroes of most novels had either fought in the Battle of Stalingrad or, better still, had made that famous progress from Stalingrad to Berlin. If he was somehow unable to do it himself, then his loved one, his brother, or his best friend did it, as it were, on his behalf.[11] The Battle of Stalingrad or the march from Stalingrad to Berlin became the hero's own ordeal, a ready-made substitute for the trials that, as initiate, he had had to undergo in a thirties novel.

These high points from World War II became new additions to History's Great Time. It seemed appropriate for Stalin to participate in them (as he did in most forties novels anyway). Very often, authors contrived to have Stalin appear in person. In Bubennov's *The White Birch Tree* (1947), for instance, the hero loses consciousness after being wounded in battle but comes to to find Stalin standing above him (then, surely, he must have reached "that other world" of the fairytale!).[12]

Since in actual fact Stalin was not very much in evidence at the front, his usual role in war fiction was to deliver one of his major wartime speeches over the radio (most often the November 7 speech before the Battle of Stalingrad). This is of course a form of "testament." In areas under occupation, the speech was run off and distributed clandestinely, in which case it is something like passing the "baton." In short, in forties novels Stalin functioned as a superior mentor.

The End of the Heroic Age and Its Implications for Literature

Because the war and Stalin's wartime speeches had been established as Great Moments, novelists were relieved of much of their obligation to show *extraordinary* feats and *extraordinary* changes. These had already occurred in the war and / or were being taken care of by a figure from outside the novel's world, Stalin. Consequently, in the forties it was possible to depict more everyday, unexceptional moments, more of the quotidian world, than it had been in the thirties. Because *kairos* was assured, *chronos* could continue.

Chronos could continue, but it had to be of a different order from what it had been before the war. After Zhdanov's speech it seemed incumbent on the literary world to formulate an explicit model for demonstrating change. The critics found one in the positive heroes. It became a cliché to remark that Pavel Korchagin (the hero of *How the Steel Was Tempered* [1932–34]) and Oleg Koshevoy (the hero of *The Young Guard*) were "worlds apart": Pavel and his comrades had been a valiant few who had tried to lead the people forward in the face of many alien and hostile social elements; the people of Oleg's generation lived in a more "conscious" and comradely environment. Now, "the socialist way of life has already entered the flesh and blood of Soviet man and is reflected in our every reaction."[13] Consequently, today one finds Pavel Korchagins reproduced "in the millions."[14] In fact, some reviewers claimed that "all are heroes."[15]

These views did not, as one might expect, sound a return to the First Five-Year Plan goal of the kingdom of the "little man." Soviet society was already very hierarchical, and the qualitative cutoff between the ordinary man and his leader was often mentioned in fiction as an assumption not requiring proof. But these doctrines did mean that if all, or most, men are "positive," they do not have to combat menacing villains, and, if their environment is superior to any known before, then their lives are, to that extent, less heroic than were the lives of the Pavel Korchagins.

As "culture" began to supplant the heroic or extraordinary as a central value of both rhetoric and literature, it was perhaps inevitable that the vogue for the pseudo-folk would come to an end. Once again, the official signal for this change was sounded in the Zhdanov lecture of 1946. What Zhdanov found most offensive in the recent works of several of the authors he attacked (including Zoschenko) was that they made Soviet reality and Soviet man seem "primitive."[16] He continued: "We have changed and grown. The time has come to raise the level of sophistication in literature. The reading public is now better educated and simply will not tolerate poor or simplistic literature."[17]

The reign of the people's bards was finally challenged. As recently as 1946 Kryukova, the famous composer of Stalinist *byliny*, had been awarded the Order of Lenin to mark her seventieth birthday, but by 1947 the situation had changed. Critics came out in strength to attack the folk bards, and with a certain alacrity, which no doubt reflected attitudes long suppressed while the bards were lionized.

They invariably cited the catch phrase from Zhdanov's lecture, "Russia is not the same," when they argued that the policy of encouraging folk-epic occasional poetry was misconceived.[18] Generally speaking, this cooling toward folk forms applied only to *Russian* folklore ("Russia is not the same," but ...). The contemporary bards of non-Russian (especially non-European) peoples continued to be feted.

The reaction against folk forms was specifically against old oral, not written, forms. In the forties the place of the *bylina* was largely taken by *The Igor Tale,* a medieval Russian epic from the written tradition, which was frequently published in a modern translation. Motifs from it were used in many war novels besides *The Young Guard.* This change was not merely formal or stylistic (e.g., contained fewer folkisms), but also thematic: the heroes of *The Igor Tale* were not spirited, fantastic folk adventurers, but princes of the Russian land. Correspondingly, the heroes of forties novels were no longer the daring youths of the thirties but older, more responsible people.

The typical hero of the thirties novel was a youth. His forties counterpart was probably between thirty-five and forty.[19] His lack of "youth" was not, however, so much a function of age as of status. He was no longer a potential member of the Soviet hierarchy but actually in it, usually as a junior executive in the Party, military, or government administration.

The forties hero was a leader (*rukovoditel'*) and an organization man. He believed that, if orders came from above, they would be in the organization's interests and therefore should be obeyed without question.[20] He tried to wear at all times the Soviet equivalent of the gray flannel suit, i.e., a neat uniform or coat and tie. Even Oleg Koshevoy, in *The Young Guard,* could not, as an officeholder in the Komsomol, be seen fleeing the Germans across the countryside in midsummer heat without wearing a coat and tie.[21] In several novels the hero was even said not to drink alcohol (in contrast to certain less worthy members of his organization).[22]

To be an officeholder in some hierarchy involved more than automatic compliance and conformism. Leadership was said to be an "art"—a part of "culture," in other words. Hence the aim of the hero's quest in both war and production novels was not to perform some extraordinary feat but to master the art of leadership.

Thus, the typical forties novel is not so much an allegorical tale of an individual's quest for "consciousness," symbolizing the greater quest of society as a whole; rather, it tells how one individual perfects himself as a leader. The metaphoric and adventure-tale elements, which were quite strong in thirties fiction, were palpably weaker in the forties. In fact, together with attacks on pseudo-folk literature came rumblings against "Jack Londonism."[23] The hero's antagonists became less like monsters, fierce beasts, or elemental hordes.

Forties fiction was also less dominated by the rite-of-passage structure than its thirties counterparts had been. Since the hero was often not a youth, the motif of initiation was in any case less feasible. Also, the hero of most novels was a Soviet official who, having usually crossed over into a state of "consciousness" already, merely had to be perfected in that state. Consequently, the initiation of the positive but "spontaneous" youth often provided a subplot rather than the central plot: it was the wife, son, younger friend, or subordinate of the hero who was initiated, not the hero himself. The central plot was often a tale of promotion or preparation to enter the Party. Indeed, the quality sought in the hero was closer to "conscientiousness" than to "consciousness." Like "spontaneity," the Russian word used for the ideological category "consciousness," *soznatel'nost'*, is polysemic and includes "conscientiousness" in its range of meanings.

In novels of this period the "last testament" or "passing of the baton" very often occurred between the hero and his superior, the local Party head, or Stalin, or, since forties novels were somewhat baroque, with all three.[24] The high point of the novel was often a mere routine promotion or reshuffling in the organization, yet it was usually attended by the same atmosphere of initiation into mysteries that was typical of the youth's rite of passage in the earlier novels. But of course the elevated tone was not merely for the promotion itself: at the moment of passage, once again, many of the conflicts and contradictions in society were resolved. There was still, in other words, a major allegorical element in forties novels, even though they were often set in the prosaic, organization-man world.

These observations do not apply equally to all forties novels. The change from heroic to organization-man novel is a trend that begins

in the late thirties and develops during the forties. Therefore, forties
novels were in part organization man and in part heroic. By the late
forties, even war novels had become strikingly less heroic.
The stock antagonist of forties novels was a bureaucratic opponent. He was an antagonist rather than a villain, because he was not
especially wicked; he was simply less perfect than the hero. This is
what was envisaged in the doctrine of "conflictlessness." The bureaucratic antagonist came from within the organization. He was not
opposed to it and was not normally even a "masked enemy" (except
in war novels); he was simply misguided. The hero's chief antagonist
was the bureaucrat who was too overbearing with his underlings,
too neglectful of human welfare, too cautious, and unable to push
the pace of the production or construction enterprise he supervised
beyond conventional limits, too much a prisoner of his bureaucratic
mentality, a so-called formalist who clung to paperwork and im-
peded results.

Such people were hardly evil. Rather, as one critic, Kovalchuk,
proposed, "In the new stage literature has reached, negative material
is more organically linked to positive examples. In fact, negative
material is itself a medium for advancing what is new and progressive."[25] In other words, the principal negative character in a forties
novel is not so much the hero's antagonist as he is his Janus face.
Rather than a villain, he is a negative example of the hero's positive
quality (primarily "consciousness" or conscientiousness), which in
his case has somehow been distorted or carried to excess. Consequently, negative characters are usually not purged but are rehabilitated in some way, usually by means of a salutary demotion
or relegation to the ranks.[26]

Thus in the forties the old political parable of how the forces of
"consciousness" triumph over the forces of "spontaneity" was expanded. Each of the two ideological categories to be represented in
the parable was split into positive and negative versions. The typical
plot involves both characters personifying positive forms of
"spontaneity" and "consciousness" and those exemplifying negative forms, such as being (instead of "spontaneous") headstrong,
self-centered, or susceptible to "elemental" passions, or (instead of
being "conscious") having a mania for red tape, being too wedded
to the office and not responsive to the world outside. Even the
conventional dual image of the mentor figure (stern but loving) was

often split up by providing two mentors, one "stern," the other
"loving."[27]

Forties Variants on the "Little Family" /
"Great Family" Pattern

In fiction, one symptom of the end of the "heroic" was the increasing role given to the hero's private life. In the thirties the hero often
had to sacrifice or transcend his personal attachments, but in the
forties he was expected to regularize his relationships as a way of
proving himself worthy of a position of responsibility in the "organization."

There are several reasons for this change. Since the hero was
usually at a later stage of the life-cycle than his thirties counterpart,
he was therefore often a husband and father, who was not expected
to abandon his wife or child. Also, the hero was now quite often a
woman, probably a wife or mother, and it was clearly even less
acceptable that *she* should neglect her duties to her nuclear family.
Dasha, a hero of Gladkov's *Cement*, had neglected her family,
and her little daughter had even died as a result. But that was in the
twenties, in an age of revolutionary extremism. Times were different now, and gestures such as Dasha's were unthinkable.

There were other, extraliterary reasons why positive heroes of
forties fiction never abandoned their families. During the forties the
government took extraordinary measures—even greater than in the
thirties—to strengthen the nuclear family as a "cell" of that greater
family, the state. It was important to increase the birth rate and
discourage sexual license. Family morality was not considered a
private matter. After all, it was pointed out, if a man's wife com-
promises him with another, this harms his work performance.[28]

In literature, the "little family" and "great family" became more
closely interrelated. In fact, although forties novels were usually set
in "the organization," many of them were set in the hero's family.

The two spheres did not overlap completely. The hero's family
was inevitably smaller in scope than the public sphere in which he
worked. But because several family members usually worked, an
author could manage, with a certain ingenuity, to squeeze quite a
large proportion of one or two families into leading roles within the

local hierarchies. Those local officials who escaped the "family" net could be coopted as structural family members. V. Kochetov's *The Zhurbins* (1952) provides a striking example example of this. Between his four-generation family of shipbuilders (the Zhurbins), their spouses, their girlfriends, and their families, Kochetov almost manages to make his one "little family," the Zhurbins, coextensive with his local "great family."

Ordinarily, however, the mentor figure (or figures) comes from outside the hero's "little family." Even so, he usually assumes the role of "structural elder" in the *private* life of the protagonist. The mentor figure will urge a young hero to marry his girl, counsel him against an impending adultery, comfort him if his loved one is lost in war, and, if a woman finds her husband unworthy, will often counsel her to try to keep living with him. In Babaevsky's second kolkhoz idyll, *Light over the Earth* (1949–50), we find not merely an avuncular "father" but a mother figure as well: the district Party secretary plays matchmaker for the young hero, Sergey, and "loves him like a son," while the secretary's wife gives Sergey's "swarthy shepherdess" advice and feels toward her "as a mother to a daughter."[29]

Conversely, dramas of the public sphere and of ideological consequence were largely played out in terms of "little family" relations. Family problems were usually patterned in terms of false and true family members who were false or true in their public roles as well. In V. Panova's novel, *Kruzhilikha* (1947), for instance, the protagonist Listopad, a factory director, is a poor and inconsiderate husband toward his first wife and, to a comparable degree, a poor administrator; both defects are corrected with the second marriage. Also in Fedin's *An Unusual Summer* (1947–48), an Old Bolshevik revolutionary's search for and discovery of his foundling son (lost due to tsarist repression and brutality) becomes the discovery of a Bolshevik revolutionary's "true" heir: he gives his "last testament" to the son.[30]

Family members who are false in blood terms will prove false in values, too. In G. Nikolaeva's *Harvest* (1950), for instance, the hero and kolkhoz Party leader Vasily Bortnikov is disturbed to find his father and brother corrupted by his (wicked) stepmother. He is even obliged to denounce his father to the kolkhoz for appropriating

wheat meant for the orphanage. His father is taken in hand by the
kolkhoz and improves but is soon stricken by cancer and dies con-
fessing to his son that he took "the wrong road" in life. The young
brother later breaks with the stepmother and becomes a dedicated
member of the kolkhoz. "The father's blood came out," triumphs the
narrator.[31] Family harmony and kolkhoz harmony are restored.

It was not just family relations that were given a bigger role in
forties fiction. Love relations were, too. As the initiation plot became more often relegated to the subplot, that is, it had a lesser
character as its subject, so, proportionately, the love plot became
not an auxiliary plot but an integral part of the main plot, an aspect
of the hero's public life. Love was no longer one of the hero's
"ordeals"; rather, it was said to enhance his work performance.
Indeed, the climax of the love plot and the novel's kairotic moment
now often come together. In P. Pavlenko's novel *Happiness* (1947),
for instance, the kairotic moment occurs when the hero, Voropaev,
sees Stalin in Yalta. Voropaev himself is a sort of updated version of
Ostrovsky's Pavel Korchagin and has been wounded in battle so
many times that he has decided he is too debilitated for love and
personal happiness. But when he emerges from his meeting with
Stalin, he feels "1,000 years younger" and goes home to start an
affair with his landlady.[32]

In some novels, by contrast, love and the kairotic moment do not
occur in rapid succession; in these, love *is* the kairotic moment. In
V. Panova's *Krukhilikha* (1947), for instance, the moment Listopad
and his future second wife spend their first night together proves to
be the turning point in all his professional problems. Being thus
renewed, he is able to solve them all.[33]

Intimations of Metaphysical Quest

In typical forties fiction, then, love helps the hero solve his management problems, and the plots commonly revolve around conflicts between positive and negative examples of the conscientious
bureaucrat. Such conventions do not, on the face of things, seem
particularly auspicious for a vital literature. These sorts of things
gave Zhdanovism its bad name. Nevertheless, it should not be pre-
sumed that the literary world of this decade was lacking in vigor
and controversy.

Surface bombast, surface adherence to Socialist Realist conventions, and homage to Stalin notwithstanding, the pervasive
concern of forties literature was with what was "false" and what
was "true." Critics spoke of false idealization, of false realism, and
of false literary forms (neofolkism, Jack Londonism, etc.). Books
depicted false leaders and true leaders, false goals and true goals,
etc. What lay beneath this interest in the false and true was not just
a need to find the "correct line." Rather, as is quite clear in the
polemics themselves, the main concern was with the *quality of life.*
In other words, although certain forties novels perhaps show undue
attention to scalloped bedspreads and other such objects, this really
represents only the philistine end of an entire spectrum of concern
for the quality of contemporary life. This concern, moreover, was
increasingly articulated in terms of present-day reality (*byt*) rather
than the myth-inspired life lived according to some heroic code.

The stress on love in forties novels (in contrast to those of the
thirties) was not only an effect of the government's insistence that
all adult citizens found "little families." It also reflects the way
people were reevaluating earlier basic assumptions about priorities
in life. In Pavlenko's *Happiness,* for instance, the retired officer
Voropaev not only learns to bring love's balm into his hard life in
the Crimea; he is also opened to new possibilities for living. The life
of the soil he encounters in his association with Crimean kolkhozes
teaches him about a richer world than that of epaulets and pro-
motions in the (military) hierarchy. There are echoes of Tolstoy as
Voropaev confounds an ambitious young officer acquaintance by
rejecting his offer of a prestigious military post, saying that he
prefers to be where he is, among the tillers.[34] Thus, even in the
forties one can find intimations of the cult of the village and the
"soil" that was to emerge more fully in the prose of the sixties and
seventies.

The questions that most troubled the literary world of the forties
came out in discussions of those aspects of Zhdanovism that have
been fairly universally condemned since then: "conflictlessness,"
idealization, and unrealistic standards of personal morality. The
doctrine of "conflictlessness" and the practice of "glossing over"
the negative were not swallowed without a murmur. All through
the forties, critics spoke out against them in articles and polemics
that were published quite freely. Many an article was published

attacking the kolkhoz idylls of Babaevsky, for instance (though critics of the Khrushchev era, who were anxious to establish that the policies of that era were new, found it expedient to claim that Babaevsky's defects were not noticed under Stalin).[35]

Many of the questions that most preoccupied forties society centered around the interrelation between one's individual, private world and one's public life and duties. For this, writers still used the schematic contrast of the "great family" and the "little family." They focused especially on an issue that was a major concern, the right of an individual to engage in adultery. But this was a narrower focus, almost a metaphor for the larger issues at stake, which were, for political reasons, more dangerous to handle. It was not, however, the preserve of "dissident" intellectuals to be concerned with these issues. As is clear from the example of Pavlenko's *Happiness,* a broad spectrum of the intelligentsia was preoccupied with them.

The more the forties progressed, the more the shadow of adultery could be sensed hovering over the lives of all fictional protagonists. Of course, this was a way of making up for the diminished role that adventure and exploit were to play (as compared with a thirties novel) and of giving a potentially dull novel some *frisson* and suspense. It was generally considered not good literary decorum to allow positive heroes actually to indulge in adultery—at least not for more than the odd "mistake" that occurred while he was meeting his "trials." The nuclear family had to be intact for the finale. A common way of motivating the reunion of husband and wife was to have the straying husband become so involved in his work that the new lease of life it gave him helped him feel closer to her.[36]

With each new batch of novels the adultery plot became more dominant, until the possibility of saving the family's purity for the finale became less and less viable. Here we find the conflict between "real" and "ideal" raging just beneath the surface. Matters were reaching the boiling point, and in fact they were able to overflow shortly after Stalin's death—and to overflow then not just on this one issue but on many others, too, which were obscured by the steam.

In a bitter article of 1951, entitled *"Truth* in Art [emphasis mine]," Aleksandr Tvardovsky provides a satirical synopsis of a hypothetical "typical" long poem of the forties. His synopsis applies equally well to many standard forties novels:

You find [in the poem] a backward kolkhoz and a model one.
There is one kolkhoz president who is a man of foremost opin-
ions and one who is high-handed and does not understand the
new conditions brought about by human development. There is a
girl Galya and a tractor driver Vanya. There is a Party organizer
as well, and his only occupation is to organize the affairs of the
heart of this young pair.[37]

So, in forties literature, "boy gets tractor" (plus girl), but, as he does
so, he increasingly tries the patience of both critics and public, who
look for a more meaningful quest. Tvardovsky here decries such
phony trash and calls for "truth in art." It was but one step further
from there to what happened during the various thaws after Stalin's
death.

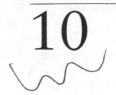

10

The Khrushchev Years

When Stalin died in March, 1953, the majority of the Soviet populace was grief-stricken. Mourners flocked into central Moscow on the day of his funeral, crowding so thickly that several people were trampled to death. But together with the people's great sadness—or so eyewitnesses tell us—came their anxiety: How can we carry on without him?[1]

Yet, before long, Stalin's work was being undone. At the September Plenum of the Central Committee, later that same year, the policies announced for agriculture implied new principles for management in general. Then began the large-scale releases of prisoners from the camps and the countless "rehabilitations."

In February, 1956, came the most climactic moment of the decade. Khrushchev delivered a "secret" speech to the Twentieth Party Congress. In this speech he indicted Stalin on the grounds that he had distorted and ignored the true "Leninist" principles of Bolshevik leadership. Khrushchev did not question the achievements of the Stalinist leadership (the development of heavy industry, collectivization, etc.) but attacked its "anti-Leninist cult of personality" (i.e., the excessive adulation of Stalin) and its breach of "revolutionary legality." As evidence that Stalin had flouted this principle, Khrushchev cited numerous instances of unjust repression, arbitrariness, and falsification.[2]

Khrushchev's "secret speech" encouraged writers to be bolder in exposing (as they had already begun to do) the absurd and counterproductive extremes to which various key Stalinist values had been taken: "vigilance," the titanic hero, the hard-driving, unflinching leader, the duty of the state to monitor the private lives of its citizens, and the Zhdanovist literary doctrines of "conflictlessness" and "glossing over" the negative. This public washing of so much of the Stalinist dirty linen, known as "destalinization," more or less reached its peak in 1962. Khrushchev "retired" from the leadership only a few years later, in October, 1964. In short, the hallmark of the Khrushchev years, 1953–1964, was destalinization.

The writers were in the forefront of this age of dizzy upheaval. Nowhere did the cry for liberalization sound more loudly than in literature. And it had its audience. When that semiofficial poet laureate of destalinization, E. Evtushenko, read his poems at the Lenin Stadium, it would be filled to capacity, as if for a soccer final.

The decade is marked by three "thaws" or high points in the process of destalinization within literature. Each of these took its cue from some recent Party convention that had marked a significant shift away from Stalinist norms. The first occurred in 1954, following the September 1953 Central Committee plenum; the second came in 1956, following the Twentieth Party Congress in February, at which Khrushchev made the "secret speech"; and the third and final thaw came in 1962, in the wake of the Twenty-Second Party Congress.

A closer look at the actual substance of the changes reflected in fiction under Khrushchev reveals that they were often not as radical as the rhetoric suggests. A novel's hero often "unmasked" a wrong that was in fact fairly commonplace in forties prose (an overbearing bureaucrat, neglect of the housing needs of local workers, abuse of privilege by officialdom, rote learning of catch phrases instead of being brought to understand the essence of communism, etc.). In so doing, the hero commonly either detected intimations of change that was to come as the result of the policies promulgated at some recent Party meeting in Moscow, usually the September 1953 Plenum, the Twentieth, or the Twenty-Second Party Congress (whichever occurred most recently), or he extolled the regenerative power of the new policies. The Party conferences enjoyed in rhetoric the status of an official kairotic moment, comparable with a meeting with Stalin in thirties and forties rhetoric.

In some ways the entire drama of destalinization can be seen as a ceremonial legitimizing of the new government. Just as the Stalinist leadership evolved rituals for marking itself off from the factions over which it had triumphed, so, too, the Khrushchev leadership found other rituals (milder and less histrionic) for marking itself off from the Stalinist—of saying, "Stalin is dead. Long live the new collective leadership / Khrushchev."

Thus, much of the ostensibly dissident fiction of this decade was in fact occasional writing, celebrating the wisdom of the leadership and its new policies. Moreover, this occasional writing was fairly formalized, as under Stalin. The great traditions of Socialist Realism were still largely intact; the new age merely demanded certain new tropes and adjustments in the master plot.

Much of the writing that made claims for a new era used the forties convention of the "true" and "false" leader (i.e., the "true" leader represents a positive form of "consciousness"; the "false" one, an excess or distortion of true "consciousness"). Now, however, the "true" leader was identified with the new age, the "false" one with the values of the superseded, Stalinist, era. Sometimes, as in Galina Nikolaeva's 1957 industrial novel *Battle en Route*, the author provided a double set of functions, i.e., "false" and "true" examples of both the mentor (Blikin, first secretary of the Regional Party Committee, as false; Grinin, the second secretary, who will replace him before the book is out, as true), and the disciple (Valgan, the factory director, as false; Bakhirev, his energetic opponent, as true). Also, fifties prose dispensed with the conventional dichotomy in the mentor between his "stern" and "loving" guises. Now the "false" mentor was often "stern," but the true mentor was rarely shown to be anything but "loving." In part this was due to a real change in values, but, under the post-Stalin leadership, it was also an act of public relations (the new leadership cares more). As such, it was the fifties answer to that forties literary sin of "glossing over" the negative.

It should be asked whether, for all the veneer of "protest" and radical overhaul, the Soviet people were not, underneath it all, getting the same sort of fiction as they got under Stalin. In other words, did the change consist merely in *different* rhetorical flourishes? Was fifties prose only a lot of occasional writing celebrating new decrees and marveling at the leadership, as before? Were the people not merely being served the "mutton" of Zhdanovist prose dressed up as the "lamb" of a new spring?

They were, and they were not. Fiction under Khrushchev was more liberal than under Stalin, although not to the degree claimed. It was also more various. Indeed, the Khrushchev years do not constitute a homogeneous era. To mark them off as a distinctive time period is to make a rather arbitrary time division, motivated by a sort of "cult of personality" of its own (Khrushchev's, that is).

On the one hand, trends that mark both ends of the period can also be found in the intellectual life of the adjacent years (i.e., immediately pre- and post-Khrushchev). On the other, the Khrushchev years were relatively volatile ones (relative to the Zhdanovist or Brezhnev years, that is), and, within the decade, there were several distinctive subperiods.

The Early Fifties to 1957: The First Wave of Reevaluation

In many ways the new values that emerged after Stalin's death represent a broadening and intensification of changes in priorities and public values that had already begun to be felt toward the close of the Stalin era. Stalin's death in 1953 and the subsequent turnover of leadership merely quickened a process that had already begun. Things finally reached (or were permitted to reach) the boiling point and then boiled over. Earlier, the issues had been expressed primarily in terms of the right of an individual to his own private life and to artistic truth. After Stalin's death, however, the right to privacy and artistic truth were expanded in scope to include, respectively, the question of where to place the point of tradeoff between the state's interests and the needs and ideas of the individual, and the issue of intellectual truth in general. In both cases, discussion was facilitated not just by the change of leadership but also by a general rescaling and shifting of priorities in the public platform, which now laid more stress on efficiency, professionalism, and human welfare and gave correspondingly less weight to such forties fetishes as political reliability and anti-Westernism.

Much of the initial post-Stalin platform seems to have come out of discussions among intellectuals during the forties. For the most part, however, these were not, strictly speaking, "dissident" intellectuals; rather, they represented minority views within the spectrum of postwar public debate. Their views did not coincide initially with the official position, but that platform came closer and closer to their position until, beginning in 1952, a marked shift in that direction occurred in the official platform itself.

In forties fiction one can find prophetic, if tentative and cautious, reevaluations of basic Stalinist values. Examples include V. Panova's *Kruzhilikha* (1947), E. Kazakevich's *The Star* (1947),

I. Ehrenburg's *The Storm* (1947), V. Kaverin's *Doktor Vlasenkova* (1952), V. Grossman's *For a Just Cause* (1952), and D. Granin's short story "The Second Variant" (1952).[3] With the exception of Kazakevich and Grossman, all these writers produced fictional works during the first half of the Khrushchev period that were in effect reruns of these forties works of theirs; the difference was that they were now more outspoken and direct.

In 1952 there were several indicators that the leadership had also begun to reappraise some of the assumptions that guided policy in the forties. For instance, in Malenkov's speech to the Nineteenth Party Congress of that year he called for managers to pay greater attention to their employees' material welfare,[4] a directive that found some echo in virtually every fictional work published through 1957 and, to a lesser extent, thereafter. Additionally, in 1952 a serious study of Western technological and scientific literature was proposed, the first major sign that the intellectual chauvinism that had been a hallmark of the forties was going to be reversed.[5] Finally, Stalin's own essay of that year, "Marxism and Questions of Linguistics," which attacked "monopolistic" authority figures in the various fields of Soviet science and learning, gave some impetus to the movement leading to the bitter attacks on dogma and on cultural authority figures that marked the first two post-Stalin thaws.[6]

In 1952 a distinct new wave began in literature, as compared with isolated earlier expressions of post-Stalin values. This trend was far from dissident; on the contrary, it was dominated by Party members. It began with the publication in 1952 of a sketch, "District Routine," written by the Party writer Valentin Ovechkin. In this sketch Ovechkin explores, in the limited context of rural management and getting the Plan fulfilled, the tradeoff between "initiative" and "discipline"—between individual and state interests. The sketch was relatively mild in its conclusions, but it was followed by an entire series of sketches, each more radical than the last, published between 1952 and 1956 under the same general heading, "District Routine." Ovechkin's views probably represent a segment of new thinking in the Party, one that would gain official support after Stalin's death. Thereafter, all of his sketches were published in *Pravda* in at least extract form, and often they were published before the Party itself passed the very measures suggested in one of the sketches.

Thus, in the early fifties, the main thrust for change came from within the system. The champions of "the new" did have their radical wing,[7] but, generally speaking, the whole movement was officially sponsored. Why this reevaluation of values—values that seemed almost intrinsic to postwar Soviet society? One answer might be found in societal changes. By the beginning of the fifties the Soviet economy had recovered from the devastation of World War II[8] and was thus in a better position to be liberal, to pay attention to human needs. Moreover, if it was to go on to create a truly advanced, technological nation, it needed more expertise, foreign know-how, and flexibility. This sort of explanation would certainly make the changes seem reasonable, but, given that element of the arbitrary in the history of Soviet policy, it could never provide a complete explanation.

If one analyzes the various changes in values that occurred during the early fifties, one will find that most of them can be accounted for as effects of yet another shift in values: in a reaction to the values of High Stalinism resulting in a return to a milder version of the First Five-Year Plan ethos. Even the reversal of anti-Westernism in science and technology can be associated with the Plan years, since, during that time, the country both imported and studied zealously a great deal of Western technology.

The main thrust of early fifties prose was, however, one of reaction against High Stalinist values rather than specifically toward the Five-Year Plan ethos. Directly or indirectly, the main target of writers, critics, and even policy-makers was that backbone of High Stalinist political culture, namely, hierarchy and privilege, and the cult of the titanic hero that went with them. Despite these assaults on the very axioms of High Stalinism, however, writers did not go to the opposite extreme of the First Five-Year Plan's cult of the "little man"; its protagonists were still largely managers and professional people, as in the forties.

The fifties saw a growing cult, not of the "little man" as a "cog" or "bolt" in society's great "machine," but rather of the ordinary person as an individual. This cult was reflected in several ways: in campaigns to reintroduce "sincerity" and "the lyric" in literature

(read: individual expression, debunking of unrealistic characterization, and paying more attention to love and other feelings) and in
concern for the right of individuals to a full and unhindered private
life. Positive heroes began to indulge in adultery, as they had not
been able to do since the early thirties. Anyone in authority who
sought to prevent it was represented not as a paternalistic figure, as
in the forties, but as a pathetic or cynical busybody, someone to be
shouted down by public opinion.

"The Year of Protest," 1956

In 1956 this cult of the individual grew in scope beyond the realms
of private life and human welfare. In this year the slogan *"Pravda!
Pravda!"* (Give us truth!) was blazoned forth in response to
Khrushchev's secret speech to the Twentieth Party Congress. For
several writers it represented not just the demand that the abuses of
the Stalin era be righted but actually that, henceforth, everyone
should not merely have but actively fight for "One's Own Opinion" (the title of a short story of that year by D. Granin).

In fiction of 1956, writers were more outspcken than before.
They not only responded to cues given them in official speeches but
often acted on their own. At the time, Western commentators became quite excited by these "protests" and calls for the exercise of
independent judgment. Harold Swayze even claimed that the discussions in 1956 literature "threatened to extend beyond, if not to
call in question, that 'great truth, the Party's truth and Lenin's.'"[9]
In fact, however, very few writers went so far in their fiction—
although it is of course always a matter of opinion as to what
constitutes "Lenin's truth."

Many Western commentators were blinded by the sight of the
word *pravda* and assumed that 1956 writing was about "truth"
when most of it wasn't, at all. They tended to assume, for instance,
that when a Soviet writer speaks of *pravda*—particularly when, in
the same breath, he vociferates against conservatism and au-
thoritarianism or expresses his disgust at Soviet "double talk" (i.e.,
saying what one is expected to say rather than what one knows to
be the case)—he is contrasting objective truth and dogma. In actual
fact, all three elements (anticonservatism, antiauthoritarianism, and

hatred of cant) can be found in a book as servile toward received attitudes as Azhaev's *Far away from Moscow* of 1948.[10] The only novelty about much 1956 writing is the actual use of the word *pravda*, which was an innovation as far as mainstream Socialist Realist fiction was concerned, although it had actually been used in some 1952 works that were harbingers of post-Stalin attitudes.[11]

In 1956, most writers insisted that there were *two* truths—the new and the old. Just as, between 1953 and 1955, they contrasted the attitudes of an "old-style" administrator with a "new," in 1956 they contrasted a cynical leader's attitudes with those of a living incarnation of the platform of February, 1956, and cried out *Pravda!* in doing so.[12] There were other writers, however, who under the banner of *"pravda"* managed to champion values that were not completely identical with those of the Twentieth Party Congress platform. Most of them identified their ideas hopefully with the spirit of the new age and, most insistently, with "Leninism."

The most radical example of fiction that championed a non-received sense of *pravda* (in this case, the author did not even bother to identify it as "Leninist") is V. Dudintsev's 1956 novel *Not by Bread Alone*. The novel treats a popular 1956 theme of struggle against careerists who have corrupted and frustrated true scientific endeavor, but it goes to unprecedented extremes in the extent of the corruption it depicts, the implication of the Party in the corruption, and the negative picture of the possibility that "truth" will prevail. This made the novel an especial *bête-noire*, and it caused quite a commotion when it was published.

Not by Bread Alone concerns an inventor, Lopatkin, who has invented a new machine for the centrifugal casting of sewer pipes. Unfortunately, to adopt this machine would mean scrapping the one slated for adoption, which, although inferior, was invented by the authority figure in this branch of engineering. Consequently, the director of the provincial factory where Lopatkin works, Drozdov, blocks the project quite cynically. Lopatkin both loses his job and has to fight his own battle against overwhelming odds to see his machine accepted. In 1956, Drozdov became an emblem for the cynical, careerist bureaucrat who lives in great material comfort himself.

In *Not by Bread Alone* the agents of authority are almost overwhelmingly corrupt, but this picture is counterbalanced by a positive account of a handful of the elect, the fighters for "truth," comprising largely Lopatkin and Nadezhda, Drozdov's wife, who soon leaves Drozdov for Lopatkin. In building up his picture of the elect, Dudintsev has essentially created a new heroic *vita* but one still modeled on that of the conventional Soviet hero. Lopatkin meets many of the standard criteria for the true revolutionary hero: he is of working-class origins and has proved himself under fire in one of the Great Moments of Soviet history (wounded in World War II, he was decorated with the Red Star).[13] The one thing missing is a Party background. Still, Lopatkin, in defying the bureaucrats who want to keep his Promethean spirit "bound," recapitulates the pattern of the Stakhanovite, who, it will be recalled, did not have to be a Party member.

Lopatkin also meets the exigencies of the Heroic Code. In his single-minded bid to get his invention adopted, he scorns "bread"—material comfort—and stands fast before the slings and arrows with which the mockers and antagonists assail him. In the tradition of the best of the Old Bolsheviks, he survives a prison term (which the wronged husband, Drozdov, organized for him) with his faith intact. Lopatkin does not, of course, attain quite the heights of Rakhmetov, the hero of Chernyshevsky's *What Is to Be Done?*, who submits himself to a bed of nails to train his will and transcend the bodily. Nevertheless, Lopatkin's rigorous asceticism and zealous guardianship of his spiritual purity (he allows himself only physical exercise and uplifting concerts of classical music; all else is work and thin gruel) make Pavel Korchagin or any other of the Soviet "new men" seem profligates by comparison.

Lopatkin's single-mindedness is not directed toward any Bolshevik or Marxist ideal of grace in some collective harmony. On the contrary, Dudintsev's novel is redolent with intellectual elitism—an elitism, moreover, that echoes the ideas of Zamyatin and Tynyanov (twenties intellectuals who stood outside the world of Party thinking). Throughout the novel Dudintsev draws a distinction between two types of people, a distinction highly reminiscent of the one Zamyatin drew in the twenties between "inquirers" (*izobtretateli*) and "acquirers" (*priobretateli*). For Dudintsev (as for Zamyatin) it is given only to a select few people (the inquirers) to make the truly radical intellectual discoveries that will bring about great changes in history. Most of mankind, basking in the benefits of the progress thus brought about, seeks only material self-aggrandizement. Unable to see beyond the present stage of human thought, they are mere "acquirers." Also, in connection with figures like Lopatkin, Dudintsev invokes some of the key terms Tynyanov used in his 1928 essay on Khlebnikov, that cult figure of certain twenties intellectual circles: Lopatkin and his like have true "vision" (*zrenie*), they have true "daring" (*smelost'*).[14] He also (through a minor character, who quotes Bryusov) talks of the "torches" of thought that people like Lopatkin carry, torches that must be hidden in the underground (the "catacombs") so that they will not be extinguished.[15]

In all these respects, *Not by Bread Alone* reiterates ideals of the twenties, but in others it prefigures the ideas of Solzhenitsyn and other intellectuals of the sixties, who bore witness to the camps and the purges in a spirit of proud defiance. Lopatkin's imprisonment is, for instance, embellished with declarations that seem to come right out of Solzhenitsyn's *The First Circle* ("A thinker is unable to stop thinking," and "Whoever has learned to think can never be completely deprived of freedom").[16] One might, however, equally well associate these ideas with the nineteenth-century myth of the martyred member of the intelligentsia—a myth coopted into Bolshevik lore as the myth of the revolutionary who defies tsarist prison and exile.

Here we are once more confronted with that great irony of Soviet culture, the fact that in many ways "dissident" and "orthodox" values form, not two opposed traditions, but different forces locked in a dialectical relationship within the one system, each feeding on the other. Moreover, High Stalinist values resemble the views of leading dissident thought during the periods of relatively liberal cultural climate that frame the Stalin years, i.e., the twenties and the fifties.

Paradoxically, then, during the 1956 thaw the one novel that is most "dissident" more closely resembles Stalinist fiction than any of the more "conformist" writings of that year. Just when the bards of the "new era," bent on dismantling the High Stalinist ideals of the Heroic Code and its titanic figures, were calling for moderation, pragmatism, and democratization, we find in *Not by Bread Alone* such salient traits of Stalinist culture as Promethean symbolism, the notion that there is a higher-order knowledge accessible only to the chosen few, and the myth of the martyred member of the intelligentsia. The only crucial element lacking is a mentor figure for Lopatkin, and Dudintsev provides vestiges of that in various "caring" designers whom Lopatkin encounters during the course of the saga. However, these relationships are not followed through.[17] There is no organization into which Lopatkin is to be inducted after instruction by an elder figure; he stands virtually alone with his muse.

Not all the writers who in 1956 championed intellectual values saw the process of truth-seeking in terms of a simple binary opposition (us / them, inquirers / acquirers, etc.). Some writers maintained that there is not a "true" and "false" truth to be sought or championed but that, rather, truth is *complex*. Their concern was not merely to champion another variety of truth from that of received truth but to show the pitfalls of insisting on any form of truth, no matter how right and "true" it might seem to be; it is up to the individual to ascertain his own beliefs.[18]

Complex truth and individual autonomy in ascertaining truth are attributes of a *Gesellschaft* world view and imply rejection of, or a superseding of, the ideal of *Gemeinschaft*. But in 1956 it was not really *Gesellschaft* values that predominated. Most writers still believed that the kingdom of *Gemeinschaft* could be theirs; they had merely taken the wrong turning on the path to it during the Stalin years. Those who maintained that truth is complex represented a small minority. The dominant group among the so-called protest writers of 1956 were actually communist idealists. Most of them were Party members who were determined that the experiment of 1917 should not come to naught. They were therefore in some ways more ruthless and zealous in their rejection of Stalinist ills than uncommitted writers (except, that is, for Dudintsev).

Ovechkin was a leading figure among the idealists. In fact, the year 1956 in some ways represented the zenith of the movement for change in administration of which he had, all along, been in the vanguard. His sketch of 1956, "A Hard Spring," is his most outspoken and ambitious expression of the call for change. In it Ovechkin explores that most problematical issue of Marxism-Leninism: how to strike a balance between allowing the people to participate in their own government and to use their own initiative, on the one hand, and, on the other, adhering to the Party principle of democratic centralism (*edinonačalie,* or one-man management).[19]

In this sketch the usual positive hero, Martynov, first secretary of the District Party Committee, breaks his leg and is hospitalized for a while. In his absence the administration is taken over by a new figure, Dolgushin, who, in his determination to rid the region of corrupt administrators, calls an open Party meeting at which the people vote to exclude all the corrupt local bureaucrats from the Party. This action is controversial, for it raises some basic issues of Party rule. As Martynov muses in his hospital bed on what has happened, he jots down the following thoughts on the matter:

> Initiative and discipline—independence and compliance with orders from above. How can they be reconciled? Where can one define "the bounds of the permissible"? Where is the dividing line beyond which one can't go if one wants to avoid creating anarchy? I don't know. As yet this is not quite clear to me. But is it clear to those comrades who have begun to bandy about the word "initiative" so often of late in newspaper editorials?[20]

It appears from internal evidence in "A Hard Spring" that Ovechkin intended to continue his discussion in later sketches. But this was the last one published in the series.

Neither Ovechkin nor any other writer pursued further the major questions of governance in a communist society raised in 1956. This was not so much because it was politically unwise (after the 1956 thaw ended) as because, in pursuing them, they had reached a sort of impasse. That this was so is suggested in the quotation from Ovechkin's "A Hard Spring": "Initiative and discipline—independence and compliance with orders from above...," Martynov mused, and he virtually concluded that no answer could be found.

In the specific context of Marxism-Leninism, an answer could not be found as yet. No true "answer" or resolution can come until the spontaneity/consciousness dialectic is resolved in a classless society. Until then, any solution must necessarily be makeshift, imperfect, and guided by the historical circumstances of the moment. But the issue itself is larger than its specific Marxist-Leninist formulation: it is a dilemma of modern society.

Not only the initiative / discipline issue, but also virtually every
other question raised in 1956 can be viewed in two contexts: in the
context of Stalinist ills and, on the other hand, in the more general
context of the problems that beset any society dominated by
bureaucracies or corporations. In that second, more general context, the problems can be seen as part of the perennial dilemma:
how is it possible to maintain the individual citizen's identity, intellectual integrity, dignity, and private life without voluntarily or
involuntarily submitting to the demands of "the organization" (in
the Soviet case, the Party or state), and how is it possible to foster
initiative while yet assuring efficient administration and achievement as the major goals? In other words, at some level of generality,
much of the 1956 "protest" was not ultimately about "Stalinism"
per se. It was rather the sort of stock-taking that was bound to occur
when the Soviet Union came of age as a modern society. The
coming-of-age had occurred in the late thirties, but the stock-taking
had largely been kept out of print hitherto. Now it could be made
public. The issues raised in 1956 were variants on the problems
endemic in all modern societies but exacerbated in a centralized and
bureaucratic state. That they were not recognized as such in 1956 is
in a sense a sign of the naivety that characterized the initial post-
Stalin period.

Ovechkin and the other idealist communists writing during these
years did not really have a solution to the initiative / discipline dilemma. The nearest Ovechkin came to it was when he periodically
implied that all would be well if administrative power were reserved
for what he called the "true communists at heart" (duševnye kom-
munisty).[21] In other words, the solutions to these various dilemmas
were ultimately not to be found in legislation or decision but in
things innate, felt ("spontaneous"?). Writers in this initial post-
Stalin period continued to wax lyrical about efficiency, technology,
rational regulation of norms, reasonable (uninflated) goals, etc., but
underneath it all there was a lurking attachment to things spiritual,
not accessible to regulation, natural.

Thus the questions raised in 1956, firmly grounded as they were
in that year's agonies of destalinization, nevertheless bring back
again the "eternal questions" of the Bolshevik experiment as an
attempt to work out traditional Russian dilemmas and intelligentsia
myths through some eschatological vision of an age when time

would stand still. At a certain level of generality, the initiative/ discipline dichotomy (itself a variant of the spontaneity/consciousness dichotomy, which has been at the center of my entire inquiry) is an expression of a basic problem of communist idealism. For those who seek to found an ideal fraternalistic community, the problem arises of how to maintain a state of ideal community in fraternity without invoking the countervailing impulse: to structure (to institutionalize, organize, hierarchize). The official Bolshevik solution to this dilemma was a form of normative community.[22] Equality and fraternity were mandated, and society was subjected to all the distortions of the ideal this mandate entailed, including, especially in this case, excessive regimentation and hierarchy. In the attempt to correct these distortions (1956 and all that), many writers suggested that what was needed was to perfect the structure that was supposed to maintain community. Yet there was, at the same time, a strongly felt impulse to go to the other extreme, to the existential sense of community that defies time, is inwardly felt, is pure and spontaneous.

For all the talk of bringing about a more rational order, the appeal of the revolution in Russia from the very beginning came from a desire to transcend human limitations, from an unwillingness to take more impersonal and "necessary" forces into account. One sees this again in the Soviet period in, for instance, the slogan that Lenin, though dead, is "more alive than the living" and in the Stalinist dictum that nothing is impossible for man—one has only to will it sufficiently. Even though much of the writing and policies of the post-Stalin fifties was directed toward deflating the extravagant claims of the Stalin era and setting more reasonable goals, their authors still wanted to deny necessity, and the necessity of structure (real structure, actual bureaucracy) above all.

Generally speaking, the Russian intellectual tradition has prized organicity and rejected, or at best felt ambivalent about, bureaucracy. Bureaucracy as a formal structure has been a traditional symbol for the inorganic (in literature especially). In 1956 Soviet intellectuals had effectively reached an impasse in the route they had taken for tackling the several ills ascribed to "Stalinism": its assaults on truth, on individual integrity, private life, etc. Of course "Stalinism" exacerbated all these problems, but, even if its particular excesses were combatted, the problem would still remain of

how to maintain traditional intelligentsia ideals in postwar, modern
society.

Ironically, it was the "necessity" of the Hungarian uprising in
late October, 1956 (a major crisis in administration), that jolted the
idealists out of agonizing over how to have "structure" without
necessity, how to have a bureaucratic society that would not
threaten such fifties values as "sincerity" and "one's own opinion."
The event itself made it politically impossible to discuss such issues;
but, even when the climate became more liberal, totally different
solutions and ideals began to emerge in fiction, solutions closer to
the mainstream of traditional intelligentsia thought.

In the literature of the last seven years of the Khrushchev era,
1957–64, the movement for destalinization was expressed primarily in two ways. On the one hand, it continued that common theme
of the early fifties, the need to pay greater attention to human
welfare; what was now especially questioned was the right to take a
human life in the name of the cause or simply because, otherwise,
one would be disobeying orders.[23] The enormous attention paid to
these issues was hailed as the new "humanism" born of the Twentieth Party Congress.[24] Under its banner came a new wave of war
literature that was antiheroic and even somewhat pacifist.[25]

On the other hand, new themes were found in the specific
Stalinist abuses cited in Khrushchev's secret speech. These include
the deportations; the excesses committed in the name of collectivization and dekulakization; Stalin's not having the country prepared
for World War II; and—a topic allowed only from 1962 on—the
camps.

Thus, after 1956, and especially after 1961, writers were able to
discuss some extremely sensitive political issues they had been unable to discuss before. Yet, except for talk of the need for bureaucrats to be more conscientious and less self-seeking (a perennial
Soviet theme), few writers returned to the ticklish questions of government raised in 1956 (initiative versus discipline, etc.).

The Heroic Revival? Fiction of the Late Fifties
and Early Sixties

In many respects, fiction of the late fifties was born of a wave of
reaction against the particular brand of idealism that had domi-

nated literature during the initial post-Stalin years. The more conservative authors (such as Kochetov in his late-fifties novels) were
reacting against what they saw as a dangerous liberalism and an
irreverence for Stalinist achievement. In general, however, the reaction was not especially political (i.e., conservative versus liberal).

The late fifties saw yet another twist in the constant dialectic of
Soviet culture, something like the thirties reaction against "machine" values in favor of "the garden." Of course, the early fifties
were not, like the First Five-Year Plan years, an age redolent of the
spirit of Chaplin's *Modern Times;* in fact, "the machine" was not a
compelling symbol for early-fifties writers. Nevertheless, the ideal of
an efficient but benevolent bureaucracy, which informed so much
of fiction through 1956, is comparable to the idea of society as a
smooth-running machine, an idea that had informed so much
fiction in the First Five-Year Plan years (in the fifties variant, "the
machine" is conceived of in explicitly less mechanistic terms). In
reaction to this, almost all novels of the late fifties and early sixties,
both "die-hard" and "liberal," there was a return to the "garden"
and "storm" romanticism of the late thirties. Many of these works
used the precise thirties ensemble of flight, struggle, and the elements as the setting for an allegorical saga of Soviet man's quest.

Of course, after Sputnik was launched in 1957, the Soviet people
again found in aviation (and space exploration) a rallying point for
national pride. Thus it is not surprising that the "heights" of the
skies and the stars became major motifs once more. But while Sputnik can probably be credited with the resurgence of the earlier
theme of flight, the resurgence of those other thirties symbols—
struggle, the elements, and the harmony of nature—has no identifiable historical cause and must be seen as yet another twist in the
nature/culture dialectic.

Nature once more appeared everywhere in novels ostensibly dedicated to the industrial theme,[26] but in late-fifties novels it was
predominantly not a garden but a place of challenging, elemental
forces. A stock hero of late-fifties fiction is the intrepid construction
chief who builds giant enterprises in wild, remote regions. But
whether Soviet man's struggle was to be fought in the skies or in
hostile climes, he would, once more, win through because of his
"stickability" and his being "hard as flint." The drift away from the
heroic, which had been going on since the forties, was finally halted.

The many "revelations" of 1956 ritually delivered a mighty blow
to the "great family," making it effectively impossible for writers to
return completely to the plot patterns of Stalinist fiction, which
were articulated in terms of "fathers" and "sons." When the great
patriarch of the Soviet family, Stalin, was discredited, a shadow fell
on the dynastic line that was at the heart of all Soviet legitimizing
myth. It might have seemed possible simply to pick up the pieces of
the shattered "great family" and regroup them on a slightly different familial line (e.g., some dynastic line stretching from Lenin to
Khrushchev while bypassing Stalin, the "false" father), and this was
effectively what was done in the fiction of the early post-Stalin
years, with its conventional opposition of the new-style leader to
the old-style administrator. But 1956 saw such sweeping de-
nunciations of the old father figure that it was really incumbent on
writers to employ positive heroes untainted by close ties to him (a
reason in itself, incidentally, for using younger heroes). Literature
was expected to present a ritual celebration of 1956's officially
engendered *Angst*. Hero after hero was heard to exclaim something
like "Given all these devastating revelations, how can I go on func-
tioning in Soviet society?" Hence, the usual way the positive hero
attained social integration—through the guidance of a father figure,
senior to him in the local Party or government hierarchy—was no
longer a viable option.

Who could play "father" for him now? Usually it was an Old
Bolshevik or an old worker, and it was always established that he
had begun his political life well before Stalin's rise to power. Often
he was wrongly "repressed" under Stalin (and therefore untainted)
but had not lost his Leninist faith. Such a figure was often used as a
deus ex machina to add the last amen when the moral of the work
was brought out in its closing pages.

Authors in the late fifties sometimes did not rest content with this
but actually generated out of the old master plot an entirely new
variant, the "youth novel," which first appeared in 1956.

The youth novel might be described as a kind of mutation, for
though most of the standard events of the plot are different from
those of the typical Stalin novel, the underlying structural impulse is
the same: a rite of passage by which the hero passes from a state of
"spontaneity" to one of "consciousness" and thus achieves social
integration. The *sequence* of events thus remains much the same as
before.

The main "mutations" are to be found in the patterns used for the symbolic dialectic between the "great family," or public domain, and the "little family," the nuclear family or private world of the protagonists. The pattern is no longer one of tension between the hero's personal and public lives (as in thirties fiction) or between characters who are "false" or "true" in fulfilling their roles in both their families and their public lives (as in the forties). Instead, the hero now lives in two completely separate worlds, one false and one true, in each of which he has both a "great family" (or public life) and a "little family" (or personal attachments).

Although the two worlds are separate, the hero participates in both. Like the fairy-tale hero, he makes a journey from the profane world (the false) to a higher reality (the true). Unlike many fairy-tale heroes, however, he ultimately chooses not to return to the profane world but completes his rite of passage in the land of "the true" and hence mediates mythically the conflict between the imperfect reality revealed in 1956 and the higher reality of Communist ideals.

This opposition between the two worlds is set up through an inversion of the typical Stalinist valorization of place. In the Stalinist novel, Moscow functioned as a place prefiguring the higher-order reality to come in Communism, while the provincial town, factory, construction site, or kolkhoz in which the novel was set was bound to be far behind Moscow on the path to perfection. In the youth novel, by contrast, Moscow (or Leningrad) functions as the "false" place, polluted by bureaucracy, careerism, insincerity, and other such "Stalinist" ills, whereas some place "far away from Moscow" (in the words of the title of Azhaev's Zhdanovist classic) and, preferably, dramatically less civilized than Moscow (or Leningrad) becomes the haven of Leninist ideals to which the hero is drawn.

This reversal of the symbolic meaning of "Moscow" and "away from Moscow" did not, however, begin with the youth novel, for it can be found in some of the earliest fiction of the post-Stalin period.[27] In other words, the disparagement of the modern metropolis began as a schematic inversion of primary Stalinist symbols, but in the earlier examples the "other" place, far away, was, if less blameworthy than "Moscow," not yet a place where ideals were practiced.

The youth novel begins with a celebration of the *Angst* of 1956.

Its hero is usually a teenager who has just left high school. Hence, he is not himself tainted by Stalinism, yet he is deeply disturbed by the revelations he has heard and the cynicism and corruption he perceives in the world around him. He is a troubled youth. Often he is a troublesome one as well; in fact, many youth-novel heroes are on the wrong side of the law, or at least on the wrong side of their parents or their schools. At the outset, then, the question is, How can the hero be integrated into adult society?

The first step is for the hero to leave his Moscow (or Leningrad) world, for the journey *away* that he makes at the outset triggers his moral/political progression. Often he does not himself *decide* to make the journey but is sent on it, or his friends are going and he joins them out of sheer inertia; in this event, the only time he decides anything is at the end, when he chooses to stay in the new place.

Usually the "other place" to which the hero goes is associated with one of the new schemes of the Khrushchev regime—for example, one of the construction sites in Siberia to which many Komsomol brigades were sent in the fifties or some settlement started as part of Khrushchev's Virgin Lands scheme. Occasionally the hero sets off for purely temporary, personal reasons but finds some pocket of "socialist production and construction" and is, against all his own expectations, drawn into work with it so that, in the end, he chooses to remain there rather than to return to the Moscow (or Leningrad) of careerists and cynics. A good example of the latter pattern would be V. Aksenov's *Ticket to the Stars* (1961), in which a group of swinging young Leningraders set off for a good time in the Baltic resort town of Tallin, which, by the end of the novella, virtually changes its identity: from being a haven for jazz and other forms of Western decadence it becomes simply the nearest town to a fishing sovkhoz in which the hero decides to follow his destiny. This radical switch on the hero's part is paradigmatic, for in the youth novel a change of identity is the basic dynamic.

The classic example of the youth novel and its official progenitor, until the author defected, is A. Kuznetsov's *Continuation of a Legend* (1957). The work opens as the hero, Tolya, recently graduated from high school, sets off with friends on the Trans-Siberian Railroad, leaving his parents, his cynical, opportunist friend Victor, and his girl friend behind. Tolya gets off at Irkutsk for no particular reason, but there he is so taken by a young worker, Leonid (young, but *older than Tolya*), that he decides to stay and work on Leonid's project, the Irkutsk power station.

Then follows a commonplace of the youth novel: the hero's first day of work is a test of suffering and endurance (a favorite spot for slipping in some of the catchphrases of Stalinist rhetoric). Tolya is put to work shoveling concrete. At first all goes well, but before long his entire body aches. "Will I hold out [*vyderžu*] or not?" is the subhead that introduces this section. At the end of the day, his hands dripping with blood, Tolya just manages to drag himself home and climb "higher and higher" up the stairs to his dormitory room.[28] He has made it.

As this suggests, the youth novel combines many of the "little man" values of the Plan era (especially the glories of manual labor and of the humble life of the lowly) with much of the heroic rhetoric (of blood and sacrifice) typical of High Stalinist writing. Predominantly, however, the youth novel is a romance and, as such, is closer to High Stalinist fiction than to that of the Plan years. What impels the hero to seek an alternative way of life in distant climes is not so much "revelations about Stalinist abuses" as the lack of idealism and adventure in the lives of those around him. Each hero of a youth novel carries with him some romantic motif that inspired him in his schooldays and that he "finds" in his new world; "fairy tale becomes reality," once again (in *Continuation of a Legend* fairy tale does become reality: one of the workers tells a local folktale in which the Yenisey and Angara rivers are united—as in reality they are in the Irkutsk project).[29] However, it is adventure rather than a fairy-tale world that is the chief allure. Mentions of Conan Doyle, Jack London, and H. G. Wells pepper the pages of Kuznetsov's book. His hero, Tolya, is haunted by a childhood vision of "red sails on a blue sea," which he finds again in the bustle of the construction site.[30]

The hardship and romance of the hero's new world are constantly contrasted with the comfort and triviality of Moscow life. Tolya continues to exchange letters with his family, girl friend, and friend Victor. He yearns for the comfort of Moscow and is often tempted to go back. But Victor's cynical letters, full of talk of imported cloth and rock-and-roll, increasingly grate on Tolya. In the end he decides to break with all that and stay where he is.

He stays because he is attracted by the people he meets on his new job, especially the mentor figure. The latter is usually an older worker, possibly the brigade leader, and probably a member of the Komsomol. In other words, while considerably lower on the administrative hierarchy than the typical Stalinist mentor, he is usually on a hierarchy, all the same. He is a person of integrity who believes firmly in the collectivist Communist ideal. But, instead of being a father figure, he is usually more like an older brother. Thus, a vertical axis can be constructed through him—a link can be forged between "the organization" and the individual—without having to use a father figure of great political power.

At the end of most youth novels the mentor dies, usually in some engagement with elemental forces or as the result of some accident. In *Ticket to the Stars* the mentor figure is actually the hero's real-life older brother, and he dies in an experiment connected with preparations for space travel. In *Continuation of a Legend,* somewhat untypically, one of the hero's mentors, the old worker Zakhar, dies a natural death from old age, albeit "at his post" (while still employed). Before his death, the mentor will, in the tradition of the Stalinist novel, either give the hero a "last testament"[31] or hand him a symbolic "baton." *Ticket to the Stars* closes, for instance, with the young hero's gazing at his late brother's Komsomol membership card, his "ticket to the stars."

Upon the mentor's death the hero crosses the threshold of uncertainty and decides to stay in his new location indefinitely. He also commonly decides to study and either joins the Komsomol or at least makes some plans for a career beyond the rank-and-file position he presently occupies. In other words, he changes his orientation from the axis of infinite brotherhood, which has characterized his stay in the new place up to this point, by acknowledging the value of hierarchy. The conflict between the ideal community and the actual structure of society, so acutely felt in 1956, is thus resolved ritually.

Besides a mentor, the hero also finds a new girl at his new place of work. She is typically humbler in origins than the girl he left behind in the big city, but she has more compassion for her fellow man. At the point when the hero decides to stay on at his new location, he also decides to break with his old girl in favor of the new one, and with this his last binding attachment to the "little family" of his old world is severed. He usually does not break with his parents, but his ties to them are now very loose.

Thus, the youth novel utilizes the basic structure, many of the motifs, and even the language of conventional Stalinist novels. Yet it cannot be called a Stalinist novel or even a revamped Stalinist novel. This is because the epic quality that was so defining a feature of Stalinist novels has been lost. There is no longer that complete consonance between the inner and outer selves of the protagonists, or between the narrator's point of view and that of his protagonists, that used to obtain.

The breakdown of epic wholeness was by no means a feature of the youth novel exclusively. Rather, it was a tendency that began in fiction in 1956, when moral conflicts were often internalized[32] and many recognized that "truth is complex." The tendency became stronger in the ensuing decade; in fact, "truth is complex" became a sort of catchphrase of early-sixties fiction.[33] In the youth novel itself, the erosion of epic wholeness can be sensed both in the vogue for first-person narration chronicling the hero's confusion and in the inordinate role that sheer chance plays in determining his fate. These were but the first signs of a breakdown that would become more widespread and characteristic as time went on. Characters were now commonly given a separate inner identity, irony was widely used (even in so-called orthodox fiction),[34] and something like stream of consciousness made its appearance.[35]

The result of these various assaults on the conventions of the Socialist Realist narrative was that, whatever superficial resemblance late-fifties fiction may have had to Stalinist novels, the latter's necessary ingredients of inexorability, predetermination, and freedom from ambiguity had been undermined if not lost.

As the fifties progressed, Soviet fiction (influenced to some degree by Western literature), began to show more and more cognizance of the *Gesellschaft* reality out of which it was written. In the Russians' traditional way, this was expressed symbolically by using the modern urban center, Moscow or Leningrad, in an updated version of the St. Petersburg myth. Increasingly, Soviet fiction was set in one or the other of these towns, something that was rarely done in mainstream Stalinist fiction. At first the hero escaped from or rejected the big city, as in the youth novel; or, although the novel was set in Moscow or Leningrad, the reality of the great metropolis impinged very little on the novel's insistently *Gemeinschaft* world. But by the early sixties the heroes of youth novels often failed to take that train out of town and stayed on, instead, in Moscow (or Leningrad). There they lolled about their apartments, gadded around with their peers, fought desultorily and pointlessly with their parents, and were quite incorrigible social deviants with no high principles or "revolt" to justify their behavior. They never went anywhere and never found wholeness.

The center for this sort of writing was, ironically, Leningrad itself. There, in the early sixties, an entire mini-movement, the self-styled "urbanists" (*gorožane*), sprang up. They were but a small part of the large movement toward more modernist and sophisticated writing, generally known as the "new prose" (Bitov and the later Aksenov were other writers in the "new prose" movement).

The urbanists themselves (Efimov, Vakhtin, Maramzin, and Gubin) were peripheral figures if we judge their importance by the volume of material they actually managed to get published. Their anthology, *The Urbanists,* for instance, was rejected for publication. But they are interesting because they have more of the attributes of a cohesive group, with its own ideology, than did any other "new prose" writers. One senses this ideology in the internal, publisher's review of one of their anthologies. This review was written by D. Dar, the group's mentor. Dar distinguishes between genuine "socialist realism," with its "inexhaustible possibilities," and that abomination of Socialist Realism, what he calls "bureaucratic realism," whose writers do not "want to see life in all its complexity, [but] prefer to squeeze reality into some desirable schema."[36]

In Czechoslovakia at this time there was a movement for canonizing surrealism as a valid form of Socialist Realism. The "new prose" writers appear as a pale reflection of the same impulse. Within their native context, however—in the land which gave birth to Socialist Realism—what they were trying to do was more radical than what their Czech brothers sought.

Socialist Realism had traditionally written of wholeness: social integration was the mandatory end point of any novel. The "new prose" writers wrote not of wholeness and harmony but of alienation, disintegration, confusion. The forms their fiction took were veritable metaphors for the protagonists' fractured psyches. Predominantly, the genre used was short—usually the short story or sketch, very occasionally the novella. The compositional method was often stream-of-consciousness narration or a series of disconnected fragments. In fact, Bitov wrote a "novel" (*The Pushkin House*) made up entirely of seemingly disconnected short pieces.[37]

In short, it would seem that the attempt at a "heroic revival" had failed, that the mighty tradition of the Socialist Realist novel had foundered on the rocks of modernity.

11   Paradise Lost or Paradise Regained?

The "new prose" (of Bitov, Aksenov, and so on) coming out of the Soviet Union in the early sixties seemed to many to be the wave of the future. It was written largely by and about young people of the urban middle class, precisely the sociological category that was now in the ascendant in Soviet society. They wrote in a way that suggested a hope that Soviet Russia would "catch up with and surpass" the West on the cultural front, that it would come to terms with the reality of the postindustrial world rather than take shelter in nostalgic revivals. Their prose was largely sophisticated and undidactic—even playful.

But this wave peaked very early and was then dwarfed by other waves. In fact, it didn't really manage to peak at all, for much of the "new prose" (including the "urbanist" anthologies) was never accepted for publication. To some extent this was due to generational conflict; established prose writers on the editorial boards were not anxious to have their way of writing superseded at the hands of young upstarts. To some extent it was due to the chronic resistance in Soviet society to literary experimentation. But not entirely. Blander versions of the "new prose" have continued to be published to this day, but they do not enjoy the same resonance as works by writers (such as Shukshin and Aitmatov) who are formally very conventional but raise topical issues.

There are several historical reasons that help to explain this. Khrushchev fell in October, 1964, an event that marked the end of cultural liberalization. Since then there has not been a single "thaw." The "Prague Spring" was forcibly ended by Soviet troops in August, 1968, and, thereafter, the cultural climate became even more conservative. This is not, however, a sufficient explanation for the failure of Soviet and Western literature to converge.

Convergence failed to occur largely because most Soviet intellectuals no longer sought it. The invasion of Czechoslovakia marks a milestone in the progressive alienation between Western and Soviet intellectuals. In the late fifties and early sixties many had believed the Soviet Union and the West might learn from each other. By 1968, however, Russian intellectuals were no longer so interested in catching up with the West on the cultural front. In part this was because it was no longer feasible to do so, given the political conditions of the late sixties; but it was largely because, as was often said at the time, they wanted to enrich and develop their own traditions rather than create a second-rate, derivative Western culture.

At the same time, the Russian literary world itself became more divided than it had been under Khrushchev. The changes in the intellectual and political climate forced a substantial minority among writers and intellectuals into the underground or into exile abroad. This group now writes predominantly for *samizdat* (clandestine publication) or *tamizdat* (overseas and likewise unsanctioned publication). In the main, they have not sought these unofficial outlets in order to publish works that are particularly experimental in form or are in some other way an outgrowth of the "new prose" of the early sixties. Most *samizdat* and *tamizdat* publications (other than manifestos, articles, or light reading matter) are either memoirs or fictional exposés of Soviet oppression (the camps, detention of dissidents in mental hospitals, etc.) or contain critiques of Soviet society presented from a religious or some other traditional Russian (as distinct from Soviet) point of view. As far as form goes, they are not markedly different from the sort of writing being published in the Soviet Union. They also resemble official literature in being heavily didactic.[1]

The majority of Soviet writers, including those who have recently emigrated or who publish through unofficial channels, have rejected Westernism and posit some counterideal embodied in what they interpret to be traditionally (or uniquely) Russian values. In some cases, both in fiction and criticism, this tendency has been taken to an extreme: some works have been colored by anti-Semitic or chauvinist sentiments.[2]

The traditional impulse characterizes most recent writing, but not all. Since Khrushchev, Soviet literature, both official and unofficial, has been much more diverse than at any time since the twenties. There is a marked pluralism, not only in literary trends but in the points of view represented within each trend.

Yet, for all the surface variety and controversy, Soviet literature of the past fifteen years or so displays some of the same pervasive concerns and dialectical tendencies as in the Stalin period; one still finds the "machine" and "garden," "fathers and sons," and so on. Recent Soviet fiction (and much unofficial writing) grew out of, rather than away from, the traditions that preceded it. Although it is, de facto, no longer mandatory to use the conventions of Socialist Realism that were standard under Stalin, fiction is not entirely independent of them. Even when writers advocate values they believe to be opposed to Stalinist values, they often articulate them against the old patterns. Thus those patterns still have some currency as a code through which meaning can be conveyed symbolically.

In the literature written in the past fifteen years there have been two primary areas of debate, in each of which there are positions both pro and contra and then subdivisions within each general position. Fiction has, on the one hand, explored the whole issue of Stalinism; hence the literature of destalinization and *its* detractors, the neo-Stalinists. On the other hand, it has been obsessed with the evils of life in the modern age; hence the fiction of the city and its opposite, the anti-urbanist, or "village prose" fiction. The two debates are far from mutually exclusive: "village prose," for instance, is often anti-Stalinist.

In anti-Stalinist fiction, the two aspects of Stalin's time that have attracted the most attention are World War II and the abuses committed in the name of collectivization. Not all fiction attacking the Stalin era is infused with liberal sentiment. A recent exposé of the excesses committed in the months leading up to collectivization, V. Belov's *On the Eve* (1976), reflects the rise of Russian chauvinism in its hints that the oppressors and zealots were the Jews.[3]

Since the mid-sixties, the advocates of destalinization have encountered strong opposition. Some authors have broken the taboo of the Khrushchev years and have praised the Stalin era and its leaders. This tendency, the so-called neo-Stalinism, must not be confused with Stalinism itself. The neo-Stalinists look to the Stalin era as a time of unity, strong rule, and national honor, but they do not necessarily want a return to the Stalinism of large-scale terror and the purges.

The neo-Stalinists have chosen for their fiction topics that might help rebuild a sense of pride in the Soviet past and present. A favorite is, as with the anti-Stalinists, World War II. For the neo-Stalinists, the twenty million lives lost in the war provide a convenient counter to the comparable number lost during the Stalinist terror. Also, the war has become a favorite example for claims of Russian superiority (since claims to superiority in space flight have fast become less viable). An alternative topic for those who seek to rebuild a sense of pride in the Soviet past and present is spy and detective fiction, a new genre as far as orthodox Soviet fiction is concerned. That veteran neo-Stalinist, Vs. Kochetov, entered into the new vogue with *What More Do You Want?* (1969), an exposé of the international anti-Soviet conspiracy.

A good example of neo-Stalinist prose is A. Chakovsky's epic novel about the 900-day blockade of Leningrad during World War II. *The Blockade* (1968–73) describes how the Russians finally triumphed through sheer determination, sacrifice, and effective, unflinching leadership, i.e., because the people and their leaders exhibited a set of distinctively Stalinist qualities. The book is full of passages that could have been lifted wholesale from a Stalinist text ("Muscovites... rarely missed an opportunity to go by the Red Square to ascertain with joy that, despite the latest air raid, the Kremlin stood firm.... Perhaps, even now, there, in one of the [Kremlin] studies, Stalin is thinking up something that will radically change the entire course of the war!").[4]

More recently it has seemed that the Stalinist hagiographic tradition is being revived at the highest levels. In 1978 the literary journal *Novy mir* published an autobiographical trilogy by the general secretary of the Soviet Communist Party, Leonid Ilich Brezhnev: *Little Earth*, about his wartime experiences; *Regeneration*, about how he guided the postwar reconstruction effort in the two regions he administered; and *The Virgin Lands*, about the Virgin Lands scheme in Kazakhstan initiated under Khrushchev, which Brezhnev likewise directed. In 1979 Brezhnev was awarded a Lenin Prize (the highest award) for these memoirs, and an oratorio "The White Bird," based on *The Virgin Lands*, was performed in Moscow.

These memoirs smack of the cult of personality, which the Khrushchev era supposedly dismantled. They remind one of the

Stalinist variety of autohagiography, where "all the threads" of the administration pass through the hands of one man, who is constantly achieving what by normal reckoning is impossible. It is not merely the elevated tone, the recurrence of the old epithets, such as "stern" and "calm," and the superabundance of heroes and fantastic feats that make these memoirs seem neo-Stalinist; it is the fact that in them the author extols certain attitudes toward governance that were meant to have been discredited in the Khrushchev era. He decries, for instance, the notion that "tempos" at work should be geared to what is "possible" to achieve rather than to what is "mandatory."[5]

Despite the fact that this trend is fostered at the highest levels, it in no way dominates the literary scene today as it did in the thirties and forties. It is really only in neo-Stalinist fiction that the Stalinist clichés live on. In most other prose there is very little of the elevated tone and the use of ritualized patterns that one associates with Stalinism. This is especially true of the most common type of urban prose, so-called *byt* prose (prose of everyday life).

Byt prose tells of unexceptional lives in unexceptional places. Its urban setting *may* be Moscow or Leningrad, but that fact is not in itself remarkable. In other words, the setting is unrelated to the conventional opposition, Moscow/far away from Moscow. The characters are, likewise, unexceptional both in terms of their standing in society and in terms of their moral fiber. They are, in the words of one work, "neither better nor worse than anyone else."[6] (Cf. the Stalinist catchphrase, "the best people.")

Byt prose deals with moral problems, primarily in a family context. Its authors bear witness to the sorry state of Soviet man, to the problems of parenthood, to rampant acquisitiveness, moral indifference, alcoholism, self-seeking, and philistinism. One typical example is V. Sëmin's *Seven in One House* (1965), a novella about a working war widow and her losing battle to keep her fatherless son from becoming a ne'er-do-well; the climax occurs when the son shoots someone in a drunken brawl. Another is Y. Trifonov's "The Exchange" (1969), about a heartless young woman who seeks to have her terminally ill mother-in-law move to another apartment in order to maximize the young couple's apartment space after the mother-in-law's death.

The authors of such works have their little quibbles with Soviet institutions and policies, and especially with the large-scale corruption and indifference that seem to be destroying Soviet society from within. But these kinds of criticism have always been around in Soviet literature, and they have been especially prominent since Stalin's death. *Byt* prose is different from fiction of the Khrushchev era because typically it finds neither Stalinism nor Soviet society itself to be the main cause of the moral quagmire depicted; death, divorce, neglect, and human frailty are frequently the major offenders.

Of course, *byt* prose does not have to be very elevated, because it does not depict leaders or important public figures. But the increasingly prosaic trend is reflected even in the most "heroic" kind of recent fiction, the neo-Stalinist. Even though A. Chakovsky's *The Blockade*, for instance, contains much of the extravagant rhetoric typical of Stalinist heroic prose, it cannot be called Stalinist heroic prose because the author pays great attention to specific historical details and to the individual roles played in the war by the commanders. He uses that time-worn Stalinist system of signs for indicating the moral and political identity of his protagonists, but these features do not dominate the narrative. Protagonists are not complete subfunctions of their traditional roles, and the plot is shaped less by History than by history—albeit a somewhat partial view of history.

Recent writing has been less schematic, not only in comparison with Stalinist fiction but with fiction of the Khrushchev era as well. It is no longer as naive as mid-fifties prose, when the way out of Stalinism seemed clear, or as glibly schematic as in the late fifties, when a quick readjustment of the master plot provided a formula for resolving the post-Stalinist *Angst*. Now the problems are less readily solved. "Who is guilty?" is a constant refrain. But the answer seems less clear. It is certainly no longer the old-style bureaucrat in the local administration. Increasingly it is not even found to be Stalinism per se (the terror and all that). This is partly because authors no longer present clear-cut situations involving good and evil, but, as often as not, what Sëmin calls it in *Seven in One House,* "senselessness." He himself concludes that, in this "senselessness," "we are all guilty."[7] But how can "we" find a way out? Since Soviet fiction of the past decade has largely abandoned the convention of using a father figure (or older brother) to show the way forward, the protagonists are left at the end still leading their prosaic, imperfect lives.

A good example of this trend is Yury Trifonov's recent novel about the Stalin period, *The House on the Embankment* (1976). This book is interesting because in several respects it represents a reworking of Trifonov's earlier novel, *Students* (1950), which, although not without ambiguous sections,[8] was written under the guise, at least, of a loyalist novel about the anticosmopolitan and antiformalist campaign in higher education. The new book has been written not to reverse the valorization of the protagonists, as would probably have been the case in the Khrushchev years, for those purged do not now become martyred victims, in contrast to their role as unworthy persons in a Zhdanovist book like *Students*. Instead, virtually *everyone* is unworthy. Accusers and accused seem to be locked in an unending game of *kto kogo* (who will get whom first), and few of the bystanders drawn into the game against their will have the moral fiber to come through the experiment with their integrity intact.

Trifonov seems to have returned to his old subject not merely to blacken the picture of society he painted before. There was a strong aesthetic motive, too. He wanted to produce a work more complex than its predecessor both structurally and thematically. For example, he flaunts the distinction between what the Formalists called "plot" (*fabula*) and "story" (*sjužet*), using flashbacks, omissions, and surmises to keep the two from converging.

In these respects, *The House on the Embankment* typifies the recent trend in fiction, which has been away from mythic writing and toward what we in the West would call "fiction." Indeed, even though Brezhnev won a state literary prize for his distinctly "mythic" memoirs, it is also true that, just two years earlier, the same prize was awarded to a work that was both totally unheroic in its subject matter and nonmythical in its approach, Valentin Rasputin's *Live and Remember* (1974).[9] This work concerns a peasant from a remote Siberian village who deserts from the army toward the end of World War II. He returns to his village and lives in the wilds nearby, carving out a sort of Robinson Crusoe existence for himself, aided by his wife, the only person to whom he reveals his presence, and who brings him the bare necessities for survival. She becomes pregnant, and, when this is discovered by the villagers, they condemn her at first as an adulteress but then suspect that her deserter husband may be the father and may still be hiding in the neighborhood. They begin to follow her. One day, when she discovers that they are trailing her as she rows across the river to see her husband, she breaks down under the strain of the moral dilemmas and subterfuges that have oppressed her for so long, and in her distraught state she drowns.

This work stands in contrast to Stalinist or neo-Stalinist fiction not merely for its sensitive treatment of its subject, a deserter, but also for its emphasis on the inner lives of the characters. Different points of view are dramatized in long quasi-direct interior monologues. Such features are becoming increasingly typical in recent Soviet fiction.

Village Prose

Even though Soviet literature has become more prosaic of late, there is, lurking not far beneath the surface of all this prose, an opposing impulse to lyricism and idealization. The collective verdict of most recent writing is that somehow the country has lost its way to the Golden Age and will not find it again merely by readjusting the present (e.g., by eradicating Stalinist practices) or by sending everyone "far away from Moscow" to some place where true revolutionary values still prevail. Moscow still stands and is, moreover, much more populous and influential than any far-flung construction site.

Writers began to recommend a journey "far away from Moscow" not in place but in time. One can see that happening even in the fifties; in 1957, for instance, the year of the youth novel, A. Soloukhin in his sketch "The Hamlets of Vladimir" waxed lyrical about his trip to a place which, though not distant geographically a mere two hundred kilometers from Moscow, went back in time to the traditional Russia of the village hamlet, to a world of forests, fields, and churches.

Not all writers of this period recommended a journey so far back in time, but most found a panacea for the age's ills in reviving the spirit of an earlier time. Fiction of the sixties and seventies provides a spectrum of nostalgia: the neo-Stalinists wanted a revival of the

heroic age of the Stalin era, a time when men were men and orders
were orders and everyone respected each other; some of the self-
styled avant-garde looked wistfully at the twenties, while others
took eighteenth-century models; and so on.

In recent years the majority of writers have, like Soloukhin,
wanted a revival of the earlier time represented by rural Russia.
Like the authors of the youth fiction of the fifties, they speak of the
possibility of regeneration in a place "far away from Moscow," a
garden world. Their garden is one of wholeness and tranquillity
rather than of storms and struggle (as in late-fifties prose), although
there is a touch of Scythianism in works by several writers, who
have revived the twenties cult of Stenka Razin as a quintessentially
Russian figure in his impulsiveness, rebelliousness, and expansive-
ness.[10]

The beginnings of this movement appeared quite early in the
Khrushchev period. Most associate it with E. Dorosh's first (1953)
sketch in his series "Village Diary," although, as I pointed out in the
chapter on the forties (chapter 9, p. 207, above), there are hints of it
even in such orthodox Zhdanovist prose as P. Pavlenko's *Happiness* (1947).

By the late fifties, writers were feeling increasingly less con-
strained to transplant their jaded urban types into a kolkhoz or
construction site in order to restore them. A vogue developed for
wild, remote settings, untouched by most aspects of twentieth-
century life. The hero could, as in Nagibin's tales, be on a hunting
expedition, or he could, as in many short stories by Kazakov, go to
the wilderness on vacation or for a quiet sojourn. Once there, he
would come into contact with essences both wild and pure. Increasingly, however, the hero found in the backwoods not so much
a primal contact with nature as spiritual regeneration. The author
no longer left the church out of the garden, and in work after work
the hero finds balm and wholeness in a setting that includes "a little
hamlet," "a white church," a "lake," a "forest," and a "bath-
house."[11] He finds, in other words, the iconic version of the traditional Russian village. If such a one is not to be found, he then goes
back even further in his symbolic quest through time and finds his
perfect peace in that home of the earliest Russian settlers, the forest
itself. This sort of writing was called "village prose."

Unlike the authors of those infamous Stalinist pastorals, the authors of village prose write out of an explicitly *Gesellschaft* world. They emphasize all the evils of the pluralistic "city" because these evils enhance (by contrast) the joys of country life depicted in their schematic opposition between "city" and "village." In other words, *byt* prose could be called village prose that never got as far as the countryside. In village prose, the city stands for pollution, corruption, ugliness, indifference, and, above all, alienation, while the village stands for the true sense of family and human bonds, for natural existence, for honest labor and craftsmanship, for that which is truly Russian, and perhaps even for closeness to God. These qualities do not necessarily obtain in the *Soviet* village, and much of village prose is concerned with the decline of the village in recent years: churches have been destroyed or misused, the old crafts have been forgotten, kolkhoz regulations frustrate farmers—they can no longer use nature's bounty for their food and warmth and are dependent on the limited supplies available in the village store, etc.

It might seem that village prose would be anathema to the Soviet government, since, potentially, it entails some form of religious revival, questions the assumption that material progress is the chief goal, deprecates technological achievement, and delivers sharp criticisms at government management of the villages. In general, however, writers of village prose have been relatively free from harassment because of the strong nationalist sentiment that guides them (one voice heard in opposition was that of V. Kochetov: in his exposé of Western infiltration into Soviet cultural life, *What More Do You Want?* of 1969, he found space for satirizing village prose as well).[12] Village-prose writers, in their capacity as lobbyists for environmental control, for restoration of churches and other antiquities, for preserving national traditions, and for paying attention to the plight of rural people, merely take particular stands in the ongoing public debates of recent years (some positive changes have in fact been made: the lot of rural folk has been ameliorated, churches have been restored, more attention has been paid to ecology, etc.). The religiosity of much village prose is of course more problematical, but it is generally expressed in muted, ambiguous, or figurative fashion.

Despite the respectable position that village prose occupies in modern Soviet literature, its purest expressions are found predominantly in underground and émigré publications. In such texts one

commonly encounters the notion that, in the Soviet Union, paradise
has been lost and can be regained only by a historical reversal,
preferably one involving a return to Christianity and the communal
way of life. A good example of this is the parable told by a priest in
V. Maksimov's novel *The Seven Days of Creation* (1971). The
parable tells of the "City" where all have lived in harmony for a
thousand years (a period of time that corresponds roughly to the
length of time Russia has been Christian). The community's peace is
disturbed when "a certain person" comes and preaches a new approach to life—one that sacrifices the present in the name of a
glorious future—and he leads the weak in spirit among the city-
dwellers to orgies of suffering, violence, and purging (clearly intended to represent the Soviet era). The parable's conclusion is that
the only way out of the debacle is to take all the children away "to
the villages," where they will not be corrupted.[13] The novel's central character, Lashkov, a Party member and retired bureaucrat, is
so troubled on hearing this parable early in the novel that he enters
into a period of doubt and quest. The novel ends with the words
"He knew and believed." Then follows the heading for a hypothetical final part of the novel (left blank): "And Then Came the Seventh
Day, a Day of Hope and Resurrection."

Such faith and certainty do not characterize most of the village-
prose writers who publish in the Soviet Union; their works are full
of doubts, ambiguities, and contradictions. Those who publish with
tamizdat have, by choosing sides (or by being propelled to one side
through involuntary emigration), opted for (or acquired) a resolution of the *Angst* that torments their brothers still wrestling with the
quandaries of Soviet reality. There is a consequent lack of tension in
much *tamizdat* fiction, a certain sameness.

Even in the early sixties, Soviet writers began to express doubts
that city-dwellers could any longer find peace in idyllic, remote
villages. In Kazakov's suggestively titled "Adam and Eve" of 1962,
for instance, a neurotic, disaffected artist travels with his girl to a
beautiful Karelian island, but its magic cannot work for him. He
sends the girl back and remains a sort of transplanted underground
man, alone with his bitterness and perversity. For such hard cases,
paradise has been lost and can no longer be regained. Perhaps if,
like the proud, troubled spirits of Dostoevsky's fiction, they were to
accept God, they might find the way back to the garden again? This

is the unanswered question that continues to hang over village prose even now.

Village-prose writers have oscillated between presenting their garden ideal and retreating from it into a self-flagellating description of the glaring reality of actual village life or even into self-parody. From time to time they confront the hard question "Where is the country and where is the city, anyway?" In modern times those ugly boxes of Soviet cities have been put up all over the countryside. There are factories everywhere you turn, too. In Soloukhin's "The Hamlets of Vladimir" the city pilgrim suddenly finds the rural garden he traverses violated by the stench and smoke of nearby metalworks.[14] Even Solzhenitsyn's emblem for the goodly people of yore, Matryona of "Matryona's Homestead" (1963), has crude Soviet posters hanging in the very heart of her traditional wooden cottage.[15]

Perhaps the presence of the city in the garden should be eradicated, resisted, ignored? Perhaps one should revive the spirit rather than the trappings of the old village? But how can it be transmitted? In story after story, city folk come back to the village to see their long-lost kin, only to find that they cannot shed their artificial ways and so gain contact with the life-force and with their fellows. Perhaps what they feel they have lost was a mirage anyway? Perhaps their imaginations have been captivated by a tableau vision of "the village" that has little relation to the dynamic reality of village life? In F. Abramov's *The Wooden Horses* (1970), for instance, a city-dweller sojourning in a remote village savors every example he can find of local crafts. For him the carved wooden horses that decorate several houses in the village, and in olden times adorned dozens more, symbolize the falling-away from the glory of old village life. But an old peasant woman tells him of the barbarity and hardship of those days.[16]

The village has become a symbolic panacea for the evils of modern life, and especially for that greatest evil of all: alienation. In the nineteenth century, Marx had proposed communism as a solution to the alienation of *Gesellschaft* society. Many Russians had been attracted by this as a "scientific" solution to the country's manifold social contradictions. Now, it seems, the intelligentsia is back at the crossroads again, only with a renewed sense of loss.

Thus, village prose tells of a fall from the garden. Most writers articulate this by either bemoaning the sad decline of the village or musing that the man of the city should—but probably cannot—go back to that simpler, purer life of country folk. The city/country opposition was not the only nexus of symbols used by writers in recent years. Another favorite was the end of innocence or the violation of the innocent (especially children and animals). But, together with the "village," the second key metaphor of this era has been, as in High Stalinism, the family.

The Family as Metaphor

In both literature and rhetoric of the Stalin era the family, with its connotations of unity, bonds, and a common cause, was a crucial symbol. In this period it was also used in literature as a metaphor for wholeness, but in a different way. Wholeness is that lost quality that writers have been seeking over the past two decades. Even the neo-Stalinists seek wholeness. What they seek to revive is the kind of certitude and unity one can see in the Stalinist statue used as an emblem by Mosfilm, in which the kolkhoz girl and the factory lad look forward as one.

Most other writers of this period seem less concerned with unity in the "great" family. Their attention is focused on the "little," or extended nuclear, family. One of their perennial themes is death in the family or some other form of separation. The reality of Soviet life in every decade has of course provided countless variations on this theme. There were deaths in the purges and in the various wars. Families were split up by the purges, by the war, or simply by members being posted to different places. Also, the changing sociological composition tended to divide families; often, for instance, one or another member went from the village to the city to study or work and formed a new, unrelated family there. Finally, there are the "deaths" and "separations" that characterize human relationships even in relatively normal times, such as separations of couples, divorce, estrangement between husband and wife, between stepparent and child, and even between parent and child. Soviet literature of the past two decades deals with all manner of deaths and separations within the "little family," but a particular favorite has been separation of a son from his father, whether through death or estrangement; there is, in other words, discontinuity in that crucial line from father to son. The son has no mentor to guide him. Thus, as in Stalinist fiction, death and figurative death have played a major role in recent Soviet prose, but death is now a divisive rather than an enabling or heroic event. Even a death that occurred in the purges is no longer mentioned simply as an instance of Stalinist heinousness and arbitrariness. Such a death is but one of the many tribulations that reflect the historical condition of the society. Fractured families are a reality of Soviet life, and the Stalinist terror is a contributing cause. But ultimately the fractured families are in themselves only a metaphor for discontinuity and alienation, for failing to find "the garden."

While much recent fiction has been concerned with exploring and diagnosing the condition of Soviet society, some has been inspired by an idealistic vision. A good example is Boris Vasiliev's *Don't Shoot at White Swans!* (1973). Vasiliev's work is almost quintessential village prose in that its theme is the ending of innocence and wholeness when the city intrudes into the village. In his chosen setting—a remote northern forest—this intrusion occurs when electricity, the factory, and the train are introduced and the forest is cut down in consequence. In other words, Vasiliev uses the conventional Russian symbols for nature and the modern age; moreover, he explicitly uses negatively that major Leninist symbol, electricity. The result of this importation of "the modern" into the forest lands is not "light," as Lenin believed, but virtual rape. It brings with it ugliness, graft, a bureaucratic mentality that does not tolerate individuality or exercise of the imagination, and, above all, senselessness. As the hero, Egor, expresses it, in poetic, folksy language: " . . . we are orphans. We are not at peace with our mother earth; we have quarreled with our father the forest, and, with our sister the river, there has been a bitter separation. We have nothing to stand on."[17]

As if to compensate for this harsh assault on fundamental Leninist values, Vasiliev uses more of the master plot's conventions than one generally finds in recent fiction. As in forties fiction, for instance, Vasiliev structures much of his moral argument in terms of false and true family members. He counterposes two families of relatives, one false and the other true. Each family comprises the same members: father, mother, and a son of the same age. The values of father and son in one family are the exact opposite of

those held by the other pair. In the "good family," Egor and his son
Kolka are unmaterialistic, good-natured, and lovers of the forest
who suffer whenever it or any of its animals is harmed; deeply
sensitive, they are, in their own way, creative people. Egor is uneducated but artistic and has a craftsman's sense of pride in his
work. Kolka does not do well at conventional school but is a natural poet. In the "bad family" of Egor's in-laws, both father and son
are mercenary, have a cynical attitude toward work, are dishonest,
cruel to animals; lovers of modern life, they scorn the primitive
ways of the village.

The conflict is not contained within the "little family" but reaches
into the hero's public life. Here Egor is almost a complete failure.
Several times he is dismissed from work because of some incident
provoked by the fact that his impulses do not coincide with the
expectations of his jaded, literalistic employers (and once because
scornful big-city types get him drunk and he loses a state-owned
motorboat in the lake). He becomes a virtual laughingstock of the
community; the general attitude is that he should learn to use the
system to his advantage.

As in Stalinist fiction, however, it is the petty *local* officials who
are corrupt and unprincipled. The hero finds more care and sympathy when he goes "higher." First he finds it in the new local
forestry officer. Then, through this forester, Egor is invited to a big
congress in Moscow. In a scene which could have been lifted from
countless books of the Stalin period, Egor is unexpectedly asked to
speak to the congress. At first he is speechless. Then, with the
encouragement of a very high government official, he begins to lose
his nervousness and to express his ideas about misuse of the forests
in recent years and about what should be done in national parks.
The official is so impressed that he has the conference resolve to
have Egor's ideas adopted.

The denouement is tragic. Egor discovers that the old name for the
local lake was Swan Lake. While he is in Moscow, he obtains two
swans and takes them back to be the foundation of a new flock for
the lake (a symbol for restoration of the beauty of antiquity). One
night, however, the same city types who had caused Egor's earlier
downfall return to the lake and in drunken jest kill the swans,
intending to eat them. An enraged Egor confronts them but is fa-
tally beaten by the revelers. In this tragic ending Vasiliev re-

capitulates the ending of Gorky's *Mother,* where the defiant mother is beaten to death by the tsarist police, but his story closes on a less elevated note. In *Mother,* readers sense the ongoing generations of revolutionaries who will pick up the mother's baton and bear it forward to the triumph of the revolutionary cause, but Egor's successor, Kolka, can no longer bring himself to go to the lake, and his poetry becomes "disjointed and unreadable." Vasiliev concludes, somewhat unconvincingly, that it is now up to the kolkhoz to change the lake's name to "Swan."[18]

A second example of fiction informed by an idealistic vision, Chingiz Aitmatov's *The White Steamer* (1970), is set in a veritable paradise, a Kirghiz settlement on the edge of virgin woods, high in the mountains. The hero is a young Kirghiz boy who is brought up by his grandfather, who feeds his imagination with Kirghiz lore. The boy's favorite is the legend about the mountain deer he sees on the nearby slopes, who saved the Kirghiz people by leading them away from adversity to the mountain paradise. For this the deer is now recognized as the sacred animal and "mother" of the Kirghiz people.

The boy's lot is not a happy one. The novella chronicles a series of affronts to his innocence: first his parents' divorce and his abandonment by his father, then the debauchery indulged in by his mother and other kin, the corruption of local officials, and even the cold officiousness at the school he had joined with such expectations. Through all this the boy is comforted by his grandfather, by the presence of the deer, and by a white steamer he can see plying the waters of a distant lake. He believes that his father is riding in the boat.

The final affront to the boy's innocence comes when his grandfather betrays him by leading hunters from the town to haunts where they can kill the mountain deer. An orgy of alcohol and eating follows. The boy is so revolted and distraught that he becomes ill. In his delirious state he walks out of the house and into a mountain stream, where he drowns. The force of the stream carries him to the lake and to the "white steamer."

Of the many "gardens" in village prose, the "garden" whose loss Aitmatov laments is perhaps closest to the original Garden of Adam and Eve, for what is lost is the purity and innocence of the child. But there are certain defining and typical constants his work shares with

Vasiliev's *Don't Shoot at White Swans!* First, both heroes die a
martyr's death at the hands of callous and indifferent people. They
instinctively reject modern life, and their one link with the past—
Egor's swans and the Kirghiz boy's deer—is destroyed. They are too
pure for this imperfect world, and without this link with the past
there is nothing to carry them through the vale; so they must die.
Even those "near and dear" are not to be trusted (Egor's son Kolka
is something of an exception). Death is the only way to escape from the forces that conspire to
destroy "the garden." Only in death can one reenter it (compare the
fate of the protagonists in Bulgakov's novel, *The Master and Mar-*
garita). Ultimately, "consciousness" does not lead one to the kingdom of *Gemeinschaft*. Rather, as nineteenth-century literature
chronicled so well, it is consciousness in the other sense—self-
consciousness, awareness—that keeps *Gemeinschaft* forever out of
reach.

Conclusion

Socialist Realism has been the dominant mode in Soviet literature for the past fifty years. No matter how "unnaturally" it was developed and maintained, it cannot, by the nature of literary systems, have been completely "inorganic." There must, therefore, have been something in Socialist Realism that was connected to the needs and drives that existed in Russian literary history before the appearance of Socialist Realism.

There are, in fact, several elements that Socialist Realism shares not only with nineteenth-century Russian literature and thought but with much of the "unofficial literature" of recent years, and these are elements, moreover, that are either absent or markedly less pronounced in Western literature. Among them is the idea, accepted by all factions, that literature must have more than aesthetic significance. In the nineteenth century this idea was reflected either in didacticism or in the outright desire to prophesy, as in Dostoevsky or Gogol. A related feature is the search for a "positive hero," which dominated Russian fiction of the second half of the nineteenth century. Although the high literature of that century never had anything remotely resembling a master plot, there are some formal similarities between its tradition and Socialist Realism, including, for example, the utopian resolution of difficulties at the end (Western readers have always deplored such "unrealistic endings" as Levin's epiphany in the apiary, which concludes *Anna Karenina,* or Raskolnikov's last-minute conversion in the epilogue to *Crime and Punishment*).

The two traditions also have much in common thematically. Socialist Realism's emphasis on the workingman can be seen, for instance, as a transformation of the traditional Russian respect for the common man, so evident not only in Tolstoy's fiction but in that of many other nineteenth-century writers. Also, many of the seeming quirks and forced situations that one finds in typical Stalinist prose have counterparts in nineteenth-century and recent "unofficial" prose. The longing for a *Gemeinschaft* world and the nostalgia for the world of "nature," the source of so many incongruities in High Stalinist fiction, are in fact common sentiments of the old Russian intelligentsia, as are the ideals of the martyr-hero and of historical self-transcendence.

Ideology is no stranger to the Russian novel in any of its manifestations. What is different about the Soviet novel is, first, the *particular* ideology that informs it, which—except in isolated cases, such as Gorky's *Mother*—was not invoked before. Second, ideology plays a particular historical role in the relationship between literature and the government.

This relationship is very different in the Soviet period from what it was under the tsars, although much of the difference is one of degree only; for several nineteenth-century writers—Goncharov, for example—worked as censors, Dostoevsky was close to the tsar's advisor Pobedonosetsov, and in the 1830s the infamous Bulgarin worked as a government agent. Thus, during the old regime there were writers who shared the official ideology, and the government itself played a monitoring role in nineteenth-century literature. The chief difference between the tsarist and Soviet situations is the fact that the Soviet government has not only censored the writers—has told them what they must *not* write; it has also told them what they *must* write.

Despite all these parallels, there is one difference between the two traditions that is fateful and decisive: the function each has served in the cultural ecology containing it is very different. Instead of doing what we have come to think of as the work of literature, Socialist Realism performs an essentially mythological task. It is mythic in the degree to which it supports and explains the main thrust of the politically dominant forces in its society. The master plot is the thread that stitches together several significant layers of culture, including its theory of history, its philosophical anthropology, and its literary presuppositions.

The conclusion to be drawn is not, however, that literature in the Soviet Union necessarily became merely an elephant's graveyard for the reigning political doctrines. It would be wrong to think that Socialist Realism was simply dictated by the demands of the government. It was, rather, a forcing bed for culturally viable rituals.

As Lotman has recently reminded us, societies act like information-processing systems; that is, literature was not only a receiver of signals but a sender of them. It has been pointed out often enough that Socialist Realism has much in common with other manifestations of Stalinism as a cultural style. This is not because the style was worked out in conference rooms and then poured into neutral literary vessels. On the contrary, as I have shown in this book, much of the cultural style, even the most dominant existential clichés of Stalinism, derived from literary models—a particular, and in some cases particularly sinister, example of what Oscar Wilde meant when he complained that "Life imitates art."

In the Soviet Union, the story in myth (Socialist Realism) informs the rituals of the culture in which it exists. There is a mutual interdependence between myth and ritual, and it operates dialectically.

When this process is looked at in terms of literary history, the evolution of Socialist Realism is seen to provide examples of Tynyanov and Jakobson's assertion, in their Theses of 1928 (*Problems in the Study of Literature and Language*), that literary history consists of a constant selection of certain possibilities and the discarding of others that are available in the tradition. The particular literary possibilities canonized in Socialist Realism were those that had power to interact with the new ideologies that had become dominant. What was kept was kept because it served a function in the new conditions; yet, as a part of the new tradition, these surviving elements of the old tradition would have an effect on literature's further evolution. Thus, as Socialist Realism was taking form in the 1920s, it adopted elements from disparate literary schools, including even Symbolism, but it did so only insofar as these elements could illuminate the unique needs of the twenties.

Socialist Realism thus played a central role in Russian cultural life, a role guaranteed by the power of its symbolic forms to encompass the major cultural forces abroad in both literature and politics. The history of Socialist Realism is, then, not only a history of Soviet literature, but is itself a constitutive element in recent Russian history.

The Master Plot as
Exemplified in the Production Novel and Other
Basic Types of Novel
of the Stalin Era

There are several different types of Soviet novel. A possible thematic division would consist of the production novel plus five other
basic types: the historical novel, the novel about a worthy intellectual or inventor, the novel of war or revolution, the villain or
spy novel, and the novel about the West. The differences between
these types are not as great as they might seem, since all involve,
minimally, a "road to consciousness" pattern and usually a "task"
as well. The historical novel, for instance, is usually a novel about
leadership (as in A. Tolstoy's *Peter the First*) or, simply, political
maturation (as in V. Kataev's *A Lonely White Sail Gleams*). The
novel about a worthy intellectual or inventor usually follows much
the same plot outline as a production novel (the hero's "task"
being, in this instance, to write or invent something or to get a new
idea approved), except that more attention is paid to the hero's
struggles with the enemies of "truth" than to his encounters with
the practical problems of task fulfillment or with natural disasters.

The three remaining categories—novels about war or revolution,
novels about villains or spies, and novels about the West—are less
conventionalized. Instead of being set in a single microcosm, they
are often somewhat picaresque. Generally speaking, the novel of
war or revolution combines a tale of moral and political growth
with a tale of task fulfillment. Both the villain or spy novel and the
novel about the West contain a higher proportion of negative material than is customary in a Soviet novel; nevertheless, they usually
entail a positive hero who is learning to be sufficiently strong to
combat the foe, i.e., Western decadence or his love for an alien.
Since he must become aloof and "ruthless," he must, in terms of the
conventions of the Socialist Realist novel, become more "conscious." In other words, these novels usually entail a "road to consciousness" also.

The Production Novel

The most common type of Stalinist novel *by far* is the production novel (the novel about how the plan was fulfilled or the project was constructed). It is also the most highly ritualized. Since it typically contains more formulaic stages in its plot than a novel like the one I analyzed in my account of the master plot in chapter 7, Fadeev's *The Young Guard* (a war novel), it deserves some attention here.

Below I have set out a general scheme for the plot stages of a typical production novel—the novel type that uses the master plot in its fullest version. My scheme is not as elaborate or finely differentiated as the one Propp presents in his *Morphology;* [1] instead of his thirty-one specific plot functions, I have provided only six broad divisions, designed to show how the production novel fuses the tale of task fulfillment with that of the hero's ritual maturation. These broad divisions are then further divided into their most customary components.

Propp asserts in his *Morphology* that any one of the thirty-one functions he lists in his table may be omitted in a given tale but that the *order* of functions is fixed. This is not so in the Stalinist novel, where not only is the sequence very flexible within a given section of the plot (Transition, Finale, etc.), but a particular function may occur in a section other than the one in which it is listed here (e.g., "death," which is listed below as function b of the Climax section, may occur in the Finale). The order in which I present them, although it is the most conventional and logical, is therefore not invariable.

The production novel more or less originated with *Cement*. It will be remembered, however, that *Cement* did not have as tightly organized a plot as the later, full-blown Socialist Realist novel; hence, some of the actions normally performed by either the positive hero or his mentor are, in *Cement,* performed by more peripheral characters of no clear moral and political identity, such as the purged bourgeois Party member, Sergey. To illustrate this divergence, the corresponding moment in *Cement*'s plot is indicated below in square brackets after each function listed.

Prologue or "Separation"

The hero arrives in the microcosm, the small, fairly closed world of the novel. This may be a factory, a kolkhoz, a machine tractor station, an army unit, or a provincial town. Often (as in *The Young Guard*) the hero's arrival in the microcosm is actually a return to a place he had been before, but it is now changed. [Gleb is demobilized from the army and returns to his factory town.]

Setting Up the Task

(a) The hero sees that all is not good in the microcosm. This most often means that the state-given plan is not being fulfilled or is being fulfilled at a lax "tempo." [*Cement* predates the era of the Five-Year plans, but the Party directive to step up post–Civil War reconstruction is equivalent to the Plan of later novels; Gleb sees the factory idle, petty-bourgeois values rampant, and the local officials insufficiently committed to reconstruction.]

(b) The hero concocts a scheme for righting the wrong, often—as it happens—thinking along somewhat the same lines as the state and local "people." [Gleb decides on a way of rebuilding the factory and solving the fuel-supply problems; his plan coincides with the deepest desires of all of the town's true workers (Brynza, Savchuk, etc.).]

(c) When the hero presents his plan to the local bureaucrats, they say it is "utopian"—that it would be impossible to fulfill it in terms of both technical feasibility and available manpower and supplies. Also, they commonly claim that the hero's plan runs counter to their orders from above. [In *Cement,* all these elements are present.]

(d) The hero mobilizes "the people" and inspires them to follow his plan by addressing them at a mass meeting, at which his powers as an orator are displayed, and / or by talking to them in smaller groups. Usually he also finds a minority group among the local bureaucrats (the noncareerists) who support his proposals [this is the pattern followed in *Cement*].

Transition (Trials, etc.)

(a) Work on the hero's project begins.

(b) Work is hampered by a series of snags, which, like the "obstacles" of folk narrative, can occur in various forms and any number of times. Since the Stalinist novel is truly a combination of "the most matter-of-fact, everyday reality and the most heroic prospects" (à la the Zhdanov formula presented in his speech to the First Writers' Congress in 1934), these obstacles are usually of two orders:

  i. *Prosaic:* Problems with supplies, manpower, or equipment; bureaucratic corruption or slackness; worker apathy or discontent. [Gleb is faced by all of these.]
  ii. *Dramatic/heroic (mythic):* Natural disasters, enemy invasions, class enemies, counterrevolutionary terrorists, struggle with an antagonistic bureaucrat. [Gleb is faced with all of these except the natural disaster. Also, it is never clear whether his bureaucratic antagonist, Badin, is a positive or negative figure.]

(c) The hero has a problem in his love life and/or in controlling his emotions. [Gleb is estanged from his wife, Dasha, and he cannot master his hatred of Badin.]

(d) The hero makes a journey (perhaps only by telephone) seeking help from more authoritative persons than are available in the microcosm; usually he goes either to Moscow or to the local "center." [Gleb goes to the "center" to seek help and approval of his plans.]

Climax (Fulfillment of the Task
Is Threatened)

(a) The hero's task seems unfulfillable, usually when a "dramatic/heroic" obstacle appears to threaten its completion. [In *Cement,* counterrevolutionaries attack and destroy the ropeway set up for moving lumber. Also, work on the factory is halted while Gleb is away at the center, and this is partly due to the connivance of his enemies.]

(b) At some point, usually in the course of the hero's encounter with a dramatic/heroic type of obstacle, an actual, symbolic, or near death occurs. This usually involves the hero. However, if an actual death occurs, some lesser figure may act as his surrogate. [In *Cement,* a local worker is killed in the counterrevolutionary raid.]

(c) The hero has a moment of grave self-doubt ("Perhaps my opponents were right, perhaps I pushed things too far, perhaps I have lost touch with the people," or even "I am responsible for *X*'s death; I should not have pushed things so far"). [In *Cement,* Gleb has such doubts after the ropeway is destroyed and a worker is killed.]

Incorporation (Initiation)

The hero has a talk with his local mentor, and this gives him the strength to carry on. [In *Cement,* the person Gleb talks to at this point is Sergey, the Party member of bourgeois origins who is soon to be purged by the Party and is therefore not appropriate for the role of mentor.]

Finale (or Celebration of Incorporation)

The finale is complex, since it involves several functions that occur more or less simultaneously but must of course be presented sequentially in the narrative. (The order in which the following elements are presented is not fixed.)

(a) Completion of task. [The factory is rebuilt.]

(b) A ceremony or celebration to mark the task's completion. There are usually speeches and rejoicing. This event may provide a frame for the entire finale, since all of the other finale functions are interwoven with an account of the celebration. [Gleb speaks at a public ceremony marking the reopening of the factory.]

(c) Resolution of the love plot and other emotional problems. [Gleb's wife, Dasha, leaves him, but he has learned to accept his pain; however, he has not mastered his hatred for Badin.]

(d) The hero transcends his selfish impulses and acquires an extrapersonal identity. [Gleb accepts the fact that his private life is unhappy by finding in the collective cause his source of self-fulfillment. However, this function is more powerfully realized when Sergey regards his being purged as a merely personal tragedy, insignificant in the greater context of History's onward march.]

(e) A funeral is held for the tragic victim killed during the climax (this funeral may occur earlier, but it is often postponed, to enhance the finale). Alternatively, the protagonists may visit their fallen comrade's grave and make speeches. [In *Cement* this function occurs during the climax sections: the comrades bear the victim's body down the mountainside, and Gleb makes a speech.]

(f) There is a reshuffling of personnel in the microcosm; some may be purged or dismissed, some promoted or transferred. Often the hero is promoted to the post formerly held by his mentor. [In *Cement* there is a reshuffling, but the significance of the fact that various local officials are sent away to other posts is not clear, and Gleb himself is not involved.]

(g) In a speech marking the completion of the task, or in some tangible form, such as the birth of a child, the theme of regeneration and of the glorious time that awaits future generations is introduced as a thematic counterpoint to sacrifice and death. [In *Cement* this motif is introduced largely in Sergey's monologues, but it is also present in the speeches by Badin and Gleb that mark the factory's opening.]

Appendix B The Official Short List of
Model Novels as Inferred
from Speeches to Writers'
Union Congresses

The following novels appeared in the *short list* of exemplars cited,
on the occasions indicated below, in official speeches made to congresses of the Writers' Union. Model novels were sometimes cited
by author, sometimes by positive hero, and sometimes by the title
itself. When only the author is cited, I have placed the biblio-
graphic reference before the titles of the novels by the author in
question and have indicated in square brackets the novels I assume
the official speaker had in mind (other than those cited at other
congresses and therefore listed without square brackets). When the
positive hero only is cited, I have indicated that with an asterisk. I
have not included model novels by non–Great Russians that did
not have a major formative influence on the Socialist Realist tradition, nor have I included model examples of poetry or drama.

Key to the Bibliographical References

II stands for A Surkov's speech to the Second Writers' Congress
("Doklad A. A. Surkova 'O sostojanii i zadačax sovetskoj literatury.'," *Vtoroj vsesojuznyj s"ezd sovetskix pisatelej 15–26
dekabrja 1954 goda. Stenografičeskij otčet* [Moscow: Sovetskij pisatel', 1956]).
III stands for A. Surkov's speech to the Third Writers' Congress
("Doklad A. A. Surkova 'Zadači sovetskoj literatury v kom-
munističeskom stroitel'stve.'," *Tretij s"ezd pisatelej SSSR 18–
23 maja 1959 g. Stenografičeskij otčet* [Moscow: Sovetskij
pisatel', 1959]).
IV stands for G. Markov's speech to the Fourth Writers' Congress
("Doklad G. M. Markova 'Sovremennost' i problemy prozy.',"
*Četvertyj s"ezd pisatelej SSSR 22–26 maja 1967 goda. Steno-
grafičeskij otčet* [Moscow: Sovetskij pisatel', 1968]).
V stands for G. Markov's speech to the Fifth Writers' Congress

("Doklad G. Markova 'Sovetskaja literatura v bor'be za kommunističeskoe stroitel'stvo i ee zadači v svete rešenij xxiv s"ezda KPSS.'," *Pjatyj s"ezd pisatelej SSSR 29 ijunja–2 ijulja 1971 goda Stenografičeskij otčet* [Moscow: Sovetskij pisatel', 1972]). VI stands for G. Markov's speech to the Sixth Writers' Congress ("Doklad G. M. Markova 'Sovetskaja literatura v bor'be za kommunizm i ee zadači v svete rešenij xxv s"ezda KPSS.'," *(Šestoj s"ezd pisatelej SSSR 21 ijunja–25 ijunja 1976. Stenografičeskij otčet* [Moscow: Sovetskij pisatel', 1978]).

Short List of Exemplars

Azhaev, Vasily N. *Far Away From Moscow* (1948), II, p. 15; IV, p. 17.

Fadeev, Aleksandr A. III, p. 12; *The Rout* (1927), III, p. 13: *The Young Guard* (1946, 1951), II, p. 15; V*, p. 17; VI, p. 9.

Fedin, Konstantin A. III, p. 12; *Early Joys* (1946) and *An Unusual Summer* (1947–48), both III*, p. 13, and V*, p. 17.

Furmanov, Dmitry A. *Chapaev* (1923), III*, p. 3; V*, p. 17.

Gladkov, Fedor V. *Cement* (1925), II, p. 15; IV, p. 17; V*, p. 17; *Energy* (1932–37), II, p. 15.

Gorky, Maksim. *Mother* (1907), IV, p. 16; V*, p. 17; VI, p. 9.

Ivanov, Vsevolod V. III, p. 12. *The Partisans* (1921); *The Armored Train No. 14–69* (1922).

Kataev, Valentin P. *Time Forward* (1932), IV, p. 17.

Kochetov, Vsevolod A. *The Zhurbins* (1952), II, p. 15; IV, p. 17; V*, p. 17.

Kozhevnikov, Vadim M. *Meet Baluev* (1960), V*, p. 17.

Krymov, Yury S. *The Tanker "Derbent"* (1938), II, p. 15; IV, p. 17; *The Engineers* (1938–40), IV, p. 7.

Leonov, Leonid M. III, p. 12; *Sot* (1930), IV, p. 17; *Skutarevsky* (1932), IV, p. 17; *The Russian Forest* (1953), V*, p. 17.

Malyshkin, Aleksandr G. III, p. 12 [*People from the Backwoods* (1937–38)].

Nikolaeva, Galina E. *Battle en Route* (1957), IV, p. 17.

Ostrovsky, Nikolai A. *How the Steel Was Tempered* (1934), II, p. 15; III*, p. 13; V*, p. 17.

Panferov, Fedor I. *Brusski* (1930–37), II, p. 15; IV, p. 13.

Paustovsky, Konstantin G. *Kara Bugaz* (1932), IV, p. 17.
Polevoy, Boris N. *A Story about a Real Man* (1946), II, p. 15;
  V*, p. 17.
Sholokhov, Mikhail A. *Quiet Flows the Don* (1928–40), III*, p. 13;
  VI, p. 9; *Virgin Soil Upturned* (1931–60), II, p. 15; III*, p. 13;
  IV, p. 13; V, p. 17.
Tolstoy, Aleksey N. III, p. 12 [*Peter the First* (1933)]; *The Road
  to Calvary* (*The Sisters*, 1922; *The Year 1918*, 1927–28; *A
  Gloomy Morning*, 1939–41), III*, p. 13.

Note: This list is an imperfect guide to the model novels of the
Stalin years, since the speeches on which it is based were all made
at post-Stalin writers' congresses. Actually, however—and this is
perhaps indicative of how entrenched the Socialist Realist tradition
is—the list includes most of the principal model novels of the Stalin
years.

At the First Congress of the Writers' Union, held in 1934, no
Soviet model novels were singled out in the official speeches. Lists
can be found in several authoritative sources of that period, how-
ever. A good example would be V. Kirpotin's official speech to the
First Plenum of the Organizational Committee of the Writers'
Union, held from October 19 to November 3, 1932. The prose
works and writers praised in Kirpotin's speech were these: M.
Gorky (p. 13); Vs. Ivanov; D. Furmanov; Yu. L. Libedinsky, *A
Week* [1922]; A. Fadeev, *The Rout;* M. Sholokhov; and F. Panferov (all on p. 14); and M. Shaginyan, *Hydrocentral* [1930],
L. Leonov, *Sot* and *Skutarevsky,* and Vs. Ivanov, *Journey to a Land
That Does Not Yet Exist* [1930] (all on p. 15). Page references
are to the printed version of Kirpotin's speech, "Doklad V. Kir-
potina 'Sovetskaja literatura k pjatnadcatiletiju oktjabrja.'," *Sovetskaja literatura na novom etape. Stenogramma pervogo plenuma
orgkomiteta Sojuza sovetskix pisatelej* [Moscow: Sovetskaja literatura, 1933]).

Afterword

So many changes have occurred in Soviet literature in recent years that several of the generalizations made in the last chapter of this book are already out of date. The new directions do not derive from Andropov's accession to power, and there was no *major* shift after Chernenko succeeded him. Just as many of the developments we associate with the post-Stalin years actually began before his death, so too the new trends which seem to define the post-Brezhnev era began during Brezhnev's lifetime. In the literature of the late seventies, one can detect a growing reaction against the standard topics and paradigms of the sixties and early seventies. The calls for change intensified in 1979 and 1980 as writers and critics strove to define a new kind of literature for the decade then beginning. Official guidelines laid down then were canonized in a speech by G. Markov, the First Secretary of the Writers' Union, in a speech to its Seventh Congress in 1981, and again in a Party Central Committee resolution on literature of July 1982. All these events predate Brezhnev's death in November 1982. After his death, the reaction intensified, as can be seen in Chernenko's two major statements on literature—his speech to a plenary session of the Party in June, 1983, and his speech marking the fiftieth anniversary of the Writers' Union, made in the Great Kremlin Palace in September, 1984. Although there have been differences of emphasis under Chernenko (i.e., since Andropov died in February 1984), the reaction has not yet changed its basic direction.

As critics and official spokesmen reappraised the seventies, they singled out for attack two of that decade's defining trends, *byt* prose and village prose. Official spokesmen have particularly decried the vogue for writing of inconsequential people and their meager achievements, and demanded that the "positive hero" be reinstated as the cornerstone of Socialist Realism. They have insisted that, in the words of the title of the July 1982 resolution, literature ". . . Increase Its Creative Ties with the Practice of Communist Construc-

tion," and that writers do more "public-affairs writing" once again.
Critics have attacked village prose as a "literature of nostalgia" and
have recommended that writers on rural themes focus on the "technological revolution" now taking place, choosing *its* agents as their
heroes. At the same time, the strains of Great Russian chauvinism,
religious quest, and Russian Orthodox philosophy which informed a
great deal of village prose and allied critical movements of the
seventies have been denounced. Writers have been told to show
greater ideological commitment, and publishing houses to give their
Party groups a greater voice in editorial decisions.

Official spokesmen are not so much advocating a return to the
classic paradigms of Socialist Realism (as they did under Zhdanov),
as asking that writers start from these earlier paradigms in creating a
new one. At the same time, to use the terms of this book, they want
writers to put the "machine" back into the "garden." But in practice
the "machine" (modernization in the economy, etc.) does not play as
great a role in Soviet literature today as it might because of the
tremendous impact which deteriorating East-West relations has had
on thematics. Soviet literature today is concerned more with international affairs and internal cohesion than it is with brute industrialization. In consequence, the main catchwords of criticism in recent
years have been (in addition to "the positive hero") "of global
scope" (*global'nost'*), "of an impressive scale" (*masštabnost'*), and
"a multinational literature." These terms are directed either explicitly or implicitly against the trend in village prose of setting works in
remote or antiquated places where people of only one ethnic group—
Russians—live. Officials have worked actively to achieve a more
"multinational" literature by instructing editors of the main literary
journals to publish more material by or about people of the ethnic
minorities.

Additionally, a spate of novels has been written in response to the
call for "global scope," but are mostly devoted to establishing the
moral bankruptcy, cult of violence, and militarism of the West.
Novel after novel has used a *topos* which has not been popular since
the years of the first Five-Year Plan—the ideological duel between a
representative of the capitalist West (usually an American) and a
Soviet acquaintance, who will of course prevail. (A typical example
would be V. Stepanov's *The Thunderers* (1983), in which two captains of atomic submarines, one Soviet and one American, meet in

the Hermitage in Leningrad as they admire the Italian masters. A lofty discussion of Lorenzetti's statue of a dolphin ensues, but before long it emerges that Americans train these delightful creatures for suicide missions to plant mines, whereas. . . .) Still another kind of writing to gain prominence in this climate (one for which special prizes were introduced in 1984) is fiction about the exploits of the police and the KGB.

This is not to imply that the movement for change was generated entirely from above. However, it is certainly true that, for instance, the weakening of the strains of Russian Orthodox thought and Russian chauvinism in literature and criticism was a far from spontaneous development. Even before the powers that be had begun to demand "global scope" and "an impressive scale" in literature, many of the more serious writers and critics had themselves begun to realize that their literature was out of date and too narrow in focus, and to aspire to enter the international literary community—or at least a section of it. In so doing they fastened on the conveniently leftist writer Gabriel Garcia Marquez, who became an emblematic figure for the direction they wanted Socialist Realism to take. (William Faulkner has also been a major, if less vaunted, influence.)

Marquez's 1967 work, *One Hundred Years of Solitude*, published in translation in the Soviet journal *Foreign Literature* in 1970, became the primary model. Its setting—a "village" or isolated region of the author's childhood—particularly appealed to Russian writers, who perceived the village both in the specificity of historical experience and in the universality of mythic truth. Obviously, in the puritanical Soviet Union, where "modernism" is still a catchword for all that is wrong with contemporary Western literature, authors could not go to the extremes of Marquez's grotesque bodily imagery, eroticism, and violence. Yet, due in part to his influence, Soviet novels have risen in recent years above the trumped up folklorico and myths of political affirmation characteristic of High Stalinist fiction, as writers strive to use elements from traditional folklore in original and creative ways to impart a mythic dimension to their texts.

This development is not confined to village prose writers, but has become a broad movement. The principal figures within the movement come from the ethnic minorities (from the Baltic Republics, the Caucases, and Central Asia) whose widely-published works today fulfill both the official demand for a "multinational literature" and the widespread demand among readers for greater sophistication and fresh topics.

There is a conflict within Soviet literature today between those who demand a variety of mythopoeic writing and those who want a literature more closely geared to "the practice of communist construction." In a sense, the old controversy of the 1920s which Socialist Realism was in part instituted to resolve (that between proletarian realism and revolutionary romanticism) still manifests itself in this tension between the would-be mythopoets and the would-be realists, although the "romanticists" are no longer so "revolutionary," and there is a new level of sophistication on both sides.

Ironically, at this time of rabid anti-Americanism, supporters of both sides of this controversy sometimes use the widely-read fiction of Arthur Hailey (*Airport, Wheels,* etc.), as a point of reference in establishing their arguments. Those who propose a kind of topical literary journalism advocate something like the Hailey model, though they hasten to point out that in Hailey's novels man is lost in his barrage of information about technology and organization, whereas Socialist Realism gives pride of place to Man. The advocates of the mythopoeic school, however, maintain that Soviet literature has outgrown the "Haileyism" (*xejlijanstvo*) of its past, that it doesn't need the tractors and other such props any more and without them it can produce works which are sophisticated, but no less ideologically committed than before. Indeed some critics maintain that is can do so even by allowing greater ambiguity, by rejecting Socialist Realism's traditional "two-dimensional" portraits in favor of writing which is "three-dimensional," "polyphonic," or at least "contrapuntal."

This claim of the would-be mythopoets and other advocates of the more sophisticated "socialist realism" found in fiction of the last two decades raises a very serious question: Has Soviet literature, by throwing out so many of the icons of Socialist Realism, effectively jettisoned Socialist Realism as such, or at least as defined by this book? In other words, can Socialist Realism be separated from the masterplot, the ritual biography, and the standard clichés for the positive hero and his mentor? The answer is clearly yes.

The definition of Socialist Realism provided in this book is really two-tiered. At one level, it describes the formal features, and at another its function. The formal features are experiencing change. With the call from official quarters for more "positive heroes," and

the frequent citing of the old model novels (*Cement*, etc.) as examples for writers to emulate once more, there has been a marked return
to the conventions of Socialist Realism in recent fiction (in contrast
to fiction of the late sixties and seventies where they were weakly
represented). The ritualized biography has ceased to be as defining a
feature as it was under Stalin, and for a decade or so after him.
Nevertheless, it can not be said that the tradition has died or is to
be found only vestigially or in the fiction of "conformist hacks."
One virtue of the model proposed in this book is that it describes
a classical norm against which any change can be perceived. In
the space that remains I will confine my remarks to a discussion
of recent developments in terms of Socialist Realism's defining
functions.

The function of Socialist Realism was to provide political alle-
gories. It became a respository of offical myths which affirmed the
status quo. This latter aspect now obtains only in the most general
sense: a major task of Soviet literature today is to evaluate the past.
Novels about history predominate not only statistically, but also in
influence: they command the most attention from readers, critics,
and the juries who award state prizes. *The* theme of Soviet literature
of the late seventies and early eighties is retrospection. In almost all
works protagonists muse over a past that is most frequently their
own. This theme has served very different purposes in fiction, rang-
ing from Cold War propaganda to philosophical explorations of the
concept of time. In fiction by writers of ethnic minorities, the theme
of retrospection has served primarily as a means of exploring the
traditions and national identity of the author's own people. Indeed,
some writers were perceived as going too far in the direction
of cultural nostalgia, and Chernenko, in his speech marking the
Writers' Union Jubilee in 1984, reminded ethnic writers that their
literature will develop "more quickly and fruitfully" if it connects its
"national culture" with others, and in particular with "fraternal
peoples that have acquired transnational importance."

The theme of retrospection is often presented with an epic sweep.
Writers typically express their reaction against the narrow parameters of time and place which characterized so much fiction of the
sixties and seventies by setting their works in a singularly broad
range of places and times. The pattern most often found in conservative fiction extends from World War II to the present, and covers
both the Soviet Union and the West; but writers increasingly push

these boundaries out to include the timeless past of folk legend or the distant future of intergalactic communication. Science fiction—a genre that was in decline during the heyday of "village prose"—has experienced a revival in recent years, and science fiction writers have begun to weave traditional elements or material from olden times into their futuristic narratives.

However broad the range of times and places used in a work of fiction, and however complex the pattern, the explicit or implicit point of reference or comparison for any time or place—and very often the frame of the story as well—is the present-day Soviet Union. There is, then, a dualistic pattern of time and place that informs most current novels (then/now, there/here). In many instances, but primarily in fiction that follows closely the old conventions of Socialist Realism, this pattern is only superficially present. There is, in addition, a significant body of writing published recently (including much of the science fiction and work of the mythopoeic school) in which a distinctive dualistic pattern of the two times and places shapes the novel to such an extent that it is possible to talk of yet another mutation having been generated in the ongoing tradition of Socialist Realism. Such fiction represents a serious attempt at working out new conventions against the dialogizing background of the old.

The most significant such work is Chingiz Aitmatov's latest novel, *The Day Lasts Longer Than An Age* (1980). The book is about life in a remote settlement of Kazakhstan, but Aitmatov has incorporated into the narrative both folk myth and a science fiction subplot dealing with East-West rivalry and a utopian civilization on a distant planet. Curiously, the work has been sympathetically received in the West and is widely read by Soviet intellectuals, even while pleasing officials in the Soviet Union to such an extent that it was elevated virtually overnight to the status of a canonical exemplar.

Aitmatov is a leading member of the mythopoeic school, and other writers of that inclination have used his novel as an exemplar for a new kind of writing. Nevertheless, Aitmatov employs not only elements from traditional folklore, but also the clichés of both pre- and post-Stalin Socialist Realism. Indeed, the novel is a veritable museum of the changing styles of Socialist Realism. The principal pattern he has used, however, is to conflate the basic *topoi* of classical Socialist Realism with those of post-Stalinist and, primarily, of village prose. He has created a work that can be read virtually as two different texts, one affirming the Great Tradition of Socialist Realism by extending it, the other fraught with ambiguities and subtleties.

Thus, Aitmatov's work points to the direction taken recently by the two aspects of Socialist Realism I have discussed in the preceding pages—its forms and its functions. The novel is eloquent testimony to the mutability, and therefore the durability, of the canon. But at the same time, Aitmatov seeks in it to understand history and identify through myth. The fate of one man in Kazakhstan stands in for the destiny of his people, of the Soviet Union, of Mankind, and ultimately of all forms of life. Insofar as this is the case, the function of treating history as parable is maintained. Socialist Realism continues, *mutatis mutandis,* to be history as ritual.

Readers will find a further elaboration of some of the above ideas in the following recent articles:

"The Mutability of the Canon: Socialist Realism and Chingiz Aitmatov's *I dol'she veka dlitsiia den'.*" *Slavic Review* 43, no. 4 (Winter 1984).
"New Trends in Literature." In James Cracraft, ed., *The Soviet Union Today: An Interpretive Guide.* Chicago: *Bulletin of the Atomic Scientists,* Education Foundation for Nuclear Science, Inc., 1983.
"Political History and Literary Chronotope: Some Soviet Case Studies." In Gary Saul Morson, ed., *Literature and History: Methodological Problems and Some Russian Case Studies.* Forthcoming in 1985 from Stanford University Press.
"Zhdanovist Literature and Village Prose." In Evelyn Bristol, ed., *Russian Literature and Criticism: Papers from the Second World Congress for Soviet and East European Studies.* Berkeley Slavic Specialties, 1983.

Katerina Clark
Bloomington, Indiana, 1985

Additional Bibliography

Brown, Edward J. *Russian Literature Since the Revolution.* Cambridge, Mass., and London: Harvard University Press. Revised and enlarged 1982.
Dunlop, John B. *The Faces of Contemporary Russian Nationalism.* Princeton, N.J.: Princeton University Press, 1983.

Glad, John. *Extrapolations from Dystopia: A Critical Study of Soviet Science Fiction.* Princeton, N.J.: Kingston Press, 1982.

Friedberg, Maurice. "Cultural and Intellectual Life." In Robert F. Brynes, ed., *After Brezhnev: Sources of Soviet Conduct in the 1980s.* Bloomington, Ind.: Indiana University Press, 1983.

Mehnert, Klaus. *The Russians and their Favorite Reading.* Stanford, Calif.: Stanford University Press, 1984.

Spechler, Dina R. *Permitted Dissent in the U.S.S.R.: Novy Mir and the Soviet Regime.* New York: Praeger, 1982.

Notes

Preface

1. Vsevolod Kochetov, *Sekretar' obkoma, Zvezda*, 1961, н. 7, p. 4.
2. Katerina Clark, "'Boy Gets Tractor' and All That: The Parable Structure of the Soviet Novel," in *Russian and Slavic Literature*, ed. Richard Freeborn, R. R. Milner Gulland, and Charles A. Ward (Columbus, Ohio: Slavica Publishers, 1977), pp. 359–75.
3. The term "Socialist Realism" was coined in 1932 as the name for the official method of Soviet literature. From then through the First Writers' Congress, in 1934, a whole series of articles and speeches was published, which outlined what was meant by the term.
4. Yury Tynianov and Roman Jakobson, "Problems in the Study of Literature and Language," in *Readings in Russian Poetics: Formalist and Structuralist Views*, ed. Ladislav Matejka and Krystina Pomorska (Cambridge, Mass.: M.I.T. Press, 1971), p. 79.

Introduction

1. See, e.g., *Aktual'nye problemy socialističeskogo realizma. Sb. statej* (Moscow: Sovetskij pisatel', 1969), and "Socialističeskij realism—znamja peredovogo iskusstva" (a discussion held in the Academy of the Social Sciences of the Central Committee), *Voprosy literatury*, no. 9, 1975, pp. 3–25.
2. It will be noted that Sholokhov has been accused of plagiarism in *Quiet Flows the Don*. See, e.g., Roy A. Medvedev, *Problems in the Literary Biography of Mikhail Sholokhov*, trans. A. D. P. Briggs (New York: Cambridge University Press, 1977).
3. P. N. Medvedev and M. M. Bakhtin, *The Formal Method in Literary Scholarship: A Critical Introduction to Sociological Poetics*, trans. Albert J. Wehrle (Baltimore: Johns Hopkins University Press, 1978), p. 154. When the Russian original was first published in 1928, Medvedev was listed as the author, but it is now generally considered that Bakhtin wrote the book and that Medvedev possibly made some additions (see Wehrle's Introduction).
4. See below, chap. 9, p. 191.
5. See V. Propp, *Morphology of the Folktale*, trans. Laurence Scott, 2d ed. (Austin: University of Texas Press, 1971).

6. Abner Cohen, *Two-Dimensional Man: An Essay on the Anthropology of Power and Symbolism in Complex Societies* (London: Routledge & Kegan Paul, 1974), pp. ix, 35, 26, 135.

7. Shalom Spiegel, *The Last Trial: On the Legends and Lore of the Command to Abraham to Offer Isaac as a Sacrifice*, trans. Judah Goldin (New York: Schocken Books, 1967).

8. Vissarion Grigorievich Belinsky (1811–48), an extremely influential literary critic, called on Russian writers to put their pens to the service of some great idea and, in doing so, to expose all the shortcomings of Russian life.

9. Karl Marx and Friedrich Engels, *The German Ideology*, in *Collected Works*, vol. 5 (New York: International Publishers, 1976), esp. pp. 31, 35–37, 43–44, 50.

10. Karl Marx, *Capital: A Critique of Political Economy* (Chicago: Charles Kerr & Co., 1909), pp. 954–55.

11. An analogous observation has been made by Leopold Haimson in his *The Russian Marxists and the Origins of Bolshevism* (Cambridge, Mass.: Harvard University Press, 1967).

12. V. I. Lenin, *What Is to Be Done? Burning Questions of Our Movement*, in *Collected Works*, 4th ed., vol. 5, trans. Joe Fineberg and George Hanna (Moscow: Progress Publishers, 1961), p. 374.

13. See, e.g., V. I. Lenin, "Russian Revolution and the Civil War" (September 1917), in *Collected Works*, 4th ed., vol. 26, trans. Yuri Sdobnikov and George Hanna (Moscow: Progress Publishers, 1964), p. 31.

Chapter 1

1. H. Ermolaev, "Roždenie socialističeskogo realizma," *Mosty*, 1968, nos. 13–14, p. 295.

2. A. Dementev, E. Mikhailova, L. Polyak, "Vvedenie," *Istorija russkoj sovetskoj literatury v četyrex tomax*, 2d rev. and enl. ed., vol. 2 (Moscow: "Nauka," 1967), p. 10.

3. L. I. Timofeev, *Sovremennaja literatura* (Moscow: Učpedgiz, 1947), p. 52; A. Volkov, A. M. *Gorkij i literaturnoe dviženie sovetskoj epoxi*, 2d enl. ed. (Moscow: Sovetskij pisatel', 1971), p. 550.

4. L. Ulrikh, *Gor'kij i Gladkov (K voprosu o gor'kovskix tradicijax v sovetskoj literature)* (Taskhkent: GIXL UzSSSR, 1962), pp. 301–2.

5. Jorge Luis Borges, *Other Inquisitions: 1937–52*, trans. Ruth L. C. Simms (New York: Washington Square Press, 1966), p. 113.

6. V. Kirpotin, speech published in *Sovetskaja literatura na novom etape. Stenogramma pervogo plenuma orgkomiteta sojuza sovetskix pisatelej* (Moscow: Writers' Union, 1933), p. 23.

7. Abram Tertz (Andrei Sinyavsky), "On Socialist Realism," in *The Trial Begins and On Socialist Realism*, trans. Max Hayward (New York: Random House, Vintage Russian Library, 1965), pp. 214–15.

8. For a fuller account of the literary polemics of the twenties, see E.

Brown, *The Proletarian Episode in Russian Literature, 1928–32* (New York: Columbia University Press, 1953), or H. Ermolaev, *Soviet Literary Theories, 1917–34: The Genesis of Socialist Realism*, University of California Publications in Modern Philology, no. 69 (Berkeley: University of California Press, 1963).

9. RAPP was short for the Russian Association of Proletarian Writers, a broad-based organization led by some "Party-minded" militants. For the history of RAPP, see S. I. Sheshukov, *Neistovye revniteli* (Moscow: Moskovskij rabočij, 1970).

10. Katerina Clark, "'Little Heroes and Big Deeds': Literature Responds to the First Five-Year Plan," *Cultural Revolution in Russia, 1928–31*, ed. Sheila Fitzpatrick (Bloomington: Indiana University Press, 1978).

11. *Pravda*, 19 April 1931.

12. Ulrikh, pp. 225–26; A. K. Romanovsky, "Partijnoe rukovodstvo literatury v period podgotovki k pervomu s"ezdu sovetskix pisatelej," in *O politike partii v oblasti literatury i iskusstva* (Moscow: Akademija obščestvennyx nauk pri CK KPSS. Kafedra teorii literatury i iskusstva, 1958), p. 110.

13. "Reč' sekretarja CK VKP(b) A. A. Ždanova," *Pervyj s"ezd pisatelej. Stenografičeskij otčet* (Moscow: Ogiz, 1934), p. 4.

14. See my article "'Little Heroes and Big Deeds' . . ."

15. Romanovsky, "Partijnoe rukovodstvo literatury," p. 113. For an early flier see *Učebno-metodičeskie materialy dlja literaturnyx kružkov i rabočix avtorov. Gotovitsja k Oktjabr'skoj godovščine*, Organ massovogo otdela Orgkomiteta Sojuza sovetskix pisatelej (Moscow: Writers' Union, 1932). Note that this list includes two First Five-Year Plan novels— Shaginyan's *Hydrocentral* and Shukhov's *Hatred*—that by 1934 were dropped from the short list of canonical exemplars.

16. This point was made by Rufus W. Mathewson, Jr., in *The Positive Hero in Russian Literature*, 2d ed. (Stanford University Press, 1975), pp. 5, 175, 231, 250.

17. Cf. Abram Tertz, "On Socialist Realism," pp. 214–15, and Rufus W. Mathewson, Jr., *The Positive Hero*, p. 4.

18. M. M. Bakhtin, "Epos i roman (o metodologii issledovanija romana)," *Voprosy literatury i estetiki. Issledovanija raznyx let* (Moscow: Xudožestvennaja literatura, 1975), pp. 447–83, esp. 463.

19. Mircea Eliade, *Cosmos and History: The Myth of the Eternal Return*, trans. Willard R. Trask (New York: Harper & Row, 1959), esp. pp. ix, 5, 9, 38–39, 106, 149.

20. See the figures published in "XVII s"ezd partii i zadača pisatelej. Sokraščennaja stenogramma doklada zav. kul'tpropa CK VKP(b) t. A. Steckogo na sobranii pisatelej 3 marta," *Literaturnaja gazeta*, 1934, no. 28 (March 8), p. 1.

21. For examples of neoclassicism, see Anon., "Privet tovariščam (Posv. administrirovannym)," *Pravda*, 1917, no. 7 (March 12), p. 4, and Kuzma Terkin, "Voždjam naroda," *Pravda*, 1917, no. 20 (March 29), p. 4. For

examples of neo-Lermontovism see Y. Berdnikov, "Vskipaet nemolčno more," *Pravda*, 1918, no. 26 (February 15), p. 2.
22. See Katerina Clark, "The Image of the *Intelligent* in Soviet Prose Fiction, 1917–1932" (Ph.D. dissertation, Yale University, 1971), pp. 87, 130–131. Gorky's role in the Party is not clear; see chapter 2, note 20, below.
23. *Cement*, for example, was written to counter specific prose works by Vs. Ivanov, Leonov, and V. Kataev (B. Brainina, *Fedor Gladkov. Očerk žizni i tvorčestva* [Moscow: GIXL, 1957], p. 37).
24. This might not seem to be the case with Furmanov's *Chapaev*, but see my remarks in chapter 3 (pp. 87–88).
25. For more on negative characters see the section "Villainy" in chapter 8.

Chapter 2

1. Cf. the example of Vera Pavlovna in *What Is to Be Done?*
2. Cf. "Russkomu narodu" in *Agitacionnaja literatura russkix revoljucionnyx narodnikov: potaennye proizvedinija 1873–1875 gg.*, comp. O. B. Alekseeva (Leningrad: Nauka, 1970), pp. 74–85.
3. Cf. S. Kravchinsky, "Pravda i krivda," *Agitacionnaja literatura*, p. 117; cf. also Rakhmetov's example in *What Is to Be Done?*
4. Cf. "Skazka o mudrice Naumovna," in *Agitacionnaja literatura*, pp. 216, 240.
5. *Xrestomatija po drevnej russkoj literature XI–XII vekov*, comp. N. K. Gudzy, 7th ed. (Moscow: Učpedgiz, 1962), pp. 98–104.
6. See, e.g., V. I. Lenin, "Zamečanija na knige G. V. Plexanova 'N. G. Černyševskij'" (*ca.* 1909–11), *Polnoe sobranie sočinenij*, 5th ed., vol. 29 (Moscow: Gos. izd. polit. lit., 1963), pp. 541–42, 601–3.
7. See, e.g., Molotov's speech at Gorky's funeral in 1936, *Stat'i i reči* (Moscow: Partizdat, 1937), p. 238.
8. I. N. Kubikov, *Kommentarii k romanu M. Gor'kogo 'Mat'*, no. 2 (Moscow: Kooperativnoe izdatel'stvo Mir, 1932), p. 45.
9. Ibid., pp. 69–71.
10. Cf. the trial transcript in the Appendix to *Maksim Gor'kij, Literaturno-kritičeskaja biblioteka*, comp. P. E. Budkov and N. K. Piksanov, 2d ed. (Moscow-Leningrad: Giz, 1929), pp. 166–73.
11. There are six different redactions of *Mother*. I am using here the final—substantially revised and canonical—version, which Gorky worked on between 1922 and 1923.
12. Kubikov, p. 71.
13. Cf., e.g., A. Serafimovich, "Bombs" and "The Funeral March," both published in 1906.
14. S. Mashitsky, *V ogne* (Geneva, 1904).
15. B. Akhundova, "Sputniki 'Materi' (tema proletariata v russkoj proze načala XXv)," in *Gor'kovskie čtenija 1964–1965. Gor'kij i russkaja*

literatura načala xx veka (Moscow: Nauka, 1966), p. 305.

16. For a fuller account of God-building, see George Louis Kline, "The 'God-Builders': Gorky and Lunacharsky," chapter 4 of *Religious and Anti-Religious Thought in Russia* (Chicago: University of Chicago Press, 1968).

17. *Mat', Sobranie sočinenij v tridcati tomax*, vol. 7 (Moscow: GIXL, 1950), p. 240.

18. M. Piksanov, *Gor'kij i fol'klor*, 2d. ed. (Leningrad: GIXL, 1938), p. 16.

19. Gorky's association with the Social Democratic Party begins around 1901, and, although he contributed both money and writings to the cause, it is not clear whether he was ever actually a Party member. The recent edition of the Soviet literary encyclopedia asserts that he joined in the summer of 1905 ("Gor'kij, Maksim," *Kratkaja literaturnaja enciklopedija*, vol. 7 [Moscow: Sovetskaja enciklopedija, 1974], p. 288), but Alexander Kaun claims that "Gorky has told me definitively that he never belonged to any political party. In the revolutionary movement he was merely a 'sympathizer'" (*Maxim Gorky and His Russia* [New York: Jonathan Cape & Harrison Smith, 1931], p. 408).

20. N. Chernyshevsky, *Čto delat'?* (Moscow: Xudožestvennaja literatura, 1969), pp. 263–64.

21. D. S. Likhachev, *Čelovek v literature drevnej Rusi* (Moscow and Leningrad: Akademija nauk, 1958), p. 34.

22. Ibid., p. 34.

23. *Čto delat'?*, pp. 74, 78.

24. T. P. Maevskaya, *Idei i obrazy russkogo narodničeskogo romana (70-e gody–80-e gody XIXv)* (Kiev: Naukova dumka, 1975), p. 81.

25. "Skazka o mudrice Naumovne," pp. 182, 184, 187.

26. *Mat'*, pp. 202, 203, 204, 206, 209.

27. Ibid., pp. 205, 219.

28. See S. M. Stepnyak-Kravchinsky, *Andrej Kožuxov, Izbrannoe* (Moscow: Xudožestvennaja literatura, 1972), p. 209.

29. See M. Cherniavsky, *Tsar and People: Studies in Russian Myths* (New Haven: Yale University Press, 1961).

30. *Mat'*, pp. 319–20.

Chapter 3

1. *Modern Russian Poetry*, ed. Vladimir Markov and Merrill Sparks (Indianapolis: Bobbs-Merrill, 1967), p. 311.

2. The word "moustache" was used as a code term for Stalin during the years when it was dangerous to criticize him.

3. See S. G. Asadullaev, *Roman F. Gladkova "Cement,"* Avtoreferat dissertacii na soiskanie naučnoj stepeni kandidata filologičeskix nauk (Moscow: M.G.U., 1959), p. 9; and B. Brainina, *"Cement" F. Gladkova* (Moscow: Xudožestvennaja literatura, 1965), pp. 17–19.

4. The most probable time during which the action was set is from spring

to late autumn (November), 1921. However, some Soviet commentators have said that the novel was set in 1920. Cf. S. V. Shuvalov, "Fedor Gladkov." Kompozicionno-stilističeskij analiz romana 'Cement,'" in *Belletristiki-sovremenniki. Stat'i i issledovanija*, vol. 1, ed. E. F. Nikitin and S. V. Shuvalov, 2d ed. (Moscow: Nikitinskie subbotniki, 1928), p. 48, and F. Gladkov, *O literature. Štat'i, reči, vospominanija* (Moscow: Sovetskij pisatel', 1955), p. 8.

5. See, e.g., N. Nikandrov, *Prokljatye zažigalki, Krasnaja nov'*, 1923, nos. 6 and 7.

6. B. Brainina, "*Cement,*" pp. 79–82.

7. Cf., e.g., P. S. Kogan, "O Gladkove i 'Cemente,'" *Na literaturnom postu*, 1926, no. 1, pp. 41–44.

8. N. Bukharin, "Tovarišč Sverdlov," *Pravda*, 1919, no. 59 (March 18), p. 1.

9. See P. S. Kogan, p. 41.

10. "Justin Žuk," *Pravda*, 1919, no. 241 (October 28), p. 1.

11. F. Gladkov, *Cement, Krasnaja nov'* (1925), no. 2, p. 79; English version, *Cement*, trans. A. S. Arthur and C. Ashleigh (New York: Frederick Ungar, 1974), p. 65.

12. Ibid., no. 3, p. 53; English version, p. 113.

13. Ibid., no. 5, p. 82; no. 4, p. 83. English version, pp. 208, 193.

14. Ibid., no. 2, pp. 99–100; English version, pp. 92–93.

15. Ibid., no. 1, p. 108; English version, p. 55.

16. O. M. Brik, "Počemu ponravilsja 'Cement'?," *Na literaturnom postu*, 1926, no. 2, pp. 31–32.

17. Yury Pukhov, *Sovetskij roman i rabočij klass ("Cement" i "Energija" F. Gladkova)* (Sredne-Ural'skoe knižnoe izdatel'stvo, 1962), p. 9.

18. B. Brainina, "*Cement,*" p. 15.

19. *Krasnaja nov'*, 1925, no. 5, p. 101; English version, p. 249.

20. Compare *Cement (Krasnaja nov'*, 1925, no. 2, pp. 96–97; English version, pp. 88–89), and Andrey Biely, *St. Petersburg*, trans. John Cournos (New York: Grove Press, 1959), pp. 233–35. Note that Cournos has translated the later (1922) redaction, which was, of course, the main source for Soviet writers.

21. See Robert A. Maguire, *Red Virgin Soil: Soviet Literature in the 1920's* (Princeton: Princeton University Press, 1968), p. 124.

22. See Appendix A.

23. *Krasnaja nov'*, 1925, no. 2; cf. p. 81 with pp. 98, 104; English version, pp. 67, 91 (section omitted), 98.

24. N. Kostelevskaja, "Dva tipa," *Pravda*, 1919, no. 264 (November 25).

25. See, e.g., Y. Andreev, *Revoljucija i literatura. Oktjabr' i graždanskaja vojna v russkoj sovetskoj literature i stanovlenie socialističeskogo realizma (20-e–30-e gody)* (Moscow: Xudožestvennaja literatura, 1975), p. 102.

26. See Y. Libedinskij, "Kak ja pisal svoju pervuju povest'," *Ob uvaženii*

k literature. Stat'i (Moscow: Sovetskij pisatel', 1965), p. 34; K. Zelinsky, *A. A. Fadeev. Kritiko-bibliografičeskij očerk* (Moscow: Sovetskij pisatel', 1956), p. 28.

27. P. Kupriyanovsky, *Xudožnik revoljucii. O Dimitrii Furmanove* (Moscow: Sovetskij pisatel', 1967), pp. 163–65.

28. D. Furmanov, *Čapaev,* 3d ed. (Moscow-Leningrad: Giz, 1925), p. 25.

29. Ibid., p. 49.

30. Ibid., pp. 88, 77.

31. Ibid., p. 169.

32. D. Furmanov, *Iz dnevnika pisatelja,* 1934, p. 3 (cited in Andreev, p. 239).

33. *Čapaev,* p. 88.

34. Ibid., p. 129.

Chapter 4

1. "VII s"ezd partii, reč' t. Lenina [continued]," *Pravda,* 1920, no. 280 (December 24), p. 2.

2. B. Kuznetsov, "Elektrifikacija i material'naja baza kommunizma," *Kommunist,* 1939, no. 8, pp. 43–52.

3. J. V. Stalin, "Industrialization of the Country and the Right Deviation. Speech to the Plenum of the C.P.S.U.(b) of November 19, 1928," *Works,* vol. 11 (Moscow: Foreign Languages Publishing House, 1954), p. 264.

4. See F. Gladkov, *Energija, Novyj mir,* 1932, no. 7–8, p. 105, and F. Panferov, *Bruski, Oktjabr',* 1929, no. 9, p. 17.

5. *Energija, Novyj mir,* 1932, no. 2, p. 112.

6. J. V. Stalin, "Speech to the Eighth Congress of A.Y.L.C.L.," *Works,* vol. 11, p. 81.

7. E.g., F. Panferov, *Bruski, Oktjabr',* 1929, no. 7, p. 29.

8. J. V. Stalin, "O zadačax xozjajstvennikov," *Sočinenija,* vol. 13 (Moscow: Gos. izd. polit. lit., 1934), p. 37.

9. L. Sobolev, *Kapital'nyj remont, Lokaf,* 1932, no. 2, p. 39, no. 11, pp. 74–76.

10. J. V. Stalin, "Talk with Emil Ludwig, December 13, 1931," *Works,* vol. 13, p. 106.

11. S. Frederick Starr, "Visionary Town Planning during the Cultural Revolution," in *Cultural Revolution in Russia, 1928–1931,* ed. S. Fitzpatrick (Bloomington: Indiana University Press, 1978), pp. 210–17, 221.

12. E. Zamyatin, "On Literature, Revolution, Entropy, and Other Matters" (1923), *A Soviet Heretic: Essays by Yevgeny Zamyatin,* ed. and trans. Mirra Ginsburg (Chicago: University of Chicago Press, 1975), pp. 108–9.

13. J. V. Stalin, "Novaja obstanovka—novye zadači xozjaststvennikov na stroitel'stvax. Reč' na soveščanii xozjajstvennikov, 23 ijunja, 1931," *Sočinenija,* vol. 12 (Moscow: Gos. izd. polit. lit., 1951), pp. 55–59.

14. See, e.g., Vs. Kochetov's *Žurbiny,* which is about shipbuilding but

ends with a flood in the factory (*Zvezda*, 1952, no. 2, p. 100).
15. Leo Marx, *The Machine in the Garden: Technology and the Pastoral Ideal in America* (New York: Oxford University Press, 1968).
16. See, e.g., V. Grossman, *Stepan Kol'čugin, God XX. Al'manax* (Moscow: G.I.X.L., 1937), pp. 28–29.
17. Compare F. Panferov, *Bruski, Oktjabr'*, 1929, no. 11, p. 38, and *Oktjabr'*, 1933, no. 1, pp. 25–26.
18. See, e.g., Geroj sovetskogo sojuza E. Krenkel', "*Četyre tovarišča*," *Znamja*, 1939, no. 10–11, pp. 87–93.
19. See, e.g., on Stalin's repeated Siberian exiles, B. Ponomarets, "Stalin v Xašin (1901–1902 gody). Nekotorye episody iz batumskogo podpol'ja," *Bol'ševik*, 1935, no. 1, pp. 88–96, and, on his exile in the Arctic, V. Shveitser, *Stalin v Turxanskoj ssylke. Vospominanija starogo podpol'ščika*, 2d ed. (Moscow: Molodaja gvardija, 1943).
20. "Čeljuskincy v Leningrade. Obrazec socialističeskogo realizma. Vstuplenie N. Tixonova na ploščadi Urlickogo," *Literaturnaja gazeta*, 1934, no. 81 (June 26).
21. Quoted in Joan London, *Jack London and His Times: An Unconventional Biography* (Seattle: University of Washington Press, 1968), p. 378.
22. Joan Carol Avins, "Modes of Contrasting Russia and the West" (Ph.D. dissertation, Yale University, December 1974), p. 7.
23. E.g., Yevgeny Zamyatin, "Theme and Plot" and "The New Russian Prose," both in *A Soviet Heretic* (see n. 12 above); V. Shklovsky, "Tarzan," *Russkij sovremennik*, 1924, no. 3, pp. 253–54; L. Lunts, "Na zapad!," *Beseda*, 1923, no. 3, pp. 259–74; and V. Kaverin's attempt at a Soviet crime novel, *Konec xazy, Kovš*, 1925, no. 1, pp. 161–236.
24. P. Kupriyanovsky, *Xudožnik revoljucii. O Dimitrii Furmanove* (Moscow: Sovetskij pisatel' 1967), p. 160.
25. V. Kataev, *Beleet parus odinokij, Krasnaja nov'*, 1936, no. 5, p. 115.
26. *Kavaler zolotoj zvezdy*, pt. 2, *Oktjabr'*, 1948, no. 5, p. 100.
27. William Empson, *Some Versions of Pastoral* (London: Chatto & Windus, 1935), p. 6.
28. Peter V. Marinelli, *Pastoral, The Critical Idiom*, no. 15 (London: Methuen, 1971), p. 3.
29. For an English translation of Ferdinand Tönnies' book *Gemeinschaft und Gesellschaft* (1887), see *Fundamental Concepts of Sociology*, trans. Charles P. Loomin (New York: American Book, 1940).
30. M. Shaginyan, "Čego ždet pisatel' ot kritiki." Sodoklad M. S. Šaginjan, *Vtoroj plenum pravlenija SSP SSSR. Stenografičeskij otčet* (Moscow: G.I.X.L., 1935), pp. 57–58.
31. F. Gladkov, *Energija, Novyj mir*, 1932, no. 2, pp. 114, 106; no. 6, p. 112; no. 3, p. 55.
32. M. Gorky, "O bor'be s prirodoj" (1931), *Sobranie sočinenij v tridcati tomax*, vol. 26 (Moscow: G.I.X.L., 1953), p. 198.
33. A. Chakovsky, *U nas uže utro, Znamja*, 1949, no. 11, p. 93.

Chapter 5

1. "Privetstvie pograničnikov. Reč' tov. Bičevskogo," "otvet tov. Kiršona," *Literaturnaja gazeta*, 1936, no. 9 (February 12), p. 1.

2. Sidney Monas has observed that the same dynamic obtained under Nicholas in the nineteenth century (*The Third Section: Police and Society in Russia under Nicholas I* [Cambridge, Mass: Harvard University Press, 1961], p. 85).

3. See, e.g., N. Krylenko, "Socializm i sem'ja," *Bol'ševik*, 1936, no. 18, p. 73.

4. A. Makarenko, *Kniga dlja roditelej, Krasnaja nov'*, 1937, no. 7, p. 15.

5. See E. Smirnov, *Pavlik Morozov. V pomošč' pionervožatomu* (Moscow: Molodaja gvardija, 1938), V. Gubarev, *Syn* (Moscow: Molodaja gvardija, 1940).

6. E.g., Y. Libedinsky, *A Week* (1922).

7. V. Kirshon, [response], *Literaturnaja gazeta*, 1936, no. 9 (February 12), p. 1.

8. N. Kuybyshev, "Zaščita socialističeskoj rodiny," *Bol'ševik*, 1937, nos. 5–6, p. 55.

9. See Paul Friedrich, "Semantic Structure and Social Structure: An Instance from Russia," in *Explorations in Cultural Anthropology: Essays in Honor of George Peter Murdoch* (New York: McGraw-Hill, 1964), p. 134.

10. A. Gurvich, "Čerty peredovogo sovetskogo čeloveka," *Znamja*, 1947, no. 11, p. 178

11. Friedrich, pp. 135–38.

12. *Veduščaja os', Oktjabr'*, 1931, no. 9, p. 15.

13. A. K., "Na proverku!," *Literaturnaja gazeta*, 1929, no. 16 (August 5).

14. J. V. Stalin, "Novaja obstanovka—novye zadači xozjajstvennogo stroitel'stva." *Reč'* na soveščanii xozjajstvennikov, 23 ijunja, 1931, *Sočinenija*, vol. 13 (Moscow, 1951), pp. 55–59, 68.

15. J. V. Stalin, "Reč' tovarišča STALINA v Kremlëvskom dvorce na vypuske akademikov Krasnoj armii, 4 maja 1935 goda," *Literaturnaja gazeta*, 1935, no. 26 (May 10), p. 1.

16. P. Yudin, "Novaja, nevidennaja literatura (Vystuplenie na moskovskoj oblastnoj i gorodskoj konferencii)," *Literaturnaja gazeta*, 1934, no. 6 (January 22), p. 1.

17. See, e.g., A. Erlich, "Sdvig," *Pravda*, 1933, December 25.

18. E.g., *Belomorsko-Baltijskij kanal im. Stalina* (Moscow, 1934).

19. J. V. Stalin, "Novaja obstanovka—novye zadači xozjajstvennogo stroitel'stva," p. 68.

20. J. V. Stalin, "Reč' tov. STALINA v Kremlëvskom dvorce na vypuske akademikov Krasnoj Armii, 4 maja 1935 goda," p. 1. In "On the Death of Lenin," a speech delivered at the Second All Union Congress of Soviets, January 26, 1924, Stalin opens with these words: "Comrades, we Com-

munists are people of a special mold. We are made of a special stuff. . . . It is not given to everyone to withstand the stresses and storms that accompany membership in such a party" (J. V. Stalin, *Works*, vol. 6 [Moscow: Foreign Languages Publishing House, 1953], p. 47).

21. On a 1937 expedition to the North Pole, over 50 percent of the expedition members were Party members ("Geroj sovetskogo sojuza E. Krenkel', *Četyre tovarišča, Znamja,* 1939, nos. 10–11, p. 35). Of the Stakhanovites, however, Aleksey Stakhanov reports that none of the original Stakhanovites were Party members at the time they performed their feats; some, but not all, joined the Party later (*Rasskaz o moej žizni* [Moscow: Ogiz, 1937], p. 54).

22. "Reč' A. Staxanova. Moj opyt," *Staxanovcy o sebe i o svoej rabote Reči na vsesojuznom soveščanii rabočix i rabotnic-staxanovcev* (Voronež: Voronežskoe knižnoe izd., 1935), p. 8.

23. J. V. Stalin, "Reč' tovarišča Stalina na pervom vsesojuznom soveščanii staxanovcev," *Literaturnaja gazeta,* 1935, no. 62 (November 24), p. 1.

24. S. Nagorny, "Geroi," *Literaturnaja gazeta,* 1939, no. 69 (December 15), p. 1.

25. "Lenin," a speech delivered at a memorial meeting of the Kremlin Military School, January 28, 1924 (*Works,* vol. 13, p. 54).

26. "Obščee sobranie leningradskix pisatelej." Ot sobstvennogo korespondenta. 'Lit-gazety,' *Literaturnaja gazeta,* 1937, no. 16 (March 25), p. 2.

27. E.g., *Sergej Mironovič Kirov. Kratkij biografičeskij očerk* (Moscow: Gos. izd. polit. lit., 1939), pp. 5–8; *Mixail Ivanovič Kalinin* (Moscow: Partizdat, 1940), p. 5; A. Mel'čin, *Grigorij Konstantinovič Ordžonnikidze. Kratkij biografičeskij očerk* (Moscow: Molodaja gvardija, 1939), p. 7.

28. "Obščemoskovskoe sobranie pisatelej. Zaključitel'noe zasedanie," *Literaturnaja gazeta,* 1937, no. 19 (April 10), p. 2.

29. S. Marvich, "S gerojami vsja strana," *Literaturnaja gazeta,* 1938, no. 16 (March 20).

30. "Geroi sovetskogo plemeni" (editorial), *Literaturnaja gazeta,* 1936, no. 45 (August 10), p. 1.

31. B. Chkalov, G. Baidukov, A. Belyakov, *Naš polët na ANT-25,* Biblioteka "Ogonëk," no. 59 (974), 1936, p. 5.

32. J. V. Stalin, "On the Death of Lenin," a speech delivered at the Second All-Union Congress of Soviets, January 26, 1924 (*Works,* vol. 6 [Moscow: Foreign Languages Publishing House, 1953], p. 47).

33. "Geroi sovetskogo plemeni," p. 1.

34. S. Nagorny, "Geroi," p. 1.

35. V. Vishnevsky, "Ivan Papanin," *Sčors. Papanin,* Biblioteka "Ogonëk," no. 33 (1020), 1937, pp. 30–38; Geroj Sovetskogo sojuza Marina Rykova, "Zapiski šturmana," *Znamja,* 1939, no. 2, p. 7; S. Nagorny, "Geroi," p. 1.

36. See, e.g., *Sergej Mironovič Kirov,* pp. 6–8; "Detstvo i junost' voždja, dokumenty, zapisi, rasskazy," comp. Vl. Kalinina, Iv. Vereshchagin, *Molodaja gvardija,* 1936, no. 12, p. 41.

37. Y. Renn, "Učitel′ i učeniki," *Lëtčiki. sb. rasskazov* (Moscow: Aeroflot izd., 1938), p. 567.

38. "Bol′ševistskij privet otvažnym zavoevateljam severnogo poljusa!" Poljus zavoevan bol′ševikami" (editorial), *Literaturnaja gazeta*, 1937, no. 28 (May 26), p. 1.

39. I. Gromov, "Lëtčiki novogo tipa," *Vstreči s tovariščem Stalinym* (A. Fadeev, ed.) (Moscow: Gos. izd. polit. lit., 1939), pp. 38, 40.

40. "Smert′ A. K. Serova i I. D. Osipenko," *Literaturnaja gazeta*, 1939, no. 27 (May 15), p. 1.

41. V. Chkalov, G. Baidukov, A. Belyakov, *Naš polët na ANT-25*, p. 12.

42. G. Stalingradsky, *Geroj Sovetskogo sojuza Valerij Pavlovič Čkalov* (Moscow: Gos. izd. polit. lit., 1938), p. 11.

43. S. Nagorny, "Geroi," p. 1.

44. "Slava gerojam" (editorial), *Literaturnaja gazeta*, 1936, no. 44 (August 5), p. 1.

45. Vs. Ivanov, *Parxomenko, Molodaja gvardija*, 1938, no. 11, pp. 45–62; no. 12, pp. 54–56; 1939, no. 1, p. 17.

46. *Vstreči s tovariščem Stalinym*, passim.

47. O. Gur, "Otto Juljevič Šmidt," *Literaturnaja gazeta*, 1937, no. 28 (May 26), p. 1.

48. A. Stakhanov, "Naš otec," *Vstreči s tovariščem Stalinym*, p. 24, describes the scene in the Kremlin where the "brother and sister" Stakhanovites are consumed with petty sibling rivalry over their achievements while Stalin looks on calmly and, "father-like," smoking a pipe.

49. E.g., *Valerian Vladimirovič Kujbyšev, 1888–1935. Materialy k biografii perioda podpol′ja* (Moscow: Partizdat, 1936), pp. 44–158.

50. Mostly this legend was cultivated semiofficially, in works such as the pseudo-epic "Skazanie o Lenine" by M. Kryukova (see above, chap. 6, pp. 149–50).

51. S. Nagorny, "Geroi," p. 1.

52. M. Rubinshtein, "Ljudi sovetskoj strany," *Bol′ševik*, 1935, no. 20, p. 32.

53. "Rešitel′no ulučšit′ rabotu sojuza pisatelej," iz soobščenija tov. V. Stavskogo na iv plenume pravlenija sojuza pisatelej SSSR, *Literaturnaja gazeta*, 1937, no. 15 (March 20), p. 2.

54. Ibid.

55. In a 1930 review of F. Panferov's *Brusski*, for instance, the author I. Mashbits-Verov devotes two pages to discussing the incredible "compositional amorphousness" and other literary defects of the novel, but these observations do not deter him from concluding that the book is more important than any other that has appeared since the Revolution ("Vtoraja kniga 'Bruskov,'" *Oktjabr′*, 1930, no. 8; see esp. pp. 197 and 208–9).

56. A. Fadeev, "Učit′sja u žizni," *Literaturnaja gazeta*, 1937, no. 20 (April 15), p. 2.

57. A. Fadeev, "Nedostatki raboty Sojuza pisatelej," *Literaturnaja gazeta*, 1938, no. 5 (January 27), p. 2.

58. Y. Andreev, *Revoljucija i literatura. Oktjabr′ i graždanskaja vojna v*

russkoj sovetskoj literature i stanovlenie socialističeskogo realizma (20–30-e gody) (Moscow: Xudožestvennaja literatura, 1975), pp. 314–19.

59. L. Anninsky, *"Kak zakaljalas' stal'"* Nikolaja Ostrovskogo (Moscow: Xudožestvennaja literatura, 1971), p. 10.

60. Ibid., pp. 11–20.

61. "Social command" (*social'nyj zakaz*), a radical theory on the relationship a Soviet writer should have to his society, was hotly debated in the early twenties but never implemented. According to this theory, topics should be mandated to writers either by the needs of the age or by authorities representing "the age's" interests. See "V diskussionom porjadke. Spor o social'nom zakaze. Pisateli o social'nom zakaze," *Pečat' i revoljucija*, 1929, no. 1, pp. 19–65.

62. E.g., Nikolai Ostrovsky, *Kak zakaljalas' stal'* (Moscow: Sovetskij pisatel', 1936), pp. 16, 35, 158–59 (English version in Nikolai Ostrovsky, *How the Steel Was Tempered* [Moscow: Foreign Languages Publishing House, 1936], pt. 1, pp. 24, 59, 283–84).

63. Ibid., p. 215 (English version, pt. 2, p. 53).

64. Ibid., p. 354 (English version, pt. 2, p. 357).

65. See, e.g., "Moral'nyj oblik pisatelja" (lead article), *Literaturnaja gazeta*, 1937, no. 53 (September 30), p. 1.

66. Cf. V. Shishkov, *Emel'jan Pugačev. istoričeskoe povestvovanie*, *Oktjabr'*, 1943, 4–5, 6–7, 8–9, 10, 11–12; 1944, 1–2, 5–6, 9, 11–12.

67. E. Veisman, "Mednyj vsadnik i Petr pervyj," *Literaturnaja gazeta*, 1934, no. 70 (June 4), p. 2.

68. A. Tolstoy, *Petr pervyj*, *Novyj mir*, 1933, no. 2, pp. 19–21.

69. See, e.g., E. Gerasimov and M. Erlikh, *Nikolaj Aleksandrovič Ščors. Boevoj put'* (Moscow: Gos. voennoe izd., 1937), where Schors is called an "orphan" when his mother dies when he is twelve (p. 6).

Chapter 6

1. Cf. P. Yudin, "Kommunizm i demokratija," *Bol'ševik*, 1936, no. 3, pp. 43–59; P. Yudin, "Svoboda i neobxodimost'," *Bol'ševik*, 1939, no. 14, pp. 43–59.

2. I. Vertsman, "Gor'kij o ložnom realizme," *Literaturnyj kritik*, 1937, no. 7, p. 117.

3. Robert H. McNeal, Introduction to J. V. Stalin, *Sočinenija*, vol. 1 [XIV] (Stanford: The Hoover Institution, 1967), p. x.

4. *Istorija vsesojuznoj kommunističeskoj partii (bol'ševikov). Kratkij kurs* (Moscow: Gos. izd. polit. lit., 1946), pp. 101–4.

5. G. Stalingradsky, *Geroj sovetskogo sojuza Valerij Pavlovič Čkalov* (Moscow: Ogiz, 1938), p. 15.

6. "Sovetskaja geroinja," *Literaturnaja gazeta*, 1939, no. 27 (May 15), p. 2.

7. V. Vishnevsky, "Ivan Papanin," *Ščors. Papanin*, Biblioteka "Ogonëk," no. 33 (1020), 1937, p. 40.

8. "Vsë vyše! (aviacionnyj marš)," lyric by P. German, music by Y.

Khait, in *Kryl'ja sovetov. Literaturno-estradnyj sbornik* (Moscow and Leningrad: Iskusstvo, 1939), pp. 6–7.
9. S. Nagorny, "Geroi," *Literaturnaja gazeta*, 1939, no. 69 (December 15), p. 1.
10. See chapter 3, above, pp. 75–77.
11. Vs. Ivanov, *Parxomenko, Molodaja gvardija*, 1938, no. 1, p. 21; Efim Dorosh, "Semen Mixailovič Budënny. Episody iz biografii," *Molodaja gvardija*, 1938, no. 4, pp. 110, 114.
12. I. Gudov, "On zovet na podvigi pered rodinoj," *Vstreči s tovariščem Stalinym*, p. 113.
13. "V SSSR socializm pobedil okončatel'no" (lead article), *Bol'ševik*, 1935, no. 20 (November 7), p. 5.
14. Henri Barbusse, *Stalin. Čelovek čerez kotorogo raskryvaetsja novyj mir* (Moscow: G.I.X.L., 1936), pp. 351–52.
15. Vs. Ivanov, *Parxomenko*, p. 52.
16. Akademik I. Vardin, "Ispolin-mudrec," in *Vstreči s tovariščem Stalinym*, p. 55.
17. See Plato, *The Republic*, Book 5.
18. Barbusse, *Stalin*, quoted in *Bol'ševik*, 1935, no. 20 (November 7), p. 73.
19. Akademik I. Vardin, "Ispolin-mudrec," p. 53.
20. Ibid., p. 56.
21. Cf. Y. Tynyanov, "O Xlebnikove," in *Sobranie proizvedenij Velemira Xlebnikova*, vol. 1 (Leningrad: Izd. pisatelej v Leningrade), p. 20; and V. Kaverin, *Xudožnik neizvesten* (Leningrad: Izd. pisatelej v Leningrade, 1931), p. 61.
22. J. V. Stalin, "Reč' tovarišča Stalina na pervom vsesojuznom soveščanii staxanovcev," *Bol'ševik*, 1935, no. 21, p. 7.
23. A. Stakhanov, *Rasskaz o moej žizni* (Moscow: Ogiz, 1937), p. 35.
24. I. Gudov, *Put' staxanovca. Rasskaz o moej žizni* (Moscow: Gos. soc.-ek. izd., 1938), p. 84.
25. "Ljudi stalinskoj epoxi" (lead article), *Bol'ševik*, 1935, no. 22, p. 7.
26. I. Smetanin, "Prostota i duševnost'" in *Vstreči s tovariščem Stalinym*, pp. 181–82.
27. I. Papanin, "Nezabyvaemye vstreči," ibid., p. 34.
28. I. Vardin, "Ispolin-mudrec," ibid., p. 49.
29. A. Khovin, "Stalinskie pitomcy," *Molodaja gvardija*, 1939, no. 12, p. 175.
30. F. Gladkov, *Cement, Krasnaja nov'*, 1925, no. 2, pp. 107–9.
31. F. Gladkov, *Cement* (Moscow: G.I.X.L., 1941), p. 88.
32. A. Stakhanov, "Naš otec," in *Vstreči s tovariščem Stalinym*, p. 26.
33. See chapter 1, above, pp. 39–40.
34. I. Vardin, "Ispolin-mudrec," p. 52.
35. "Socializm, uničtoženie klassov i rassvet sovetskoj demokratii" (lead article) *Bol'ševik*, 1936, no. 8, p. 2.
36. "Reč' sekretarja CK VKP(b) A. A. Ždanova," *Pervyj s"ezd pisatelej. Stenografičeskij otčet* (Moscow: Ogiz, 1934), p. 4.

37. "Doklad A. M. Gor'kogo o sovetskoj literature," *Pervyj s"esd pisatelej,* p. 6.

38. N. Piksanov, *Gor'kij i fol'klor,* 2d ed. (Moscow: G.I.X.L., 1938), pp. 141–47.

39. See, e.g., "Detstvo i junost' voždja. Dokumenty, zapisi, rasskazy," comp. Vl. Kalinin and Iv. Vereshchagin, *Molodaja gvardija,* 1936, no. 12, p. 28.

40. J. V. Stalin, "Zaključitel'noe slovo tovarišča Stalina na plenume CK VKP(b) 5 marta 1937 g," *Bol'ševik,* 1937, no. 7, p. 25.

41. M. Gorky, "O skazkax," *Pravda,* 1935, no. 29 (January 30).

42. "Strana ždet knig. O gerojax socialističeskogo truda," *Literaturnaja gazeta,* 1935, no. 61 (November 5), p. 1.

43. O. Dimin, "Živye tvorcy bylin i skazok," *Literaturnaja gazeta,* 1937, no. 15 (March 20), p. 6.

44. C. M. Bowra, *Heroic Poetry* (London: Macmillan, 1952), pp. 443–51.

45. Y. M. Sokolov, *Russian Folklore,* trans. Catherine Ruth Smith (Hartboro, Pa.: Folkore Associates, 1966), p. 697; Al. Dymshits, "Geroičeskaja tema sovetskogo fol'klora," *Zvezda,* 1937, no. 10, pp. 228–29.

46. Dzhambul, "Uničtožit'!," *Molodaya gvardija,* 1938, no. 3, pp. 17–18.

47. M. S. Kryukova, "Skazanie o Lenine," *Krasnaja nov',* 1937, no. 11, pp. 97–118.

48. M. Gorky, "Doklad A. M. Gor'kogo o sovetskoj literature," p. 6.

49. M. Gorky, "O literaturnyx zabavax," *Sobranie sočinenij v tridcati tomax,* 27, p. 255.

50. M. Gorky, "O jazyke," *Literaturnaja učeba,* 1934, no. 3, pp. 3–9; "O proze," *Literaturnaja učeba,* 1933, no. 1, p. 125.

51. E.g., Valentin Kataev, *Ja syn trudovogo naroda, Krasnaja nov',* 1937, no. 11, p. 86.

52. See, e.g., A. Stakhanov, "Moj opyt," in *Staxanovcy o sebe i o svoej rabote. Reči na pervom vsesojuznom soveščanii rabočix i rabotnic-staxanovcev* (Voronezh: Voronežskoe knižnoe izd., 1935), p. 7.

53. Felix J. Oinas, "Folklore and Politics in the Soviet Union," *Slavic Review,* 1973, no. 1, p. 52.

54. Robert C. Tucker, *Stalin as Revolutionary: A Study in History and Personality* (New York: W. W. Norton, 1973), pp. 79–82, 98, 111, 114.

55. M. Gorky, "Čelovek," *Sbornik Znanie za 1903 god,* no. 1, p. 212.

56. See, e.g., "Vperëd i vyše, komsomolec!," *Pravda,* 1933, no. 299 (October 29).

57. M. Gorky, *Ispoved', Sobranie sočinenij v tridcati tomax,* vol. 8 (Moscow: G.I.X.L., 1950), p. 288.

58. Ibid., p. 351.

59. M. Gorky, "O malen'kix ljudjax i o velikoj ix rabote," *O literature* (Moscow: G.I.X.L., 1955), p. 339.

Chapter 7

1. Walter Benjamin, "The Storyteller: Reflections on the Works of Nikolaj Leskov," *Illuminations*, trans. Harry Zohn (New York: Shocken, 1969), p. 96.
2. S. Preobrazhensky, "Poema o sovetskoj molodeže (predislovie)," in A. Fadeev, *Molodaya gvardija* (Moscow: Detskaja literatura, 1963), p. 5.
3. "Molodaja gvardija v romane i na scene," *Pravda*, 1947, December 3.
4. S. Preobrazhensky, p. 13.
5. *The Song of Igor's Campaign*, trans. Vladimir Nabokov (New York: Random House, Vintage Books, 1960), p. 12.
6. A. Fadeev, *Molodaja gvardija,* rev. and enl. ed. (Moscow: Molodaja gvardija, 1951), pp. 55, 56–57, 161, 199, 423.
7. Ibid., p. 153.
8. Ibid., p. 58.
9. Ibid., p. 155.
10. Ibid., p. 434.
11. Ibid., p. 52.
12. Ibid., pp. 80–81.
13. Ibid., p. 438.
14. Ibid., pp. 126–32.
15. Ibid., p. 127.
16. In Stalinist fiction the epithets used as signs of positiveness were almost the same as those Gorky used in *Mother,* but there were the following changes, which can be ascribed to the different ethos of the Stalin years: (*a*) an entirely new epithet, "merciless" (*bespoščadnyj*) was added to the register; (*b*) since Soviet society had become more hierarchical, epithets more appropriate to an august figure—"serious," "calm," "stern," "intent"—were used mostly for the "father"; they were applied to the "son" only in proportion as he acquired "consciousness." On the other hand, epithets that indicate action and vitality—"brave," "determined"—were now used only for the son.
17. A. Fadeev, *Molodaja gvardija*, pp. 160–61, 438.
18. Ibid., p. 80.
19. Ibid., pp. 319–20, 550–54, 681–82.
20. Ibid., pp. 252–55, 554.
21. Ibid., p. 255.
22. Arnold Van Gennep, *The Rites of Passage*, trans. Monika B. Vizedom and Gabrielle L. Caffee (Chicago:,University of Chicago Press, 1960), pp. 11, 75.
23. A. Tolstoy, *Petr Pervyj, Novyj mir*, 1930, no. 6, pp. 19–22.
24. A. Fadeev, *Molodaja gvardija*, p. 681.
25. See, e.g., Vasily N. Azhaev, *Daleko ot Moskvy, Novyj mir*, 1948, no. 9, p. 107, and Leonid M. Leonov, *Sot',Novyj mir*, 1930, no. 4, p. 27.
26. J. V. Stalin, "O zadačax xozjajstvennikov," *Sočinenija*, vol. 13 (Moscow: Gos. izd. polit. lit., 1951), p. 37.

27. A. Fadeev, *Molodaja gvardija*, pp. 666–69; S. Preobrazhensky, p. 20 (see n. 2, above).
28. *The Song of Igor's Campaign*, pp. 40, 54, 55.

Chapter 8

1. N. K. Mikhailovsky, quoted in T. P. Maevskaya, *Idei i obrazy russkogo narodničeskogo romana (70-e gody–80-e gody XIX v)* (Kiev: Naukova dumka, 1975), p. 45.
2. Maurice Merleau-Ponty, *Humanism and Terror: An Essay on the Communist Problem*, trans. John O'Neil (Boston: Beacon Press, 1969), esp. p. xxxii and chap. 1, "Koestler's Dilemmas."
3. Mircea Eliade, *Birth and Rebirth: The Religious Meaning of Initiation in Human Culture*, trans. Willard R. Trask (New York: Harper & Row, 1958), pp. xii–xiii.
4. M. R. Allen, *Male Cults and Secret Initiations in Melanesia* (Melbourne: Melbourne University Press, 1967), p. 4.
5. Moses Hadas and Morton Smith, *Heroes and Gods: Spiritual Biographies in Antiquity* (London: Routledge & Kegan Paul, 1965), pp. 10–11.
6. Leopold H. Haimson, *The Russian Marxists and the Origins of Bolshevism* (Cambridge, Mass.: Harvard University Press, 1967), p. 216.
7. Jack Goody, *Death, Property and the Ancestors: A Study of Mortuary Customs of the Lodagaa of West Africa* (London: Tavistock Publications, 1962), p. 29.
8. A. Fadeev, *Molodaja gvardija*, rev. and enl. ed. (Moscow: Molodaja gvardija, 1951), p. 682.
9. E.g., from nineteenth-century texts: "Skazka o mudrice Narumovna," in *Agitacionnaja literatura russkix revoljucionnyx narodnikov. Potaennye proizvedenija 1873–1875 gg.* (Leningrad: Nauka, 1970), p. 240, and S. M. Stepnyak-Kravchinsky, *Andrej Kožuxov* (Moscow: Xudožestvennaja literatura, 1972), p. 321. From Bolshevik texts: M. Gorky, *Mat'*, *Sobranie sočinenij v tridcati tomax*, vol. 7 (Moscow: G.I.X.L., 1960), p. 402.
10. John Bayley, *The Characters of Love: A Study in the Literature of Personality* (London: Constable, 1960), pp. 3–4.
11. F. Panferov, *Bruski*, pt. 2, *Oktjabr'*, 1930, no. 1, p. 131.
12. See, e.g., V. Kirpotin, "Reč'," *Sovetskaja literatura na novom etape. Stenogramma pervogo plenuma orgkomiteta sojuza sovetskix pisatelej* (Moscow: Ogiz, 1933), p. 24.
13. S. Babaevsky, *Kavaler zolotoj zvezdy*, pt. 1, *Oktjabr'*, 1947, no. 4, pp. 35–38.
14. A. Van Gennep, *The Rites of Passage*, trans. Vizedom and Caffee (Chicago: University of Chicago Press, 1960), p. 74.
15. See, e.g., A. Fadeev, *Molodaja gvardija*, p. 289.
16. See N. Ostrovsky, *Kak zakaljalas' stal'* (Moscow: Sovetskij pisatel', 1936), pp. 190–91.
17. V. Kaverin, *Doktor Vlasenkova*, pt. 2 of the trilogy *Otkrytaja kniga*

(Moscow: Molodaja gvardija, 1959), p. 349. Cf. also Lusha in Sholokhov's *Virgin Soil Upturned* (1931–60).
18. Hugh Dalziel Duncan, *Symbols in Society* (New York: Oxford University Press, 1968), p. 23.
19. D. S. Likhachev, *Čelovek v literature drevnej Rusi* (Moscow and Leningrad: Akademija nauk, 1958), p. 37.
20. Ibid.

Chapter 9

1. Cf. S. Babaevsky, *Kavaler zolotoj zvezdy*, pt. 1, *Oktjabr'*, 1947, no. 4, pp. 47–55, 121, and F. Gladkov, *Cement, Krasnaja nov'*, 1925, no. 1, pp. 105–8; no. 5, pp. 96, 104.
2. E.g., P. Pavlenko, *Ščast'e, Znamja*, 1947, no. 2, pp. 8–11.
3. V. Kataev, *Za vlast' sovetov*, rev. ed. (Moscow and Leningrad: Detskaja literatura, 1951), p. 190.
4. Vera Dunham, *In Stalin's Time: Middle-Class Values in Soviet Fiction* (Cambridge, Eng.: At the University Press, 1976), p. 42.
5. Vit. Vasilevsky, "Geroj našego vremeni," *Literaturnaja gazeta*, 1948, no. 49 (June 19), p. 1. This trend did not originate in the forties. Its basic philosophy can be found in Stalin's "Speech at a Reception for Workers in Higher Education, May 17, 1938" (J. V. Stalin, *Works*, vol. 1 [XIV], ed. Robert H. McNeal [Stanford: The Hoover Institution, 1967], pp. 275–78).
6. "Reč' A. M. Gor'kogo." Plenum pravlenija SSP SSSR, *Literaturnaja gazeta*, 1935, no. 13 (March 6), p. 1.
7. *Kavaler zolotoj zvezdy*, pt. 2, *Oktjabr'*, 1948, no. 4, pp. 34, 46, 100.
8. "Doklad t. Ždanova o žurnalax 'Zvezda' i 'Leningrad'," *Literaturnaja gazeta*, 1946, no. 39 (September 21), p. 2.
9. See Nikolai Tikhonov, "Pered novym pod''emom. Sovetskaja literatura v 1944–45 gg." Reč' na desjatom plenume pravlenija SP SSSR, 15 maja, 1945 (Moscow: izd. Literaturnaja gazeta, 1945), p. 4.
10. E.g., Grunya in Elizar Maltsev's *With All Our Heart* (1948).
11. E.g., the hero's wife in V. Azhaev's *Far Away from Moscow* (1948), the hero's love in Pavlenko's *Happiness* (1947), and his comrades in B. Polevoy's *Story about a Real Man* (1946).
12. Mikhail Bubennov, *Belaja berëza*, pt. 2, *Oktjabr'*, 1952, no. 5, p. 69.
13. A. Gurvich, "Čerty peredovogo sovetskogo čeloveka, *Znamja*, 1947, no. 11, p. 167.
14. "Vysokaja otvetstvennost' sovetskogo literatora" (lead article), *Literaturnaja gazeta*, 1947, no. 4 (January 25), p. 1.
15. Aleksandr Gutovich, "Gvardija Korčaginyx," *Zvezda*, 1950, no. 6, p. 137.
16. *Oktjabr'*, 1946, no. 9, p. 3.
17. Ibid., p. 19.
18. See, e.g., Nikolaj Leontiev, "Zatylok k buduščemu," *Novyj mir*, 1948, no. 9, pp. 248–66.

19. See M. Chudakova, *Besedy ob arxivax* (Moscow: Molodaja gvardija, 1975), pp. 92–93.

20. See, e.g., V. Azhaev, *Daleko ot Moskvy, Novyj mir,* 1948, no. 7, pp. 12, 20, 36.

21. A. Fadeev, *Molodaja gvardija,* rev. and enl. ed. (Moscow: Molodaja gvardija, 1951), p. 54.

22. E.g., in S. Babaevsky, *Svet nad zemlëj,* pt. 1, *Oktjabr',* 1949, no. 9, p. 22.

23. V. Goltsev, "Boris Polevoj 'Povest' o nastojaščem čeloveke'," *Znamja,* 1947, no. 3, p. 180.

24. E.g., V. Azhaev, *Daleko ot Moskvy.*

25. E. Kovalchuk, "Čerty sovremennoj literatury," *Novyj mir,* 1948, no. 9, p. 242.

26. E.g., Khokhlakov in S. Babaevsky's *Kaveler zolotoj zvezdy,* pt. 2 *Oktjabr',* 1948, no. 4, p. 7.

27. E.g., the hero Kovshov in *Far Away from Moscow* has a "stern" mentor in his immediate boss, Batmanov, the manager of a construction project, and a "loving" mentor in Zalkind, the head of the Party in the town.

28. A. Koptyaeva, *Ivan Ivanovič, Oktjabr',* 1949, no. 6, p. 88.

29. S. Babaevsky, *Svet nad zemlëj, Oktjabr',* 1949, no. 9, p. 60.

30. K. Fedin, *Neobyknovennoe leto, Novyj mir,* 1948, no. 10, pp. 84–85.

31. G. Nikolaeva, *Žatva, Znamja,* 1950, no. 7, p. 64.

32. P. Pavlenko, *Ščast'e, Znamja,* 1947, no. 2, p. 12.

33. V. Panova, *Kružilixa, Znamja,* 1947, no. 12, pp. 48–62.

34. P. Pavlenko, *Ščast'e, Znamja,* 1947, no. 2, pp. 4–6.

35. Cf. V. Vasiliev, "Zametki o xudožestvennom masterstve S. Babaevskogo," *Zvezda,* 1951, no. 11, p. 181, and F. Abramov, "Ljudi kolxoznoj derevni v poslevoennoj proze," *Novyj mir,* 1954, no. 4, pp. 217–21.

36. V. Vasilevskaja, *Kogda zagoritsja svet, Zvezda,* 1946, no. 11, pp. 57–64.

37. *Literaturnaja gazeta,* 1951, no. 36 (March 25), p. 3.

Chapter 10

1. E. Evtushenko, *Autobiografija* (London: Flegon Press, 1964), pp. 97–99.

2. Bertram D. Wolfe, *Khrushchev and Stalin's Ghost: Text, Background, Meaning of Khrushchev's Secret Report to the Twentieth Congress on the Night of February 24–25, 1956* (London: Atlantic Press, 1957).

3. Possibly also L. Leonov's *The Russian Forest,* which was published after Stalin's death in 1953 but written largely before it. This novel presents an attack on the terror and purges written in Aesopean language (it is wrong to cut down the Russian forest, i.e., people).

4. N. Malenkov, in a speech to the Nineteenth Party Congress, *Pravda,* 1952, no. 280 (October 6).

5. Gustav Wetter, "Dialectical Materialism and the Natural Sciences," *Soviet Survey*, 1958, no. 23 (January–March), p. 51.

6. J. V. Stalin, "Marksizm i voprosy jazykoznanija," *Works*, vol. 3 [XVI] (Stanford: The Hoover Institution, 1967), pp. 144–48.

7. One example would be I. Ehrenburg's *The Thaw* (1954).

8. G. Grossman, "Thirty Years of Soviet Industrialization," *Survey*, no. 26 (October–December, 1958), p. 16.

9. See Harold Swayze, *Political Control of Literature in the U.S.S.R.,* *1946–1959* (Cambridge, Mass.: Harvard University Press, 1962), p. 144.

10. V. Azhaev, *Daleko ot Moskvy, Novyj mir,* 1948, no. 7, p. 74 (anti-conservatism); p. 94 (antiauthoritarianism); pp. 46–47 (anti doubletalk).

11. E.g., Vasily Grossman, *Za pravoe delo, Novyj mir,* 1952, no. 7, p. 30.

12. See, e.g., A. Chakovsky, *God žizni, Oktjabr',* 1956, no. 9, pp. 91–99, 275.

13. V. Dudintsev, *Ne xlebom edinym, Novyj mir,* 1956, no. 8, p. 52.

14. Ibid., no. 9, p. 96.

15. Ibid., no. 8, p. 88. It is interesting to note, in this connection, that the underground Orthodox Church in the Soviet Union is called the "True-Orthodox Catacomb Church."

16. Ibid., no. 8, p. 88; no. 10, p. 56.

17. Ibid., no. 8, pp. 85–88; no. 10, p. 67.

18. See, e.g., M. Bremener, *Pust' ne sošlos' s otvetom, Junost',* 1956, no. 10, p. 51.

19. For a definition of the concept "democratic centralism," see Edward Hallett Carr, *The Bolshevik Revolution 1917–1923,* vol. 1 (London: Macmillan, 1950), pp. 190–92.

20. V. Ovechkin, "Trudnaja vesna," *Novyj mir,* 1956, no. 9, p. 124.

21. Actually, Ovechkin used this expression even in his first sketch in the series, "District Routine" (*Novyj mir,* 1952, 9, p. 13).

22. See Victor W. Turner, *The Ritual Process: Structure and Anti-Structure* (Chicago: Aldine, 1969), esp. pp. 112–13, 128–33.

23. See, e.g., V. Tendryakov, *Ruts* (1962).

24. See the discussion in *Voprosy literatury,* 1964, "Černy literatury poslednix let," nos. 2, 4, 5, 7, 9, 10, and 12.

25. E.g., Yury Bondarev, *Batal'ony prosjat ognja* (1957) and *Poslednie zal'py* (1959); Grigorij Baklanov, *Pjad' zemli* (1959).

26. E.g., G. Nikolaeva, *Bitva v puti* (1957).

27. E.g., I. Ehrenburg, *Ottepel',* pt. 1 (Moscow: Sovetskij pisatel', 1954), p. 76.

28. A. Kuznetsov, *Prodolženie legendy, Junost',* 1957, no. 7, pp. 25–27.

29. Ibid., p. 38.

30. Ibid., p. 52.

31. Ibid.

32. E.g., D. Granin, "One's Own Opinion."

33. In, e.g., V. Nekrasov, *Kira Georgievna* (1961), V. Tendryakov, *The Trial* (1961), G. Medynsky, *Honesty* (1958).

34. E.g., in V. Kozhevnikov's *Meet Baluev* (1961), which is otherwise a conventional novel about a construction hero.

35. E.g., in V. Semin's *Seven in One House* (1965).

36. D. Dar, "Rekomendacija" [to the publishing house Sovetskij Pisatel'], (1964).

37. *The Pushkin House* has not been published in toto in the Soviet Union, though several parts of it have appeared in assorted journals. It has, however, been published in the United States, by Ardis Press (1978).

Chapter 11

1. This statement is something of an oversimplification. It applies to most unofficial writing that treats anti-Soviet themes, but it does not apply to so-called "third literature," an underground literature that seeks to be neither polemical nor topical but to explore the possibilities of the word.

2. See, e.g., Ivan Shevtsov, *Vo imja otca i syna* (Moscow: Moskovskij robočij, 1970).

3. V. I. Belov, *Kanuny* (Moscow: Sovremennik, 1976), pp. 196, 198.

4. A. Chakovsky, *Blokada*, pt. 3, *Znamja*, 1968, no. 6, p. 24.

5. Leonid Ilich Brezhnev, *Vozroždenie* (Moscow: Detskaja literatura, 1979), p. 18.

6. V. Sëmin, *Semero v odnom dome*, *Novyj mir*, 1965, no. 6, p. 118.

7. Ibid., p. 119.

8. See, e.g., Y. Trifonov, *Studenty*, *Novyj mir*, 1950, no. 10, p. 135; no. 11, pp. 89–91.

9. V. Rasputin, *Živi i pomni*, *Naš sovremennik*, 1974, no. 10, pp. 2–99.

10. E.g., Boris Vasiliev, *Ne streljajte v belyx lebedej*, *Junost'*, 1973, no. 6, p. 21; V. Shukshin, *Ja prišel dat' vam volju* (Moscow: Sovetskij pisatel', 1974).

11. E.g., V. Shukshin, *Kalina krasnaja*, *Naš sovremennik*, 1973, no. 4.

12. V. Kochetov, *Čego že ty xočeš'*, *Oktjabr'*, 1969, no. 9, pp. 50–52.

13. V. Maksimov, *Sem' dnej tvorenija*, *Sobranie sočinenij*, vol. 2 (Frankfurt: Posev, 1976), pp. 28–32.

14. V. Soloukhin, *Vladimirskie prosëlki*, *Novyj mir*, 1957, no. 9, p. 113.

15. A. Solzhenitsyn, *Matrënin dvor*, *Novyj mir*, 1963, no. 1, p. 46.

16. F. Abramov, *Derevjannye koni*, *Novyj mir*, 1970, no. 2, pp. 78–79.

17. B. Vasiliev, *Ne streljajte v belyx lebedej*, *Junost'*, 1973, no. 6, p. 16.

18. Ibid., no. 7, p. 55.

Appendix A

1. V. Propp, *A Morphology of the Folktale*, translated by Lawrence Scott, 2d ed. (Austin: University of Texas Press, 1971).

Select Bibliography

The works I have consulted in preparing this book are too numerous for complete citation. I am therefore confining this bibliography to the principal general studies of Soviet literature by Western writers and the theoretical works that have most influenced my ideas.

Western Studies of Soviet Literature

Brown, Deming. *Soviet Literature since Stalin.* Cambridge, Eng.: At the University Press, 1978.

Brown, E. J. *The Proletarian Episode in Russian Literature.* New York: Columbia University Press, 1953.

————. *Russian Literature since the Revolution.* New York: Collier Books, 1969.

Dunham, Vera. *In Stalin's Time: Middle-Class Values in Soviet Fiction.* Cambridge, Eng.: At the University Press, 1976.

Eng-Liedmeier, Jeanne van der. *Soviet Literary Characters.* The Hague: Mouton, 1959.

Ermolaev, H. *Soviet Literary Theories, 1917–34: The Genesis of Socialist Realism.* University of California Publications in Modern Philology, no. 69. Berkeley, University of California Press, 1963.

Gasiorowska, Xenia. *Women in Soviet Fiction, 1917–1964.* Madison: University of Wisconsin Press, 1968.

Gibian, G. *Interval of Freedom: Soviet Literature during the Thaw, 1954–1957.* Minneapolis: University of Minnesota Press, 1960.

Hayward, M. "The Decline of Socialist Realism," *Survey* 18, 1 (1972): 73–97.

————. "Themes and Variations in Soviet Literature." In Milorod M. Drakhovitch, ed., *Fifty Years of Communism in Russia.* University Park, Pa.: Pennsylvania State University Press, 1968.

Holthussen, Johannes. *Twentieth-Century Russian Literature: A Critical Study.* New York: Frederick Ungar, 1962.

Hosking, Geoffrey. *Beyond Socialist Realism: Soviet Fiction since "Ivan Denisovich."* London: Granada Publishers, 1980. New York: Holmes & Meier, 1980.

Johnson, Priscilla, and Labedz, Leopold, eds. *Khrushchev and the Arts: The Politics of Soviet Culture, 1962–1964.* Cambridge, Mass.: M.I.T. Press, 1965.

293

McLean, H., and Vickery, W., eds. *The Year of Protest, 1956*, New York: Random House, Vintage Books, 1961.

Maguire, R. *Red Virgin Soil: Soviet Literature in the 1920's.* Princeton: Princeton University Press, 1968.

Mathewson, Rufus W., Jr. *The Positive Hero in Russian Literature.* 2d ed. Stanford: Stanford University Press, 1975.

Struve, G. *Russian Literature under Lenin and Stalin, 1917–1953.* Norman: University of Oklahoma Press, 1971.

Swayze, Harold. *Political Control of Literature in the U.S.S.R., 1946–1959.* Cambridge, Mass.: Harvard University Press, 1962.

Thomson, Boris. *Lot's Wife and the Venus de Milo: Conflicting Attitudes to the Cultural Heritage of Modern Russia.* Cambridge, Eng.: At the University Press, 1978.

————. *The Premature Revolution: Russian Literature and Society, 1917–1946.* London: Weidenfeld & Nicholson, 1972.

Vaughn, J. C. *Soviet Socialist Realism: Origins and Theory.* New York: St. Martin's Press, 1973.

Vickery, Walter N. *The Cult of Optimism: Political and Ideological Problems of Recent Soviet Literature.* Bloomington: Indiana University Press, 1963.

Works That Have Influenced My Theoretical Approach

M. M. Bakhtin. "Epos i roman (o metodologii issledovanija romana)." In *Voprosy literatury i estetiki. Issledovanija raznyx let*, pp. 447–83. Moscow: Xudožestvennaja literatura, 1975.

Eliade, Mircea. *Birth and Rebirth: The Religious Meaning of Initiation in Human Culture.* Translated by Willard R. Trask. New York: Harper & Row, 1958.

————. *Cosmos and History: The Myth of the Eternal Return.* Translated by Willard R. Trask. New York: Harper & Row, 1959.

Haimson, Leopold H. *The Russian Marxists and the Origins of Bolshevism.* Cambridge, Mass.: Harvard University Press, 1955.

Likhachev, D. S. *Čelovek v literature drevnej rusi.* Moscow and Leningrad: Akademija nauk, 1958.

Medvedev, P. N., and Bakhtin, M. M. *The Formal Method in Literary Scholarship: A Critical Introduction to Sociological Poetics.* Translated by Albert J. Wehrle. Baltimore: Johns Hopkins University Press, 1978.

Propp, V. *Morphology of the Folktale.* Translated by Lawrence Scott. 2d ed. Austin: University of Texas Press, 1971.

Tertz, Abram. [Andrei Sinyavsky]. "On Socialist Realism." In *The Trial Begins and On Socialist Realism.* Translated by Max Hayward. New York: Random House, Vintage Russian Library, 1965.

Turner, Victor W. *The Ritual Process: Structure and Anti-Structure.* Chicago: Aldine, 1969.

Van Gennep, Arnold. *The Rites of Passage.* Translated by Monika B. Vizedom and Gabrielle L. Caffee. Chicago: University of Chicago Press, 1960.

Index

Index